THE MAGIC OF THE MANY

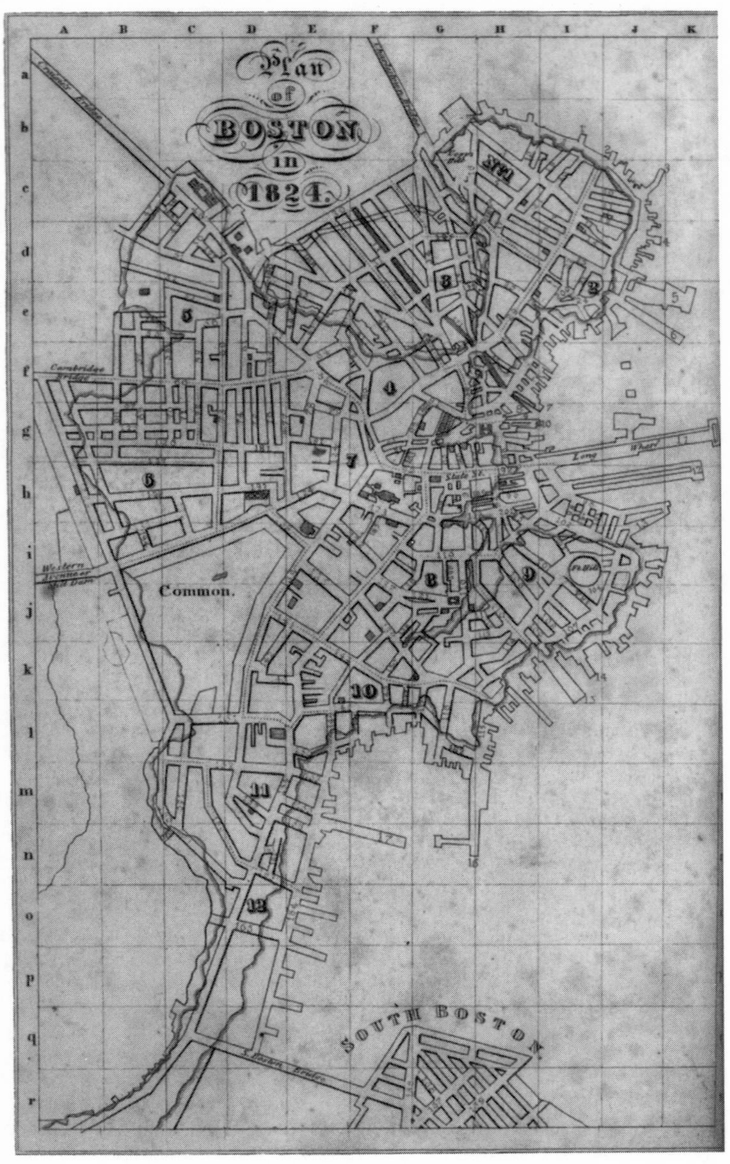

Plan of Boston, 1824, showing the twelve wards. From Caleb H. Snow, M.D., *A History of Boston, The Metropolis of Massachusetts, from Its Origin to the Present Period: with some account of the environs* (Boston, 1825)

THE MAGIC OF THE MANY

Josiah Quincy and the Rise of Mass Politics in Boston 1800–1830

MATTHEW H. CROCKER

University of Massachusetts Press
Amherst

Printed in the United States of America
LC 99-15158
ISBN 1-55849-222-4
Designed by Milenda Nan Ok Lee
Printed and bound by Sheridan Books, Inc.
Set in Adobe Caslon by Graphic Composition, Inc.

Library of Congress Cataloging-in-Publication Data

Crocker, Matthew H., 1962–
The magic of the many : Josiah Quincy and the rise of mass politics in Boston, 1800–1830 / Matthew H. Crocker.
p. cm.
Includes bibliographical references (p.) and index.
ISBN 1-55849-222-4 (alk. paper)
1. Boston (Mass.) —Politics and government—1775–1865.
2. Political Culture—Massachusetts—Boston—History—19th century.
3. Quincy, Josiah, 1772–1864. 4. Mayors—Massachusetts—Boston
Biography. I. Title.
F73.44.C9 1999
974.4′6103—dc21 99-15158
CIP

British Library Cataloguing in Publication data are available.

To my Mother and Father,
Elinor Winslow Crocker and John Crocker Jr.,
and
the community of North Haven, Maine

CONTENTS

PREFACE

This is a book about the growth of democracy in an American city during the early nineteenth century. It is an account of a politically disabled citizenry demanding and gaining inclusion in a political structure that, up until then, functioned more like a restrictive private club than an engine for democracy. Through grass-roots activism and political realignment, this discontented urban citizenry fought for and won an influential voice in the workings of government. While, in essence, this book explains how democracy worked in one city during one period of time, it also provides insight into a larger national phenomenon—the rise of popular Jacksonian politics. Indeed, the forces discussed in this work proved to be the harbingers of Jacksonianism.

Yet, as much as this illustrates the triumphs of popular democracy, it also demonstrates many of democracy's failures. Coinciding with populist victory, the process of democratization immediately began to deteriorate at the hands of many of the movement's most ardent champions. The political solidarity that had been forged from a common democratic vision and put into motion to subdue a limited democracy—replete with exclusionary practices, procedures, and traditions—broke apart at the very moment of its success. With the advent of a more inclusive democratic system came the democratization movement's unraveling. A once unified campaign for inclusive democracy shattered under the very weight of its success. The consequences were the complete transformation of an American city's political structure and, ironically, an American city whose government looked remarkably undemocratic.

The city I have focused on is Boston between 1814 and 1829. I have chosen Boston because democratization erupted there with such acceleration and speed that within three years (1819–22) the guardians of the political status quo found themselves shaken, overpowered, and their party dismantled. Part and parcel of this remarkable political reorganization was an economic, cultural, and demographic transformation that radically altered Massachusetts and Boston. Arguably, the flurry of activity during this period is as significant in defining the region as the Revolution or, later, massive European immigration during the 1840s. Like past and future Bostonians, the Hub's citizens of the 1810s and 1820s often viewed the changes they experienced through the matrix of politics, and it was in the political realm that they acted upon what they saw. What average Bostonians would have seen during this period was the complete transformation of their city and state. While some of these events helped ignite the process of democratization, others were the result of such democratic action. In this sense, these events serve as beacons that help shed light on activist motivation. Also, they represent the fruition of the struggle for a more inclusive democracy—a democracy that would help usher in the political activism of the Jacksonian Age.

In 1820 the Maine district of Massachusetts was severed from the state and granted independent statehood, more than halving the state's total land mass and cutting its population by a third. In 1821 a state constitutional convention convened, and a new state constitution was written, accepted, and adopted in 1822. That same year, Boston's population rose to over 44,000 people, many of whom came from the New England countryside seeking jobs in the city. Beginning in 1819 and continuing for five years, Bostonians, along with the rest of the nation, faced a devastating depression that undercut the Hub's robust economy. As a result, by 1822 Boston's only prison was filled to capacity with insolvent debtors. This was also the year that Boston gained a city charter and abandoned its traditional town meeting form of government for a more centralized municipal authority. In Boston's first mayoral election in 1822 a third-party candidate defeated one of the state's most prominent politicians. And in the next year the state's dominant political party lost the gubernatorial race for the first time since the War of 1812, marking the final demise of a party that had dominated the state.

Shadowing these concrete events, a less tangible phenomenon was unfolding within the city. Bostonians began to radically change their political attitudes. Popular opposition to various "oppressive" local and state laws led to accusations that the city and state's traditional political leadership represented an oligarchic "monied aristocracy"—a "cabal" solely committed to maintaining its cultural, economic, and political sovereignty at the expense of the common people. In such an atmosphere, many Bostonians began to believe that the precepts of representative democracy were being undermined by a small group of elites. It was this antiaristocratic sentiment, reinforced by discernible disagreements with the established leadership over specific policy issues, that generated an overwhelming popular mandate for expanded democratization in the metropolis. Ordinary Bostonians spoke in unison through the ballot box, achieving their goal of a democracy devoid of aristocratic pretension, inherited prestige, and authority.

Yet, with its enemies vanquished, Boston democracy immediately faced a perplexing problem. Activist cohesion and unity had been predicated on a palpable enemy: the omnipresence of an antidemocratic, aristocratic political cabal. With the cabal defeated and disgraced, the forces of democratization lost much of their cohesion and self-definition. The clarity that had once driven the movement was quickly overshadowed by the disorientation that came with success. Thus, at the very moment of popular democracy's most striking victory, its internal divisions were revealed. Making matters worse, once in positions of power, some of the movement's leaders used their new prestige to benefit themselves in ways Bostonians rejected as dishonest and fundamentally undemocratic. These leaders showed themselves to be as corrupt as the old political regime. With its traditional villains purged from political power and facing betrayal from within its own ranks, the democratic movement foundered and broke apart. In its place, a fractured, confused, and disheartened Boston turned to a trusted populistic leader who would dominate the city for close to a decade—Josiah Quincy.

To many Bostonians, Quincy best symbolized the early struggle for democratization and seemed its logical beneficiary. Over time, though, and in an ironic twist, the leader who Boston thought exemplified the movement's best, developed into an imperious ruler who eventually stretched his popular mandate to its breaking point. Because of his dictatorial actions, he would force many of his most enthusiastic supporters to turn against him. At the decade's twilight, Bostonians expelled him for his excesses. Exhausted by his fierce activism, angered by his dictatorial methods of command, and bankrupted by his grandiose plans for the modernization of Boston, the city looked to its past for a more subdued and malleable leader.

In yet another paradoxical twist that connotes the complexities of both the city and the process of democratization it struggled through, Boston gave itself to a once hated chieftain of the old regime, Harrison Gray Otis. Though this politician survived long enough to experience a political rebirth, the oppressive regime in which he had once flourished had not. Under the watchful eyes of the people, his every action was scrutinized and his power hobbled. After the dictatorial rule and frenetic pace of its last leader, what Bostonians wanted most was someone who gave the appearance of a leader but would accept a subordinate role and follow the will of the people. By reinstating a politician who had consistently voiced his objections to the zealous activism of Boston's prior leadership, and who promised to restore tranquility and order to the city, Boston seized upon a controllable strawman from its past.

Boston's process of democratization was a long one. Despite the ordeals that Bostonians went through in their journey toward a more democratic society, by the decade's end the city had finally reached its goal. By 1828 Boston sustained and fostered an enriched form of advanced democracy.

ACKNOWLEDGMENTS

If it were not for the support and encouragement of numerous friends and colleagues in the history department at the University of Massachusetts Amherst this book would never have been completed.

First and foremost, my deepest thanks go to Jack Tager. Jack diligently read countless drafts of this manuscript and offered me invaluable advice and direction. As my dissertation director and friend, Jack always asked the right questions at the right times. By challenging me intellectually and proving a constant source of reassurance and motivation, Jack went far beyond the call of duty and I am utterly indebted to him. Thanks also go to Bruce Laurie, who has served both as a perceptive reader of my work over the years and as a highly competitive fly fishing comrade. Often Bruce's sagest advice would come when we returned from a long day fishing the streams of western Massachusetts. His guidance and support (both of my work and on the finer points of fly selection and gear) have been indispensable. Ronald Story was the first who inspired me to focus on nineteenth-century Boston. Ron carefully read an earlier draft of this book and graciously shared with me his immense knowledge of nineteenth-century Boston. This is a better book because of his help.

William Fowler, director of the Massachusetts Historical Society, and Peter S. Field of Tennessee Technological College scrupulously read the entire manuscript and offered perceptive insights and recommendations. Many of their suggestions were taken and the result is a much improved and more comprehensive study. Clark Dougan, senior editor at the University of Massachusetts Press, gracefully guided this work through the process of publication. Clark's unique blend of candor and humor reinforced by conviction that my manuscript was in good hands. This was never more apparent than when Barbara Palmer was assigned to copy edit this book. A consummate professional, Barbara caught countless errors, both large and small. Any mistakes found within this volume are mine and mine alone. The staff members of the American Antiquarian Society, the Massachusetts Historical Society, the Rare Book and Manuscript Room at the Boston Public Library, the John Hay Library at Brown University, and the W.E.B. Du Bois Library at the University of Massachusetts Amherst all deserve to be acknowledged for their indispensable assistance to me over the course of my research. These librarians and archivists have a mastery over the materials in their respective archives that is truly mind-boggling. As most historians will (or at least should) admit, we would be at a loss if it were not for the knowledge and talent of specialists like these.

My thanks also to those friends and colleagues who consistently provided me with humor and, often, much needed perspective: Eric Hamel, Robert Surbrug, Mark Voss-Hubbard, Graham and Jackie Warder, Michael Ross, Cathy Verrenti, Kathleen Banks Nutter, Dan Hewins, Peter Cabot, Chris and Fanny Minot, Richard Bortz, Andrew Anderson-Bell Jr., Allan Rosenblatt and Maisy. The loyal friendship these people (and one dog) have shown me over the years continually serves as an anchor. Also, thanks to those friends and family who opened their homes to me while I was researching in Boston: John and Mimpy Brooks, Charlotte Cleveland, and Aggie Littlefield.

Finally, I would like to thank those teachers who persuaded me never to give up: Jack and Mary Crocker (my grandparents), Tim Devlin (the first to get me excited about anything relating to the academic side of school), Joe Zeliner (the first to get me jazzed about history), Clair Lockheart (my first tough English teacher), Carl Reimers (who showed his students the merriment that can be found in intellectual pursuit), Ron Ross (who disciplined my writing), Patricia Kane (who showed me the potential beauty and clarity in language), and Julius Lester (who never balked at telling me the truth).

Northampton, Massachusetts, 1999

THE MAGIC OF THE MANY

I • THE SETTING FOR INSURGENCY

. . . nothing is so unequal as equality.
—Samuel Lyman, 1800

. . . the duped and deluded mob whose hosannas and execrations are as much mechanical and responsive as the pipes of an organ.
—Harrison Gray Otis, 1801

No other political organization more overtly epitomized and championed Massachusetts' patrician class than the Federalist party. Unlike its structure elsewhere, Boston Federalism developed a highly sophisticated, centralized, and effective machine that promoted, reinforced, and maintained what historian Ronald Formisano identifies as "deferential-participant politics." While in other states the party atrophied after the "treason" of the Hartford Convention, Federalism's political infrastructure in Massachusetts forestalled its demise and provided the party an unusually long and somewhat anachronistic life. Until the early 1820s, ordinary voters continued to participate in a variety of elections, following the lead of their cultural and economic "betters"—voting, often, against their own interests. Although, as early as 1814, Federalism on the national level was dead and buried, in Massachusetts the party continued to enjoy significant appeal and experienced a rebirth of sorts in its opposition to the Missouri Compromise. Yet the party's "Indian Summer," as historian Samuel Eliot Morison once described it, was short lived.[1] By 1822 Federalism had lost the city of Boston, and with it the party's last stronghold. The decisive blow, ironically, not only occurred in the party's most loyal stronghold of Boston but was delivered by ranking members of both the party leadership and the Boston patriciate. With the support of thousands of ordinary Bostonians, these apostates helped upset Boston's traditional "deferential-participant" style of politics, reshaping it to allow ordinary Bostonians much more participation, autonomy, and independence in their voting behavior. As a result, Boston became significantly more democratic.

What began as a set of seemingly innocuous demands for moderate reform in Boston and the state abruptly developed into a full-fledged populist assault on the traditional political establishment of Massachusetts. By 1821 the Boston-based Federalist state leadership found itself under siege by an urban electorate that, only a few years earlier, had been thoroughly devoted to Federalism. Although popular discontent was voiced concerning a myriad of diverse issues, in the winter of 1821–22 the most significant grievance that brought many Boston citizens together was the people's demand that Boston abandon its traditional town meeting system of governance for a more modern, municipal city system. This primary objective best illustrates the disposition of a popular political movement that would dramatically alter the nature of Boston politics for the future. The question over whether Boston should remain a town or institute a city system provoked in many Bostonians an intense hatred of their own past deferential voting behavior. As many saw it, democracy itself was at stake. Would ordinary voters continue to participate in politics "while maintaining deferential attitudes toward a recognized elite of wealth, [and] status," as the traditional Federalist leadership demanded and expected? Or would they, as one insurgent demanded, "claim from our Constitutional agents *deference* to the known will of the majority"?[2] With Boston's incorporation as a city, the issue of political independence was played out in its first electoral contest.

During the city's first mayoral race in 1822, a curious nonpartisan coalition formed between estranged members of the Boston Federalist elite and a diverse urban electorate, containing a majority membership of poor-to-middling Bostonians. This unconventional fusion mustered the energy to cause the collapse of Federalism in Boston, thereby signaling the party's final demise.[3] The party disloyalty shown by some of the Boston elite in 1822 also indicated that the normative sociopolitical precepts in Boston had changed. No longer could Federalism bank on Boston's elite to follow in lockstep. As the events from 1819 through 1823 indicated, the democratic tide not only flowed through to the lower and middling classes in Boston but rose into the bastions of Boston's elite society. In this sense, the political events that began in the early 1820s transcend conventional political history and illuminate a cultural crisis among Boston's once homogeneous elite. These activities expose the precariousness of an elite class structure that has traditionally been seen as one of the most durable and unified political and economic structures of its kind in America.[4]

The most visible member of this insurgency in Boston was patrician Josiah Quincy. Quincy was a scion of Boston wealth and lineage. John Adams once described him as "a rare instance of hereditary eloquence and ingenuity in the fourth generation. . . . He comes into life with every advantage of family, fortune and education." A graduate of Andover and Harvard, buttressed with a hefty inheritance in real estate, he chose a life in politics, serving in the U.S. House of Representatives as a reactionary Federalist for most of his early adulthood.[5] Yet, in his first run for mayor, Quincy dramatically broke with his party and led an insurgent campaign that resulted in the uprooting of Federalist hegemony in Boston. This was hardly the presumed role of a man whom Boston patrician and diplomat John Lothrop Motley hailed as "the head of the Brahmins of America."[6]

As the popular mayor of Boston for six years between 1823 and 1829, Quincy ushered in a new form of politics that centered almost solely around himself. Operating much like future Boston political impresario and mayor James Michael Curley, Quincy remained unfailingly confident in his right and ability to consolidate municipal power within the mayor's office. He presided over a rambunctious assortment of bristling political factions, while promoting a wide array of public service activities that consistently satisfied a general electorate that annually reelected him. Ever the individualist, and seemingly above the narrowness of party and class loyalty, Quincy manipulated, cajoled, and appeased Boston's variegated political forces into acceptance of his ambitious agenda of urban growth. With the Federalist party demolished and Boston's Republicans ineffectual, Quincy took advantage of the political void, filling it with his commanding personality and his unprecedented activism as the new city's chief executive. The Quincy mayoralty was dictatorial, as some have accused. Nevertheless, his rise to political power in Boston and his mayoralties should also be viewed as a transitional phase that positively imbued ordinary Bostonians with a new sense of political empowerment and stability during a turbulent period of change and political dissent.[7] Many factors combined to produce this moment of political transformation. Besides the men and their motivations, the historical setting was all-important.

Three years before Quincy made his first bid for the mayor's office, depression hit the nation. What began in the cotton export markets of New Orleans and Charleston in early 1819 quickly spread east, causing financial panic and chaos in virtually every sector of the American economy. No region of the country was immune. Not even the strong economy of Boston, some 2,000 miles away, withstood the tremors.[8]

Cotton prices steadily rose after the War of 1812. British textile manufacturers, deprived of American cotton during the war, hankered for product and were willing to pay for it. Between 1815 and 1818 the price per pound of raw cotton in the export markets of the South nearly doubled from 16.5 cents to 32.5. Running parallel to the remarkable increase in cotton prices, northern-controlled shipping rates quadrupled between 1817 and 1818. The cotton boom of the postwar years not only benefited established southern cotton planters and northern merchants but also sparked the greed of speculators who gobbled up virgin cotton lands in the old Southwest for resale at inflationary prices. Those who bought the speculators' land happily mortgaged themselves to the hilt to northern bankers betting on the continued rise of the cotton market.[9]

By 1818 English cotton importers found their market could no longer withstand the high price of American cotton and began tapping other sources for the staple crop. British manufacturers began importing East Indian cotton, nearly doubling its Far East importation between 1817 and 1818. The price of cotton in the South plummeted, taking with it the value of newly bought, underdeveloped producing land in the Southwest. The ambitious farmer who had recently bought land in the Southwest saw property values plunge by 50 to 75 percent within one year. The same pound of cotton that had sold in foreign markets for 32.5 cents in 1818 went for less than 14.5 cents in 1819; and after the New Orleans or Charleston trading house got done with him, the actual planter took home only 9 cents per pound of cotton. Just as commercial shipping rates had followed cotton's upward trend during the boom years, so did they fall during the panic. The maritime interest of New England had lost its primary customers on both sides of the Atlantic.[10]

The seaboard towns of Massachusetts were not the only areas hit by the depression. Fledgling manufacturers also felt the sting. The strict trade restrictions on British importation into the United States during the War of 1812 had served as an air-tight protective tariff for youthful American industries. Boston-financed industry developed during the war from an embryonic state into a viable and largely healthy toddler. With peace, Great Britain's burgeoning warehouses opened and flooded the American market, undercutting Massachusetts manufacturers. The protective tariffs imposed on British goods in 1816 proved ineffective against unscrupulous exporters with falsified documents. Custom agents were easily fooled or bought, rendering the tariffs ineffectual in defending home industry. A steady stream of British imports continued to deluge American ports.[11]

Directly affecting Boston's small merchants, jobbers, and importers was an ingenious new method of retailing conjured up in the boardrooms of England's manufacturing headquarters. Not only would Britain manufacture finished products, it would now sell them directly to American consumers in open auction. A full-bellied ship would anchor in Boston Harbor stockpiled with goods; word would spread on the street, and its cargo would sell at the highest bid to Boston's consumers. All local importers, jobbers, and retailers were undercut by the open bidding. Although this clearly benefited Boston consumers, the system drained money out of American coastal cities and into the coffers of British industry.[12] The auction system only further intensified the economic pressure Boston already faced due to the national depression.

During a three-month period in 1822, 100 businesses in Boston failed. Shipping rates fell and dock workers were laid off in unprecedented numbers. Credit was frozen and banks, reported Boston's *Evening Gazette,* began to "demand immediate repayment of the debtors." Between 1819 and 1820 prices for goods tumbled; yet, as one observer explained, money was "tighter than the skin on a cats back." So who could pay? "[T]he industrious mechanic," warned the *Boston Patriot,* "may not be able to earn enough money by his labor to supply the natural wants" of himself or his family. Between 1820 and 1822, more than 3,500 Bostonians were imprisoned for debt. Governor John Brooks declared the state to be in "times of peril and extreme pressure." In 1819 alone, Massachusetts lost 25 percent of its commercial capital. According to the *Boston Patriot,* the city had become "a dull and uncheery spectacle—silence reigns in the streets and gloom and despondency" rule. "[M]oney is so scarce," sardonically reported the Boston *Castigator,* "that a gentleman has offered his *character* for sale."[13]

For many Bostonians, the *Castigator*'s report directly illustrated the problem. Boston's traditional Federalist leaders did nothing to ease the burdens of depression and, as a result, fell under suspicion of selling their "character" to maintain economic and political supremacy. For the city's established leadership, such attacks on its benevolence and honor had devastating consequences. Before the insurgent challenges of the 1820s, the elite's strong grip on the "lower orders" depended upon Boston's collective reverence for patrician "character." As historian Ronald Formisano explains the predepression culture of the city, "Boston was once an oligarchy. . . . It was a world in which deference to one's social betters did not necessarily imply servility or obsequiousness, and in which respect for social rank was quite compatible with integrity, self-respect, and one's own sense of importance." Such a social order depended on traditional arrangements of reciprocal obligations between the classes. During the panic of 1819, this arrangement fell into disrepair, and community leaders quickly became viewed as uncaring, aristocratic, and corrupt.[14] Old party alliances fell by the wayside as the character of Boston's leadership faced blistering attacks.

In the one-party town of Boston, such a new political consciousness could mean only one thing: an attack on the Federalist establishment. The Massachusetts Federalist Central Committee was controlled at the time by Harrison Gray Otis, William Sullivan, and Thomas Handasyd Perkins. These men ruled their party with a dictatorial iron hand. Having total control over the party's purse-strings, its caucuses, and its press, the committee was perceived as using its resources to implement its class interests at the great expense of the people.[15]

All three of these men were seasoned and wily politicians. Although Sullivan tended to stay in the shadows, preferring to avoid public office, his devoted and active administration of the Central Committee proved essential to the day-to-day operations of the party. His low-profile status was hardly the result of a lack of personal political ambition. Instead, his shadowy role within the party was probably due more to the fact that his father, James, had allied with the state's Jeffersonians who elected him governor in 1807. Also, Sullivan had been raised in the faraway Maine district. Thus, in Boston, he seemed quite a strange commodity. Perkins, on the other hand, had served either in the house or the senate of the Massachusetts General Court pretty much nonstop between 1805 and 1822. Without question, Otis's record proved the most impressive of the trio and made him its natural leader. In 1796 his political career began with a boom. In that year alone, he received an appointment by John Adams to head the U.S. district attorney's office in Massachusetts; he was appointed to the director's seat of the U.S. Bank in Boston; and he ran for and won a position in the lower house of the

General Court where he stayed for a year before taking over Fisher Ames's coveted spot in the U.S. House of Representatives. Leaving Washington in 1802, he returned to his seat on the Massachusetts General Court, serving as Speaker of the House between 1803 and 1804. In 1805 Otis rose to the state senate where he stayed, despite a one year foray in the House, until 1817. In the state's upper house, he wielded immense power as its president for four of his eleven years there before returning to the U.S. Senate and making a failed bid for the governorship of Massachusetts in 1823.[16]

Each of these men epitomized what Boston's oppositional press identified as an undemocratic "monied aristocracy" that subverted the authority of the electorate.[17] The Central Committee's key leadership was politically dominant and fabulously wealthy. Unlike most Bostonians, Perkins, Sullivan, and Otis maintained sufficient capital to easily weather the depression. In fact, both Otis and Perkins significantly expanded their business ventures during the height of the financial panic. Taking advantage of a falling market, Otis expanded his Boston real estate holdings during the depression years, while continuing to extract high rents from his tenants. In 1819 Perkins took advantage of the economic chaos and his large cash reserves to invest $765,000 in a shipping venture to the Far East while his competition's ships languished in their slips.[18] These facts did not go unnoticed by the ordinary citizens of Boston whose financial affairs were thrown into chaos by the depression.

Before the depression, Otis had acquired a real estate empire by successfully speculating (often with the aid of inside information) in Boston and Maine lands. By 1822 he had branched out into manufacturing. With Otis's encouragement, Sullivan became his partner in the lucrative real estate syndicate, the Mount Vernon Proprietors, which developed Beacon Hill. Sullivan also had inherited stock in the Middlesex Canal, which had languished until the creation of the Lowell mills in 1813 reinvigorated its profits, adding to his personal wealth. Perkins was the richest of the group—a merchant prince who had made a fortune in the illegal opium trade. Receiving an estimated profit of $50,000 on each shipload of opium sold in Canton, China, Perkins accumulated massive sums which he successfully reinvested in manufacturing and, later, railroads.[19]

These men controlled huge amounts of capital and were members of an intricate network of interlocking financiers who were virtually in command of the wealth of the state. Meeting each Saturday night with various others of their ilk, Otis, Sullivan, and Perkins established the Saturday Fish Club, a highly secretive social fraternity estimated to have a total membership of six. Here these powerful men enjoyed Madeira together and schemed over politics and business. As historian Peter Dobkin Hall argues, by the first two decades of the nineteenth century, this elite "had been thoroughly transformed. . . . Its power now derived explicitly from . . . possession of wealth. . . ." The marriage between political and economic interests—one consummated within the arena of local politics—proved bountiful.[20]

Heightening public awareness of the inequality of Boston's class structure, the depression of 1819 fostered a rebellious spirit in the electorate that rejected the fiscal foundations for the Federalist leadership's authority and dramatically altered Boston's traditional power structure. Overstating the situation, yet betraying a common anxiety among many upper-echelon Massachusetts Federalists, Harrison Gray Otis described the new political temper of Boston as "revolutionary."[21] And in many ways it was.

After the Revolution, "the Boston political and economic elites merged," explains historian Frederic Cople Jaher, "and government service advanced class power as well as class . . . honor."[22] Business and the politics that Federalism bred went hand-in-hand in defining the Boston elite to itself. To challenge the validity of one was to denigrate the status of the whole. As one historian of Massachusetts explains, a Federalist of the first class "was expected to adhere to the Federal[ist] standard and the acceptable conservative creed. To renounce one's past political behavior, if one was a Federalist, was tantamount to admitting a serious character flaw."[23] Besides this particular aspect of the Federalist party culture, there was a practical side to blending political and economic interests—that of fusing Federalist policy with the affairs of elite enterprise. Not only could such a combination be easily justified by following the pragmatic logic of Alexander Hamilton that trumpeted the benefits of binding capitalism with government, but in a much more utilitarian sense it ensured Federalist oversight of economic policy in the state. As Oscar and Mary Handlin have demonstrated, Federalist command of the Massachusetts General Court advanced enterprise and capital accumulation.[24] Clearly, those who benefited most from the legislature's patronage were those with established wealth. Thus the Federalist policy makers and the Massachusetts economic elite worked in tandem, advanced the same agenda, and, as the Federalist Central Committee's membership suggests, were often one and the same.

By 1822 Federalism, with its firm directive requiring obedience from its members, its elitist overtones, and the economic interests the party blatantly championed, was under siege by a new party with the innocuous name of the Middling Interest. Surprisingly, the candidate to lead the insurgency's charge had spent most of his life as a self-described "raving Federalist."[25]

To understand the transformation in political culture that occurred in Boston during the early nineteenth century, the political odyssey of this "raving Federalist" turned insurgent, Josiah Quincy, must be examined. Quincy's political career had many ups and downs which resulted in his remarkable political transformation from Federalism to third partyism. Whether he led the political and cultural realignments that occurred in Boston's ordinary citizenry, or whether it led him, is less important than acknowledging that the two became inseparably linked and were widely associated with each other. The political journey of Quincy reflects not only his personal odyssey but that of all the Bostonians who supported him.

Josiah Quincy stood at the epicenter of every contentious political battle waged in Boston and the state during the first three decades of the nineteenth century. Never hesitating to voice his often irreverent opinions, he maintained a reputation throughout his career as an individualistic and independent politician who did not fear retribution from any party elders. He first earned this reputation while serving as a member of the U.S. House of Representatives.

II • NEW ENGLAND FEDERALISM ON THE ATTACK

The Washington Benevolent Society and Turning Gardens into Republican Farms, 1800–1819

Federalism takes opium; Jacobinism gunpowder and rum.
—Fisher Ames to Thomas Dwight 1804

The morning after the devastating defeat of John Adams by Thomas Jefferson in the election of 1800, Federalism awoke to the disarming reality that it was powerless on the national level. The party lost its chief executive and both houses of Congress. Jefferson stalwart Albert J. Beveridge gloated that those remaining Federalists in Congress were simply a bunch of "grumbling . . . out of date gentlemen . . . mournful of a glorious past." Jefferson himself christened the lingering partisans "mere obstructionists," who would challenge his mandate in vain.[1] And in many ways both Beveridge's and Jefferson's appraisal of the battered Federalists was right. Even Federalist party warhorse from Dedham, Fisher Ames, scolded his party fellows after the election, professing that "Federalism takes opium; Jacobinism gunpowder and rum."[2] Indeed, during Jefferson's first term, congressional Federalists were reduced to complaining bitterly about the Louisiana Purchase and the wholesale reversals of the Adams administration's policies.

When Federalist Josiah Quincy began his eight-year tenure as Suffolk County's congressional representative in 1805, Jefferson savored his second term victory and seemed more popular than ever. Both the Senate and the House remained in the hands of the Republicans, and there seemed little the Federalist freshman from Boston could do. As his wife, Eliza, confessed to Abigail Adams in 1806, her husband confined his ambitions to "enjoy[ing] the satisfaction of preventing evil," but said that to "produc[e] good [was] beyond [his] power."[3]

Eliza's assessment of her husband's role in Congress proved overly optimistic. As a Congressman, Quincy failed and failed dramatically. Perhaps if "the little band of federalists," as Eliza described the minority position in Congress, had been more united the "evil" of Jeffersonian policies could have occasionally been checked; but internal differences within the party caused resentments between the younger and the older generations, dividing congressional Federalists.[4]

Having learned a harsh lesson from the Republican victors in 1800 and 1804, young Federalists began to practice oppositional politics in a much more pragmatic manner than their party elders had ever imagined. Quincy sided with this vanguard and its new approach to politics. As Harrison Gray Otis explained, Quincy was "the only man among us who had intended . . . to pursue politics as a profession."[5] This seemed vulgar to older members of the party, who thought government service should be restricted to benevolent, disinterested amateurs. The old guard distrusted the very notion of established parties. Although many were the beneficiaries of their own party's state and local organizations, these crusty old men despised what they saw as the corrupting influence party spirit inflicted on the great united family of America's revolutionary past. "Let not party-rage, private animosities, or self-interested motives succeed that religious attachment to the public weal which has brought us successful thus far," pleaded Boston traditionalist Jonathan Mason. If conspicuous partisanship became the primary basis for Federalism, what would distinguish it from the "Jacobin" Republicans? With Jefferson's reelection, younger Federalists rebelled and openly disagreed with the very premise of such a question. Harrison Gray Otis articulated New England's interest in the fresh Federalist approach: "If we mean to preserve the commonwealth and New England . . . our organization must be more complete and systematic. It must extend through every county and town, and an ample fund must be provided for the distribution of political truth." Old-guard Massachusetts stalwarts like George Cabot, Stephen Higginson, John Lowell, and Theodore Lyman looked on in utter dismay as younger Federalists like Otis and Sullivan established a highly effective party structure that would send the confirmed nontraditionalist Josiah Quincy to Washington.[6]

After serving only one year in the Massachusetts senate, Quincy, at age thirty-two, entered the House of Representatives with little political experience. His opinion of the Federalist traditionalists he met there was unmistakably negative. Writing to John Quincy Adams, he severely criticized the old guard as "cautious politicians, who are always prophets by retrospect; men who neither devise nor execute," and who were altogether ill equipped to challenge the majority position in Congress.[7] Often single-handedly, Congressman Quincy would overtly defy the old guard's party regimen and follow his own political instincts into uncharted and often dangerous waters. The result was a botched and embarrassing congressional career.

Three notable incidents point out his political naivete, his impetuosity, and his enthusiasm to stir still waters in order to strengthen his minority position. The first occurred in 1809. Characterizing Jefferson as a "dish of skim milk curdling at the head of our nation" on the House floor, Quincy demanded the president's impeachment just five weeks before Jefferson was to step down from office. In his January 25 speech before the House, Quincy accused Jefferson of corruption, directly linking the president to staffing problems in the Boston Custom House. Even House Federalists were appalled by the audacity of the charge, and Quincy's proposal was overwhelmingly defeated by a vote of 117 to his 1. Four years after the House vote, Henry Clay predicted that the Federalist from Suffolk County's act "shall live only in the treasonable annals" of history.[8]

When Quincy took to the floor to speak against Louisiana statehood on January 14, 1811, he was once again charged with treason, this time by his Republican opponents in Congress and much of the Boston press. "If this bill passes," Quincy threatened, "I declare it my deliberate conviction that the bond of this union is virtually dissolved: that the states are freed from their moral obligation: that as it will be the *right of all,* so it *will* become the *duty* of some, to prepare for a separation—*amicably* if they can: *forcibly* if they must."[9] In Boston, the Republican press promised that "the people of [Quincy's] own state would crush any rebellious movement . . . as quick and as effectively as they did the insurrection of Shays."[10] Despite Quincy's menacing claim, New England refused to secede from the Union once Louisiana was granted statehood.

Later that year, in the fall, Quincy concocted an ambitious scheme to reestablish Federalism as a national political force. Believing that the recent Republican clamor for war with England was merely saber rattling designed "to embarrass [New England] commerce and annihilate its influence," Quincy decided to push the issue by coming out in favor of war. His strategy rested on the assumption that war with Great Britain was an impossibility. By strengthening the position of the Republican "war hawks," as he dubbed them, Quincy believed he could drive a deep wedge between the prowar and the antiwar Republicans. This, he believed, would irreparably shatter Republicanism. On January 25, 1812, he supported a Republican war bill to strengthen the navy. In February, he voted with the war hawks to step up appropriations for armed conflict. On June 1, 1812, prowar Republicans achieved what Quincy had not believed possible—by a vote of 79 to 49 the House approved the president's declaration of war. Much to Quincy's horror, the war hawks' clamor for combat had been sincere. By severely underestimating the genuine prowar feeling in the House, Quincy contributed to provoking an armed conflict that would prove devastating to his region.[11]

As Fisher Ames sadly predicted for Quincy before Ames's own death in 1808, "I declared to you, I fear Federalism will not only die, but all rememberence of it be lost. As a party, it is still good for everything it ever was good for; that is to say, to cry 'fire' and 'stop thief,' when Jacobinism attempts to burn and rob. [Yet], [i]t never had the power to put out the fire, or to seize the thief."[12] Despite trying to defy Ames's judgment by employing Machiavellian techniques to strengthen his minority position in Congress, Quincy finally absorbed the fact that Ames's assessment of Federalism was accurate. Federalists had no place in Washington.

They had become exactly what Jefferson predicted—"mere obstructionists." "I feel ready . . . to throw myself out of the window, or into a horse pond, when I think of coming here [Washington] again," Quincy confessed in utter dismay to William Sullivan.[13]

In the fall of 1812, Quincy informed the Central Committee that he would decline a Federalist nomination to Congress if it was offered. Disregarding his wishes, the committee reassigned him to the post, but Quincy refused to accept. For eight miserable years in the House, he had been one of Federalism's most explosive and reactive operatives. His intricate and unsuccessful political stratagems had caused him to be ridiculed and spurned by his own party as well as the opposition. He had few friends in Washington, and the capital, during the early nineteenth century, was no more than a frontier town that Quincy and his wife hated. Writing to his wife on the eve of the War of 1812, he explained his "odd" position: "By some I am thought such a raving Federalist as to be shrewdly suspected of [treason]; by others that I am . . . in danger of turning Democrat [Republican]."[14]

Clearly, Quincy's congressional career merited such confusion. He had called for a popular president's impeachment; he had threatened New England secession over Louisiana's constitutional right to enter the Union; and he had gone against the antiwar sentiments of his constituents in a failed political scheme to destroy the Republican party. Quincy had always thought of himself as a professional politician in the Federalist cause, but his impulsive and erratic behavior in the House belied any sense of professionalism. Henry Clay's summation of Quincy's career held more truth than falsehood when he stated before the House that "[t]he gentleman from Massachusetts . . . has entertained us with Cabinet plots, Presidential plots which are conjured up in the gentleman's own perturbed imagination," and done little else.[15] Quincy's covert partisan adventures marked a man whose stubborn refusal to surrender his independent and often self-righteous personal campaigns for more reasonable solutions to the problems Republicanism caused in New England resulted in a highly unsuccessful and humiliating congressional career. "I left Washington," Quincy wrote in his 1813 personal journal, "with the feelings of a man quitting Tadmor in the Wilderness, 'where creeping things had possession of the palace, and foxes looked out the windows,' and sought the refuge in home, and in family."[16]

In March 1813 Quincy escaped from Washington and seemingly found more refuge in his family estate's gardens than with his family. According to both his son Edmund and his daughter Eliza, the ex-congressman transferred his enthusiasm for congressional partisan politics to an obsession with experimental farming. "[W]ith all the zeal of his ardent temperament," as Edmund put it, his father poured money and time into his agricultural experiments. Soiling cattle (a topic he wrote a book on), cultivating hedges, using root crops as cattle feed, and growing carrots were Quincy's particular specialties. As one historian argues, Boston's early-nineteenth-century elite often turned to the farm to resolve their contradictory notions of aristocracy and republicanism as embodied in the image of the sturdy New England farmer. Revolutionary ideals of equality clashed with the reality of an established, postrevolutionary ruling class based in the urban setting of Boston. Boston elites desperately tried to resolve the contradictory nature of their existence within a democracy by dabbling in the soil.[17]

If one of the most visible symbols of elite control—the country estate—could be manipulated to represent something more democratic in the popular mind, then the hypocrisy of a dominant "seated" gentry within a democratic society could be better hidden. The rub for Boston's landed gentry was how to go about implementing the perceptual change. George Cabot, the director of the Massachusetts Bank and leading old-guard Federalist, found the solution in cultivating potatoes instead of rare flowers on his Brookline estate; Thomas H. Perkins took time out from his work on the Federalist Central Committee and in the opium business to begin growing fruit; when he wasn't tallying his profits from the East Indies and China trade or raving against the atrocities of one Republican administration or another, Theodore Lyman experimented with bananas and pineapples at "the Vale," his estate in Waltham. And Josiah Quincy grew a particularly hardy breed of carrots.[18]

The idea was to shift the purpose and meaning of the country seat from a place of leisure to one of utility. The country estates, with their beautifully extravagant but useless gardens, were transformed into working farms. With the establishment of the Massachusetts Society for Promoting Agriculture and the Massachusetts Horticulture Society, patrician farmers institutionalized their new self-perception and pursued a bucolic form of noblesse oblige. The stated purpose of both the MSPA and the MHS was to provide Massachusetts' yeomanry with advanced farming techniques that were being discovered on patrician estates. In an ironic twist, Boston's Federalist aristocracy would return to the soil under the guise of Jeffersonian, agrarian democratic principles.[19]

Most of Boston's "book farmers" clearly were insincere about their conversion to functional agriculture. They gleaned a living not from the soil but from maritime commerce or manufacturing. True to the Hamiltonian economic agenda for progress and as high-ranking Federalists, the book farmers consistently fought America's agricultural interests. Most Boston elites involved in experimental farming saw it as a way to stave off popular criticism and, at best, to shore up the state's yeomanry for Federalism.[20]

Josiah Quincy viewed his estate differently. Perhaps because he was trying to gain some success as a farmer after his miserable failure as a congressman or, perhaps, sincerely driven by a passion to revolutionize hedge technology, between 1813 and 1820 Quincy dumped the family fortune into his experiments. Being "wholly occupied with thoughts of agriculture," as he explained himself, Quincy seriously jeopardized his family's financial security as he plowed more and more cash into his carrots, hedges, and root-crop cattle feed. As his son Edmund gently explained, his father had lost "more than it was at all convenient to him to lose," claiming the only profits culled from the family estate came from selling salt to the local fishermen—a venture his father had no interest in. Quincy's daughter Eliza, somewhat distressed, confessed to her dairy in 1820: "upon settling his account [her father] found that his expenses were exceeding his income. A fact that caused him anxiety with regard to future independence." Summing up the situation, Eliza declared: "farming experiments were the cause of this difficulty."[21]

By April, the Quincy's financial situation became so grave that they could no longer afford to lease their posh Boston home on Summer Street. Eliza was aghast. "[T]he only plan to be pursued," she reported to her diary, "was to reside at Quincy all the year now." Horrified because this meant "the exit of us from Boston Society," Eliza and her family prepared for a new, more isolated life as fallen gentry. However, Quincy's uncle, John Phillips, upon hearing the news, came to the family's rescue and provided them, free of charge, with a "modest" house on the corner of Hamilton Place and Tremont Street. Although Edmund remarked that their new residence "was not, in itself, so large or so good as that [they had] left," the Quincy family was spared the public mortification of social exile from the Hub of New England society and culture.[22]

Although Quincy spent much of the five years after his unfortunate congressional career in convalescence with his hedges, roots, and carrots, to the surprise of many he did remain engaged in politics. "I thought you would have died a peaceful political death, but I see it is not in your nature," Philadelphian Richard Peters noted as an aside to Quincy in a long letter detailing the proper uses for a particular variety of Newcastle thorn bushes.[23] When he had first returned to Boston in 1813, the Central Committee rewarded Quincy with a nomination to the state senate. "He is proverbial industrious," explained Harrison Gray Otis, "and though an occasional expression or two have served as catchwords to injure his popularity, I have no doubt that in th[e] Senate he would soon efface any petty prejudice existing against him, and be a very useful member."[24]

"Useful" may not be the most appropriate word. As Edmund Quincy explained, his father's "duties [in the senate] were confined to a few months out of the year, and were not of a very engrossing nature."[25] Instead, when not in his gardens, Quincy occupied himself with much more exciting extralegal party affairs. First as vice-president of the Washington Benevolent Society (WBS) from 1812 to 1815 and then as its president in 1816, he remained active in and contributed greatly to local Federalist party business.[26]

With the inevitability of war with Britain, the Boston chapter of the WBS was established in the downtown Exchange Coffee House on March 6, 1812. Although it had taken eight years and a declaration of war since he had first suggested such an organization, Harrison Gray Otis's proposal in 1804 for a "more complete and systematic" method to "extend through every county and town" the gospel of Federalism had finally been institutionalized and set into motion with the WBS. Its founding members—Nathan Appleton, Henry Dwight Sedgwick, Nathan Hale, Samuel Livermore Jr., Benjamin Russell, Thomas H. Perkins, Josiah Bradlee, Francis J. Oliver, and Lemuel Shaw, represented the local vanguard of Boston's Federalist Young Turks.[27] Influenced by their opposition to the war, the 1811 losses of the governors' seat and the General Court to Republicanism, and the ineptitude of Federalism's past organizational structure, these men astounded the Bay State's old guard by mimicking Republican political fraternities such as New York's Tammany. Under the auspices of "benevolence," the Boston chapter of the Washington Benevolent Society constructed a highly organized and effective arm of the Federalist party.[28]

The WBS's primary goal was to broaden the social base of party membership. Since 1800 Boston's population had steadily grown. By 1810 the town held 33,250 people, an increase from 1800 of over 9,000 people. The vast majority of Boston's new arrivals were young, semiskilled-to-skilled native men from the countryside who came to the Hub seeking their fortunes. Although the political persuasion of these men is not known, clearly the WBS was partially established to ensure that these new Bostonians would come into the Federalist fold. Indeed, society members tended to be young and semiskilled or skilled. The Boston chapter contained 44 laborers, 68 clerks, 296 shopkeepers, 153 professionals, and 309 mechanics. Codified into its constitution under Article 17, those who could not afford the modest initiation fee of two dollars were exempted and given free membership. Over one third of Boston's membership in 1814 were designated by the society as "Free Members."[29]

The WBS constitution declared that the society would "oppose all encroachments of Democracy, aristocracy or despotism . . . and with all our strength to oppose the establishment of any usurped power therein [we pledge to] alleviate the sufferings of unfortunate individuals, within the sphere of our personal acquaintances."[30] The "sphere of personal acquaintances" of the society proved extremely limited. In 1813 the WBS gave only $10 out of its total yearly expenditure of $1,721.70 to the widow of society member W. Reynolds. When Fred W. A. Brown applied for charity from the society in 1812, "it was found," according to the WBS minutes, "that he is not a member of the Society & consequently not entitled to relief."[31] According to the WBS's annual budgets, the income of the society either paid for partisan propaganda or went to speculative business ventures to turn a profit. The WBS managed its money in a fashion similar to a bank. It made loans and charged interest much more often than it issued charity. Many investments were lucrative but in 1815 the WBS found itself in financial trouble, running a deficit of $1,398.33 after one of its companies, Austin and Blanchard, went bankrupt.[32]

Fluid in structure, the WBS's administrative positions often rotated annually. Its leadership included a president, six vice-presidents, a treasurer, a vice-treasurer, a secretary, two assistant secretaries, and a standing committee of sixteen that decided upon who would and would not be accepted as members. Underneath this superstructure lay the heart and soul of the organization. Each of Boston's twelve wards held a committee of four who circulated WBS information, collected membership dues, recruited potential members, oversaw elections for the society's leadership, and reported relevant information from each ward to the standing committee. In turn, the standing committee reported to the WBS leadership, which relayed information directly to the Federalist Central Committee.[33]

By 1813 the Boston WBS boasted a membership of 1,500. That same year, it formed a committee to centralize and coordinate the efforts of all the WBS chapters throughout the country. Boston's highly organized system proved so effective that Federalists from all over New England began writing to the Boston chapter for copies of its constitution, advice, and organizational blueprints. A letter from Khilborn Whitman of Pembroke is typical of the flood of communications arriving at the Boston WBS headquarters: "[I]t is my wish to have a copy of it [the constitution] and . . . I will thank you for your opinion, on this kind, in every town in the County, the Officers of which, shall be the organs of communication to the county Society, & they the medium of intelligence to the Head Quarters of Good Principles—I am seriously of the opinion, that if this plan could become universal in each County in the State by next year, good men would be restored to their standing."[34] The Boston chapter sent organizational material to towns as close as Salem and as distant as Hallowell, Maine. One year after its founding, voter participation in the state gubernatorial race swelled by 13 percent, the majority of which voted Federalist. In 1812 Federalism recaptured the governor's seat—a position the party would hold until 1823.[35] In Portsmouth, New Hampshire, a budding Federalist, Daniel Webster, waited for his copy of the Boston chapter's constitution so he could draft one of his own.[36]

Partially due to the WBS's success, the society provoked the wrath of Boston's Republican press. The *Independent Chronicle* charged that "the '*Washington Benevolent Societies,*' so called, were established to answer the purpose of a political party, and that they are in direct opposition both to *Washington* and *Benevolence,* must be evident to every one who will give himself the trouble to review their conduct. The *fund,* said to be raised for *benevolent* purposes, is . . . expended in paying for *banners, votes, ribbands* [*sic*], and other vapid trumpery, to make up a show."[37]

The *Chronicle*'s assessment of the WBS's allocation of society funds proved accurate. In 1813, $101.61 went to pay the Federalist-leaning Boston Washington Artillery Company for firing cannons during a society festival. Other militias often employed by the WBS were the Boston Light Infantry, the Boston Hussars and the Winslow Blues. These militias provided WBS functions not only with great color but also with protection. After the 1812 prowar riots in Baltimore, where mobs attacked and killed several society members, the Boston branch heeded the advice of G. S. Steuart, the Maryland WBS secretary. Steuart, fearing for his life during the rioting, fled Baltimore for exile in Philadelphia. He provided the Boston branch with a detailed description of the Baltimore rioting and urged the Boston chapter to hire protection. Baltimore, Steuart claimed, had been "shamefully troddened under the foot by a brutal and licentious mob who exercise an alarming tyranny over the good people of Baltimore and its vicinity. [Society members] have fallen victims to the fury of a mob, and the treachery of the civil authority. The reign of terror and confusion," Steuart heralded, "still continues to agitate that infested city, where scenes of massacre and bloodshed have of late occurred." Taking no chances, the Boston chapter of the WBS had various militias on its payroll and placed WBS members in leadership positions. Certainly the militias would prove loyal to the WBS since they were well paid, but also, as Fisher Ames once had suggested, "let the popular and wealthy Federalists take commissions in the militia, and try to win the men [for Federalism]."[38]

The WBS functioned solely to broaden and deepen the Federalist party's social base. The *Boston Patriot* accused it of attracting "the neediest and meanest people."[39] WBS celebrations featured liquor, mummery, and rowdiness. After one Boston banquet, drunken society members stumbled through the streets causing havoc. "[T]hey were exceedingly noisy and sang songs and swore oaths, and did commit other acts of folly and wickedness," explained one observer. "Yea, they took the vessels of glass which contained the wine and other liquors, and did throw them at the heads of each other. . . . And the watchmen who guarded the city, hearing the uproar, rushed in among them. . . . And some fled one way and some another, and some were lying motionless on the ground like men slain in fighting—passed-out drunk."[40]

Although old-guard Federalists were disgusted by such unruly behavior, in many ways such political antics were exactly what was needed to reinvigorate the party. The founders of the society understood this from the WBS's inception. As the preamble of its constitution declared, "We hold it to be always a right & sometimes a duty, to assemble & deliberate upon the state of public affairs to acquire & impart knowledge & to increase the ardor of our patriotism by the warmth of our social attachments."[41] In the rough-and-tumble urban culture of early-nineteenth-century Boston, what could be more effective in "increas[ing] the ardor" of Federalist-style patriotism than a boisterous party? Here the lowly mechanic met the silk-stocking merchant on the common ground of gluttony. In this, at least, they were equals.

To judge by the reaction of the Republican press, the party of Jefferson genuinely feared the society. According to Federalist operatives outside of Boston, Republicans had begun intercepting and destroying communications between various New England societies. WBS member Otis Williams of Easton Massachusetts warned the Boston chapter's first president, Arnold Welles, that "owing to the treachery of some of our political opponents [s]ome person has stopped the papers [sent by you] by some means or other as there is very violent opposition to the formation of the Society in this town." Refusing to trust the mail service for matters so important, Williams sent his warning to Welles via courier. William Gordon of Keene, New Hampshire, had similar problems and also refused to use the mail. Instead, he sent his own son all the way from Keene to request a copy of the Boston chapter's constitution.[42]

When the WBS contacted Quincy in 1812 after its first meeting at the Boston Exchange Coffee House, he still served in Congress and had not yet heard of the organization. "Although I have no previous delineation of the plan of the institution, of which you inform me, I am elected Vice President," Quincy explained to Lemuel Shaw; "the object expressed in its designation and the venerable and ever cherished name associated with it permit no hesitation. I therefore accept the honor."[43] The Washington Benevolent Society would gradually lure Quincy out of the isolation, safety, and protection of his beloved gardens and into the public arena again. The society's inclusive approach to politics meshed well with Quincy's pragmatic style of politics. The Washington Benevolent Society would provide Quincy with the confidence he had lost in Congress. More important, his involvement with the WBS would expose him to an urban constituency of lower-to-middling folk who would supply him a popular base for new and untried political ventures.

Although rain threatened to ruin the Washington Benevolent Society's April 30, 1813, celebration, the heavens held as some 2,000 disciplined but joyous WBS members and their supporters paraded through Boston's streets. Just weeks before the celebration, Federalist Caleb Strong, running on a "peace ticket," thoroughly thrashed the Republican candidate for governor, Joseph B. Varnum, by 10,421 votes. The 2,000-member WBS parade was a show of force demonstrating the potency of Federalism and antiwar sentiment in the state. Members from throughout Massachusetts converged on Boston to participate in the ceremonies that honored Washington's inauguration. Marching ahead of 270 uniformed "school boy Federalists," as Edmund Quincy remembered, were 328 armed militia-men of the Winslow Blues, the Boston Light Infantry, the Boston Washington Artillery Company, and the Boston Hussars. Behind them, some 1,000 loyal Federalists and WBS members from the rank and file marched four abreast, waving banners to the Boston throng who watched from sidewalks and balconies. Eliza Quincy vividly described the broad social composition of the typical WBS parade: "[R]epresentives of all the Trades drawn on sleds with appropriate standards, and carrying their tools [marched]. The bricklayers were building a house, they broke their bricks and worked busily. The carpenters were erecting a temple of Peace. The printers worked a small press, struck off handbills . . . and threw them among the crowd. The bakers, hatters, paper-makers, blockmakers, etc., etc. had each their appropriate insignia." At the head of the procession, mounted on a white stallion and serving as the Boston Hussars' newly elected captain, Josiah Quincy led the column to the Old South Church for a huge banquet and orations.[44]

Trying to discredit the parade, the Republican *Independent Chronicle* reported that the WBS parade was racially integrated, "including the gentlemen from [Boston's] Negro-Hill." The report chastised Quincy, likening him to his horse, Bayard. The children of the parade, argued the equally Republican *Boston Yankee,* had been "educated like Colts to the menagerie, to be bridled with restraints, to be saddled with prejudices, and jockeyed about by party spirit. When trained sufficiently in this charity school, they are to be bound out to Faction to learn the trades of Sedition and Treason."[45]

The *Yankee*'s charge of treason, though perhaps a bit overstated, held some truth. William Sullivan privately explained that the WBS was created in 1812 to block prowar fervor throughout the country and promote antiwar sentiments as well as to buttress Federalist partisanship. Indeed, the Boston Hussars were trained by a member of the WBS's standing committee, Michael Roulstone, a local riding instructor, and were founded during the early stages of hostilities between the United States and Great Britain in 1810 by wealthy antiwar Federalists. Their loyalty to the Madison administration was in doubt. Many wondered which side the militia would take if Britain invaded Massachusetts, and the Hussars did little to allay such suspicions. The symbolic pageantry employed by the militia clearly delineated its political leanings. Hussar uniforms were modeled after those of the French Imperial Guard, and the militia's most prized possession (which it shared with the WBS) was the gorget Washington had "heroically" worn as a British officer during the French and Indian War. According to Edmund Quincy, the Hussars costume represented "their dislike [of] Bonaparte and all his works." In April of 1813, with the United States at war with Great Britain, the people of Boston undoubtedly interpreted the WBS's great procession as a massive demonstration of the antiwar, antiadministration, and anti-Republican sentiment in New England.[46] If the symbolic message of the parade was missed by those who observed the procession, after Josiah Quincy's partisan speech in Old South Church any misunderstanding would be put to rest.

"This war, the measure that preceded it, and the mode of carrying it on, are undeniably Southern and Western policy," Quincy announced to a full audience. "[I]n the eyes of reason and common sense we [of New England] are slaves, . . . slaves to no very desirable masters. . . . The new States govern the old, the unsettled, the settled; the interests of the emigrants prevail over those of the ancient natives; a black population overbalances the white. . . . [W]ilderness legislators . . . control . . . the destinies of [New Englanders], paralyzing all their interests and darkening all their prospects." According to Quincy, "this great and ancient and once proud, but now . . . humbled Commonwealth, has absolutely no more weight in the national scale than a specie of beings [black slaves]." "Remember," Quincy reiterated, "the very blacks of the Southern States are equal in weight, in the political scale, to the whole State of Massachusetts."[47]

By drawing direct connections between national policy and local anxieties,

Quincy had designed his speech brilliantly. Populated with African slaves and European immigrants, the South and West had pushed the nation into war against the wishes and interests of New England. Not only was this an assault on the region's honor and authority, but the war, Quincy charged, would transform each household economy in New England from one of happy prosperity to a "darkening [of] all their prospects." Hardworking and free New England would be forced into economic subjugation by western and southern slaveholders. With one major exception, the ideology Quincy articulated would, in fifty years, prove remarkably similar to the foundations of the second Republican party's free-labor outlook. The exception rested in Quincy's skeptical opinion of manufacturing which future free-labor doctrine embraced. Throughout his life, Quincy staunchly refused to invest in manufacturing and remained tied to the state's maritime interests.[48] Also, Quincy's WBS speech hinted once again at New England secession.

Although the speech predictably received favorable reviews from Boston's Federalist organs, the Republican press lambasted him. "Can any man of sober reflection," asked the *Independent Chronicle*, "attend to a declaimer acting in the character of a disciple of Washington, while he [Quincy] exhibits himself in the boisterous attitude of a manic?—Foaming, . . . beating the air, . . . acting the part of a *mad Tom*, and exposing his folly by rant and arrogance." How could he have so insulted the Bay State by claiming "that the Representatives from Massachusetts were no more weight in Congress than so many *black* cattle?"[49] Despite such harsh criticism, the average Bostonian in 1813 probably would have disagreed with the *Chronicle*'s assessment of Quincy's speech. The congressional vote for war had fallen sharply along regional lines, all of New England's representatives, including twenty Republicans, having voted against the war.[50] Also, the effect of war would, in fact, be damaging to New England's economy, just as Quincy claimed.

The war made some Boston ship captains wealthy as privateers and hastened the transfer of New England maritime money into new manufacturing ventures. Also, Boston banks with sound money made profitable war loans to the federal government. Nevertheless, the Bay State's main enterprise, maritime commerce, dramatically declined because of the war. Beginning in 1810, and not recovering until the war's end in 1815, the actual tonnage of shipping in custom houses in Massachusetts and Boston dwindled to new lows that would not be matched until 1855. Fishing, a lucrative pursuit for many coastal Massachusetts towns since the 1790s, also found itself in serious trouble. The collapse of Boston's largest sector of the maritime enterprise significantly touched the lives of many average Bostonians.[51]

As Bostonian George Ticknor explained, "Commerce and trade were dead; the whole population was idle." According to Francis Bassett, Boston "industry was paralyzed, the music of the saw and hammer was no longer heard, and a general gloom seemed to hang over the town." In Governor Strong's assessment, "the influence of *Massachusetts*, and of the Eastern States . . . is lost, and the systems of commercial restriction, of War, and conquest, fatal to their interests, and outrageous to their feelings, are founded in ruins." Editor Joseph T. Buckingham, who went bankrupt during the war, reminisced that, in the "business of publishing, *fifty* barely live above poverty and die in possession of little more than enough to pay the joiner for a coffin and the sexton for a grave." Although his problems had little to do with the war, the 1811 imprisonment of Boston's premier architect and chairman of the town selectmen, Charles Bulfinch, for debt symbolized for Bostonians their vulnerability. "[T]hose, who are benefitted by the enormous abuses [of the war policy]," heralded the *Boston Spectator,* "are so few, compared with the great mass of the community, who are suffering beyond calculation or endurance. . . . [The war] arrests their . . . necessary pursuits, robs them of their property, and exposes even life to peril."[52] Clearly, prewar impediments to commerce and the war itself intensified laboring Boston's uncertainties about its future. Politically, these insecurities were easily exploited by the Washington Benevolent Society to attack Republicanism while strengthening the ranks of Federalism in Boston and throughout the state.

In October of 1814 every Bostonian in the General Court unanimously voted in favor of an antiwar convention to be held in Hartford. Suffolk County's representatives adamantly opposed the war, convinced as they were that the conflict sucked the lifeblood out of the state. Overall, the General Court decided 260 in favor of the convention to 90 opposed. Only the Norfolk County delegation unanimously voted against the resolution. The majority of every other district's representative delegation to the state legislature voted for the convention. In the November state elections, a month before the Hartford Convention met, the Federalist slate swept the state. John Holmes, the Republican leader of the senate and the most vocal against the resolution and for the war, was defeated at the hands of a Federalist.[53] As the General Court's overwhelming support for the Hartford Convention indicates, the antiwar and sectional appeal that Federalists such as Quincy espoused significantly strengthened the party throughout the state.

In December of 1814 Massachusetts sent twelve Federalist delegates to Hartford with the overwhelming approval of the General Court and the governor. Although Quincy voted in favor of the convention in the senate, he was not chosen as a delegate. As Quincy's son recalled, the Federalist leadership was "afraid to trust his [Quincy's] impetuous temperament and fiery earnestness." Such fears were justified. In one of his first acts as a state senator, Quincy challenged what he saw as the blatant hypocrisy of his Federalist colleagues. Before Quincy's arrival in the senate, the General Court routinely bestowed official state honors on naval commanders who successfully protected American waters from British warships. Quincy viewed such actions by his fellow antiwar Federalists as two-faced. When the senate attempted to pass a resolution honoring the "gallantry and good conduct of Captain [James] Lawrence, in the capture of a British brig of war," Quincy rose from his chair. "[I]n a war like the present, waged without justifiable cause and prosecuted in a manner which indicates that conquest and ambition are its real motives," Quincy explained, "it is not becoming a moral and religious people to express any approbation of military or naval exploits."[54]

Predictably, the Republican papers charged Quincy with "moral treason." John Holmes, having not yet been displaced from the General Court, demanded that Quincy's remarks be struck from the minutes. Even some leading Federalists found Quincy's purist stand irritating. These legislators saw no harm in tipping their hats to American bravery when it was merited while still maintaining an antiwar position. Thus, when the delegates to the Hartford Convention were chosen, as Edmund Quincy explained, the Federalist leadership "thought that [Quincy] would represent too well the spirit of those who demanded the Convention. He always described the Convention," Edmund remembered, "as 'a Tub to the Whale,' as a dilatory measure to amuse the malcontents [like himself] and make them believe that something was doing for their relief, and keep them quiet." Nothing would come of the convention, Quincy told a friend, except an insignificant "GREAT PAMPHLET."[55]

With General Andrew Jackson's unnecessary victory in New Orleans and the Treaty of Ghent, Quincy's prediction proved only half true. Vilified after the war, those who took part in the Hartford Convention became marked men—seen by most of the nation as secessionists and traitors. In this sense, the convention *had* done something of great significance: it severely damaged the reputation of the Federalist party throughout the nation. After 1815, throughout most of the country, to be called a Federalist was a dire insult. An Indiana man successfully sued for $1,000 in damages after being accused by another of being a Federalist. "Indeed," explained a friend of North Carolina Federalist Duncan Cameron, "the word Federalist alone without the aid of expletives represents to [the people's] affrighted imaginations every thing that is base and infamous."[56] Only in New England did the party continue to enjoy success, but within four years of the Treaty of Ghent even the stronghold of Boston would waver.

During the economic crisis generated by the War of 1812, the Federalist party had proved highly effective in exposing the root cause of the Commonwealth's financial problems. Employing the Washington Benevolent Society, as we have seen, the antiwar, anti-Republican party message resonated throughout the state, strengthening Federalist partisanship. In addition to this, in Boston, the decline in commerce was augmented by a rise in urban development largely funded by wealthy Federalists like Harrison Gray Otis and William Sullivan. Merchant ships may have been rotting in Boston Harbor, but new improvement projects were underway in the town. During the Embargo of 1807, workers began to rebuild India and Long wharfs; the erection of Central Wharf started in the midst of the war and proved so extravagant that it was not completed until 1816; and Harrison Gray Otis's Mill Pond Corporation began filling in the northern cove of the Shawmut peninsula in 1807.[57] Such development helped offset the negative effects of the embargoes and the war for the town's population and had direct political implications. Spreading its wealth, Federalism's Boston leadership appeared sensitive to the broader population's financial needs.

Some three years after the war, with the depression of 1819, Federalist rhetoric would seem stale and its coffers fastened tight. Unlike its response between 1807 through 1815, the party proved ill equipped to deal with the economic and political turmoil of Boston in 1819. Although the WBS persisted until 1824, the organization suffered from financial mismanagement, and its overt partisanship seemed anachronistic during the "Era of Good Feelings." As the newly elected president of the WBS in 1816, Josiah Quincy successfully reduced the deficit the society incurred in 1815, yet membership levels steadily declined. Nevertheless, the WBS's ability during the War of 1812 to reenergize the Federalist party by capitalizing on Massachusetts' antiwar sentiments and forging an activist anti-Republican coalition proved to be a great political success. The WBS proficiency illustrated the power to be gained by inclusionary politics.[58] By 1819, in the midst of economic and political chaos, the Federalist leadership seemed to have forgotten this and came to be regarded by many Bostonians as an exclusive "junto" set on maintaining its political and economic dominance at the expense of the people. Josiah Quincy would be spared such condemnation.

III • MILITIAMEN, DEBTORS, DOWNEASTERNERS, AND "DEMIGODS"

The Ingredients for Insurgent Activism and Federalism on the Defensive

I always told you, Mr. Lincoln, that I was the most of a *republican*.
—Josiah Quincy to Levi Lincoln Jr., 1821

The financial panic of 1819 affected Bostonians much more severely than the economic problems the town faced during the embargoes and the war. As a consequence of the depression hundreds of businesses failed, causing widespread unemployment in Boston. In 1823 the *North American Review* reported that "thousands [of] mechanics" were out of work due to the numerous bankruptcies within the city's mercantile and manufacturing sectors.[1] In June 1822 alone, forty-two petty merchants in Boston stopped payment on their debts and faced jail time. In May, June, and July of that same year, 100 Boston businesses, estimated to be worth a total of $4,000,000, went under.[2] More and more people were being sent to Boston's almshouse, and many, for the first time, were "respectable" citizens who had fallen on hard times.[3]

In 1820 the first copy of the *Debtor's Journal* circulated around town. The "Association of Gentlemen" who edited the *Debtor's* announced that their overall goals were "to subdue aristocracy and promote our freedom and happiness, as Americans." The *Debtor's* demanded a political response to the growing numbers of people imprisoned for debt. It attacked the state's debtor's laws through the press and in petitions to the General Court. According to the journal, "our debtors' laws are extremely oppressive to the poor debtors. . . . [T]hey only serve as rods in the hands of tyrants to torture the unfortunate, while the more independent debtors have it in their power to escape the lash." "Viewing this," announced the *Debtor's* editors, "as a growing evil, and as repugnant to the laws of liberty and equality, [we] deem the subject worthy of legislative action."[4]

Accumulating a remarkable total of 4,000 signatures, debtor advocates twice petitioned the state legislature for reform. They asked that work furloughs for imprisoned debtors be extended to include the whole of Boston instead of the traditional one- or two-block circumference around the debtor prison. The General Court responded by debating the issue but refused to act. On September 23, 1820, the *Debtor's* reported that "[t]he inhabitants of this town, or a majority of the legal voters, have petitioned for the limits of the prison to be extended over the whole town. By the influence of a petty remonstrance of 120 names, the petition has been rejected." Having no other recourse, debtor advocates filed suit against the town. "The petitioners, finding themselves attacked by a small, though spirited opposition [in the General Court]," reported the *Debtor's*, "immediately employed two gentlemen of the bar to defend their cause; and, (what is uncommon for Americans) were conquered by an *inferior* force." The debtor advocates had employed lawyer, Republican operative, and future coeditor of the *Jackson Republican* Henry Orne to represent them in the Court of Sessions for the County of Suffolk in September of 1820. The attempt to reform the laws failed in the courts, yet the *Debtor's Journal* continued to be printed for another year, keeping the issue of debtor's law in the public eye.[5]

The debtor movement in Boston is significant because of its advocacy for legislative reforms and its identification of an oppressive moneyed aristocracy that threatened popular conceptions of democracy. "The rich man," heralded the *Debtor's Journal,* "is pondering over hoarded wealth, and devising means to save and increase it, while the real patriot, the man of honesty, is meditating upon . . . the means . . . to make men equal and happy." The debtor movement focused on class inequity—a particularly timely and popular theme for many trying to survive in depression-ravaged Boston. "With a sincere desire to . . . subdue aristocracy and promote . . . freedom and happiness," the movement helped redefine Boston's political standard by injecting class issues into the political dialogue—issues that, unlike the economic crisis surrounding the War of 1812, the Federalist leadership refused to address.[6]

As the numbers of those imprisoned for debt grew in Boston, the conservative Federalist organ, the *Columbian Centinel,* found it could no longer completely ignore the debtors. The paper gave the issue credence by running an editorial debate. Although the *Centinel* stated that the existing laws "favored the honest and enterprising merchant, and show no mercy to the rogue and [are] therefore much needed in this country," the paper also ran a countereditorial, which described "the present severe laws against insolvent debtors as remnant of *barbarism,* as *un-Christian,* and as *ineffectual.*" The *New England Galaxy*'s editor, Joseph T. Buckingham, no stranger to bankruptcy and debt, actively supported the movement in his paper.[7]

Having been born in Windham, Connecticut, to a poor family, Buckingham was an autodidact who aspired to become a master printer. In 1796, at age seventeen, he secured a printing apprenticeship in New Hampshire before moving to Massachusetts where he worked for the *Greenfield Gazette* and then in the printing offices of Andrew White and William Butler in Northampton. Being dissatisfied with his position and filled with ambition, Buckingham left for Boston in 1800 to make his mark in the state capital. Within weeks of his arrival, Buckingham landed a job working for the city's largest printing press, Thomas and Andrews. Impressed with Buckingham's printing skill, Thomas and Andrews in 1805 handed the firm over to Buckingham to manage. That same year, Thomas and Andrews offered to sell their press to him. Buckingham jumped at the chance but quickly fell into debt. Soon he lost his press and resorted to teaching school and overseeing the printing firm of West and Richardson to make ends meet. Despite his failure, he had worked in publishing for twenty-one years and had become an expert printer, editor, and writer. These were the qualities that led prominent freemason Samuel L. Knapp to come to Buckingham when he wanted to establish a weekly in Boston. In 1817 the first copies of Buckingham's new venture, the *New England Galaxy and Masonic Magazine,* were distributed throughout Boston. The paper catered to the city's large numbers of skilled workers and mechanics. Although the *Galaxy* promised to avoid "all partizanship [*sic*]," with the panic of 1819 and fears of going bankrupt once again Buckingham refused to stay silent. Between 1820 and 1822, in a flurry of editorials, the *Galaxy* attacked the Federalist-dominated legislature for its stubborn support of the old debtor's laws, which the paper described as reminiscent of the "barbarism of former times."[8]

Picking up the crusade when the *Debtor's Journal* went bankrupt, the *Galaxy* kept debt reform alive in the public mind. On national issues, the *Galaxy* was decidedly Federalist, but Buckingham took great care to keep his paper out of the hands of the Federalist Central Committee. On local issues, such as debt reform, Buckingham assumed a decisively independent and individualistic view. As one appreciative reader explained in a letter to Buckingham, "You have not only been bold enough to assail the central committee—a knot of aristocrats—but you have ventured to attack aristocracy itself. . . . Your paper remains alone unsubdued. Bribery, flattery, cowardice and corruption are the means by which your editorial brethren have been drawn into the monied aristocracy." Buckingham's commitment to maintaining an independent voice proved so successful that the *Galaxy* held a remarkably high subscription rate of over 1,000 and enjoyed a loyal readership.[9]

Buckingham imitated the innovative class-based editorial approach of the *Debtor's Journal,* charging that the General Court "is so lost to humanity and common sense as to wish that the poor man should be punished for his poverty by even a single hour's imprisonment. . . . Let the swindler who hides his wealth for the rightful owners and laughs at [the debtor's] disappointments and losses starve, die and rot in his dungeon." The "*knavish rich,*" the *Galaxy* argued, who live "in affluence, [and] bring up a son or two at college, and a daughter in *elegant* and *fashionable* idleness," were unfairly protected by the current laws, while the "*honest poor*" suffered imprisonment.[10]

As more and more Bostonians failed to make ends meet in the depressed economy, popular opposition to the debtor laws heightened political awareness and galvanized Boston against what it viewed as an unjust Federalist aristocracy that ruled from the cold towers of the General Court. Although the debtor movement had discerned a politically charged and consequential concern in Boston, this one-issue movement proved too narrow to construct a viable oppositional third party that could disrupt Boston's traditional Federalist political structure.

The depression spawned another reform movement that emerged largely from the same social base as the debtor advocacy. In the midst of depression, many artisans, journeymen, mechanics, truckmen, and laborers began to call for the abolition of the state's militia requirement laws. These skilled and semiskilled laborers relied on a steady stream of task-oriented work to maintain economic solvency and independence. To be forced to leave the shop or a contracted job for militia duty could mean financial disaster for this sector of Boston's independent labor force—especially in the hostile economic environment caused by the depression. Reminiscing, Buckingham described the deep resentment the law provoked and the extent to which poorer people tried to avoid service. Describing Henry Emmons, a journeyman friend, Buckingham explained that "[a]t a time when every man in Massachusetts between the ages of eighteen and forty-five were obliged to perform military duty, or suffer the penalty of refusal, he [Emmons] suffered imprisonment for his obstinacy, and in order to escape further annoyance for similar cause he assumed the dress and probably adopted the doctrines of the Friends."[11]

Men such as Emmons were deeply insecure about their solvency, and popular opinion mounted against the Massachusetts militia laws that they believed to be oppressive, unnecessary, and a profound economic burden. Serving in the militia required one to have a functional rifle, pay for powder and shot, and buy uniforms (many of which were quite elaborate and expensive), as well as train for days at a time with no financial compensation and take orders from an officer corps that was accurately perceived as being exclusively composed of wealthy elites. The militiamen correctly suspected that the militias were used by the Federalist party to indoctrinate them to the Federalist cause.[12]

Adding to both the frustration of those forced to serve and the energy of the movement was the militia law's class-based exemption policy. All clergy, doctors, schoolmasters, those in public service (elected and appointed), justices of the peace, secondary school and college students, as well as anyone the governor deemed, were not required to serve or pay for their exemption. "Every dandy," complained the *Galaxy,* "who is afraid of a gun [and] can push himself into the governor's presence, and help himself at his table, gets a commission as a justice of the peace, and laughs at his neighbor, who has to shoulder the musket. . . . The truth is," the *Galaxy* concluded, "there is nothing *reasonable* in the system; and there never will be til the whole is renovated, and established on principles of equality."[13] The requirement to serve in the military during peacetime and while a national depression gutted Boston's economy angered the militiamen. Families suffered while sons and fathers, forced to postpone work often for weeks at a time, drilled far away from home. With little or no income during these periods, family debt naturally accumulated and fears of imprisonment loomed.

Identifying a direct link between debtors and militiamen, Buckingham adopted the militia reform movement and used his editorial skill to splice it with the debtor's movement. According to his *Galaxy,* "performance of military duty is considered a hardship. . . . It is a tax, which is most unwillingly paid . . . [T]he military tax is paid by the poor" only. Then, squarely linking the debtor's plight with that of the militiamen, and employing the antiaristocratic rhetoric inherent in both movements, the *Galaxy* charged that "[t]he laborer, whose daily tasks suppl[y] but a pitiful morsel for the support of his family, is called upon for the same sum as the nabob who is worth million[s]. He is driven from his employment, and trained to the use of arms [and] for the defence of what? Of nothing that he can call his own—of the palace and treasures of his rich neighbor."[14]

The Federalist *Columbian Centinel* responded in 1820 to attacks on the militia system, stating that "[f]ree men ought ever to consider the privilege of bearing arms an *honor* not a *tax.*" Few if any lesser Bostonians had the financial luxury to agree. In a three-month period during that same year, 100 businesses failed in Boston and the prisons were filling up with debtors.[15] By spring 1820, the militia reform movement organized a statewide petition drive and presented its recommendation for the abolition of the law to the General Court. Much like its response earlier that year to debt reform petitions, the legislature ignored the citizens' call for reform.[16]

Although the Federalist party's *Centinel* continued to defend the existing law, widespread criticism steadily mounted within Boston. In part due to the General Court's consistent refusal to even address the instructions of the people—let alone follow them—political tensions based on lower-class animosity toward the "FEW" heightened over both militia reform and debt imprisonment. By the opening months of 1821, Boston's political landscape was ripe for an insurgency that could integrate both issues within an overarching doctrine that heralded the injustice of popular subjugation to aristocratic rule.

Since the state was solidly Federalist, simply being a Federalist no longer automatically defined a legislator's position on a given policy. Internal squabbles notwithstanding, the last word always came from the Central Committee, which demanded compliance with its final ruling. When Quincy and other younger Federalist party operatives had challenged the conventional wisdom of the party elders with the Washington Benevolent Society, the Central Committee eventually accepted the idea and sanctioned the WBS due to its effectiveness in strengthening the popular appeal of the party—something it desperately needed at the time. Had the committee rejected the society, the whole idea would have been scrapped and those Federalists who supported it, had they not fallen in line, drummed out of the party. Massachusetts Federalism proved flexible, but only to a point—and that point rested with the Central Committee.[17]

By 1819 trouble brewed not only in the Federalist party's popular base but also within sectors of its elite-based, partisan foundation. The political activities initiated by Josiah Quincy in 1819 are representative of the predicament Federalism faced. Quincy's role within the Federalist party drastically changed once he returned from Washington and began focusing on local issues as a state senator. When serving in the United States Congress, Quincy could clearly define his enemies along partisan lines. During the "Virginia Dynasty's" rule in Washington, the Federalist party was clearly the underdog, and Quincy enjoyed the luxury of reacting against Republican policy. Once in the General Court, the issues for Quincy became much more complicated. Although, at first, he did not distinguish himself from other partisan Federalists in any significant way as a state senator, the issues that arose in 1819 led him to a role of activism, one at loggerheads with the party leadership.

By 1819 Quincy had alienated himself from the committee and lost its support over Maine's separation from the state of Massachusetts. The Central Committee's Otis, Sullivan, and Perkins viewed separate statehood for Maine as an effective means to purge the state of the meddlesome problem of downeast Republicans in the General Court. Without Maine, one Federalist chieftain privately remarked, Massachusetts would become "a snug little Federal[ist] state for the rest of our lives."[18]

Quincy strongly disagreed. "On the question of the Separation of Maine," his daughter explained, "he was begged to vote with his party, but he chose to stand alone, against a measure which reduced Massachusetts from the rank of a great State" to a minor one. Indeed, Quincy worried that significant national representation within the U.S. House of Representatives would be lost if the state split in two. According to Quincy, if the Maine district was allowed sovereignty, Massachusetts on the federal level would lose its flagship status as the premier northern state in "opposition to Southern predominance." Quincy also thought abandoning Maine's loyal Federalists was an act of irresponsibility on the part of the Central Committee. The downeast minority Federalist position would be pointlessly served up and quickly devoured by the ravenous appetite of Maine's Republican majority. To Quincy, the Central Committee's unilateral decision to sponsor the Maine bill reeked of excessive partisanship. To profoundly weaken the power and status of Massachusetts, making it more vulnerable to its southern enemies, simply to reinforce Federalism locally seemed to Quincy a reckless and perilous act. He even doubted whether Federalism would be strengthened by the move. Would not the people interpret Federalism's adamant support of the bill as he did—as a dangerously petty partisan gambit? Would not, in the end, the Massachusetts citizenry reject the party when it recognized the true motivation behind splitting the state in two? For Quincy, the very substance of his party was at stake. Disturbed by what he saw as the wrongheaded course his party was taking, Quincy privately warned the Central Committee that its scheme to fortify the party would backfire. His counsel was ignored. The leadership would continue to work for Maine's separation. When the question came to the senate floor, according to Quincy's son, he "resisted the passage . . . with all the energy of his character," which was formidable.[19]

In June 1819 Quincy stood with the Republican leadership by actively leading the legislative opposition to the Maine bill in the General Court. First, he unsuccessfully tried to bury the proposal in a senate committee that would review the question of whether any bill advocating separation should first be approved by referendum before reaching the General Court. His motion was defeated by a senate vote of 24 to 12. Doggedly pursuing his position, Quincy changed tactics by presenting an amendment to the measure that would require two thirds of the Maine district's electorate to vote in favor of separation before the bill returned to the legislature for final consideration. This too was rejected. Despite his efforts, the Maine bill would come to a final vote in the senate on June 15.[20]

Having exhausted all parliamentary tactics to prevent the measure from reaching the floor, Quincy fell back on personal persuasion. He spoke against the bill for two hours. The Boston *Daily Advertiser* reported that the speech was "able, clear and forcible" but did not sway the senate. Quincy's major problem was the Central Committee's strong support for the bill, which it had a hand in drafting. Finding its plans complicated by Quincy's obstinacy, the Central Committee found a worthy proponent in Federalist operative from Essex, Leverett Saltonstall, who rose to the senate floor in response to Quincy's appeal and delivered an equally long and more persuasive oration for the bill. When the bill finally came to a vote, Quincy stuck to his convictions and cast his vote with a bizarre coalition of Maine Federalists and Massachusetts Republicans that lost to an even more peculiar coalition of bitter traditional enemies; Maine Republicans and Massachusetts Federalists outvoted Quincy's forces by a margin of two to one. In a last-ditch effort, Quincy persuaded a Boston representative to introduce his amendment for a downeast referendum to the lower house when the bill arrived there on June 16. By a vote of 83 to 168, the motion for Quincy's amendment died in the house, and the next day the representatives voted overwhelmingly in favor of Maine's separation. With Federalist Governor John Brooks's endorsement of the bill on June 19, not only had Maine gained its first step toward statehood but Quincy, by his persistent opposition, had forfeited his standing within the Federalist party.[21]

At the time of legislative debates, the general electorate seemed largely apathetic to Maine statehood. Within two years of separation, however, the Boston press ran editorial after editorial chastising those individual Massachusetts legislators who had so easily allowed their downeast brethren to break off. According to one observer, "the general feeling was one of regret at a decision which it had become too late to reverse."[22] Some three years after separation, the independent *Bostonian and Mechanics Journal,* which rivaled only the *Galaxy* in its lower-to-middling-class readership, argued, as Quincy had during the debates, that the Central Committee of "the 'federal[ist] party' . . . favored the separation of Maine, in order that the Government of Massachusetts might longer remain in their hands." The *Bostonian* accused "the ranks of aristocracy" of tricking the people for their own selfish, partisan interests and—though after the fact—it now stood with Quincy against separation.[23]

The immediate political ramifications of Quincy's energetic and stubborn defiance of the Central Committee's standing orders were severe and came at great personal cost to his political ambitions. Before the Maine bill debates, he had been slated by the Central Committee to fill Eli P. Ashmun's U.S. Senate seat once Ashmun retired. After his stand on the Maine bill, the committee was so angered by Quincy's defiance that it rejected his nomination to the Senate. Quincy's punishment did not end there. For the first time since 1813, the committee's nominating list for the state senate in 1820 did not include Quincy's name. In his place, the Federalist leadership nominated one of its own, insider William Sullivan. The committee publicly justified dropping Quincy on the grounds that he "has not received for several years as many votes as the other senators had who were on the federal[ist] Ticket." Onetime Federalist lieutenant governor and Quincy's uncle, William Phillips, was outraged and expressed "strong indignation at the ingratitude of the party." "I declare," Phillips confided to Quincy's wife, "if I was Mr. Quincy I would go out of Boston and shake its dust from my feet."[24]

By so doggedly positioning himself against the Central Committee and allying with the Republican opposition during the Maine debates, Quincy found himself ostracized by the party leadership. Harrison Gray Otis revealed that the fissure between Quincy and the Central Committee could have been easily avoided "[i]f he [Quincy] had always voted at his party's call, and never thought of thinking . . . but he had an inveterate habit of thinking for himself." As Quincy's son remembered, the Central Committee "look[ed] upon his father as one whose political zeal might out run his discretion, and who could not be depended on in . . . partisan emergenc[ies]." This, according to his daughter, "rendered him unacceptable to the Federal[ist] managers. . . . [T]hey could not calculate on his obedience to them," so he was purged.[25]

Coinciding with these events, in the spring of 1820 the antiaristocracy rhetoric of the debtor and militia movements', with Buckingham's help, was laying the groundwork for viable third-party challenges to the Central Committee's stranglehold on Boston and the state. Before the April elections, the Federalist *Columbian Centinel* warned its readership of third-party activity in Boston. "[B]eware of *mixed tickets,*" it cautioned. In Essex and Salem counties attempts were made to establish a third party against Federalist domination.[26]

A month before the state elections, in March, the Central Committee fell under severe attack. Buckingham's *Galaxy,* on March 10, made its position clear: "We despise . . . the federal[ist] and all other juntos—and we should like to see the [end of the] central-committee, which has so long been the scourge and disgrace of Boston."[27] The *Galaxy*'s next issue suggested a radical plan for the restructuring of Boston politics, devoid of the Central Committee's influence. "At this important crisis, when the incompetency of our *Central Committee* and *Primary Caucus* are so glaring, and when we are smarting under the disgrace which has recently been fixed upon us in consequence of their former folly and obstinacy, I would suggest," heralded "Vox Populi" in the pages of the *Galaxy,* "the expediency of taking measures for establishing a new Committee and Caucus, on the principle of a *real representation of the wards;* the *ward delegates* to be *actually chosen* by the . . . voters in each ward. . . . [For] the junto . . . are only lovers of themselves [and] manage to monopolize those offices, which, for the honor of the town [Boston] and the good of the nation, should be given only to men of talent and patriotism."[28] "For one caucus to determine the . . . future," the *Galaxy* argued in April, "is too absurd and ridiculous for the serious consideration of any but self-created dictators."[29]

Responding to the assaults, the Federalist press argued that "[t]he Central County Committee, in Boston, have existed ever since parties began; and have the same political origin, and been organized to advance the cause of Federal[ism] the same as the old Jacobin Club. . . . Is it because the former have been so successfully frustrating all the plans of the latter," questioned the Federalist *Centinel,* "that they have become so obnoxious to their virulence and abuse?"[30] Despite repeated batteries from the *Galaxy* and the Republican press, in the April elections the Federalist party ticket held the state, holding a majority of eleven in the state senate.[31]

The events of 1820 generated an initial movement based on the legitimacy of a new third party committed to ward voting. Within two years, the ward voting issue would grow in popularity and the political party it nurtured would effectively serve as the umbrella under which the debtor and militia movements coalesced into a powerful alliance of popular interests. The *Galaxy*'s charge that the Federalist Central Committee acted as selfish, "self-created dictators" supplied the common ground for all three movements to merge into a single insurgent party.

For Josiah Quincy, the Federalist "wire-pullers'" overt rejection in 1820 caused him great bitterness and understandable anger.[32] But Quincy also saw opportunity. His remarkably bold and independent actions over the Maine bill prompted many ordinary Bostonians to view him differently from Federalism's regular operatives. To many Bostonians, Quincy seemed to possess something quite unique for a Federalist leader—a highly independent character consistently unafraid of the Central Committee and the immense political power it wielded.

Some in the Federalist and independent press seemed confused by the Central Committee's draconian measures. The Boston *Daily Advertiser* asked, "why

[has] the name of Mr. Quincy [been] withdrawn?" Buckingham's *Galaxy* viewed Quincy as one of the "few of our statesmen [who is] entitled to the esteem of [our] fellow citizens. . . . [H]is friends, even those who disapproved of his warmth and impetuosity, refuse to acknowledge that he was an honest and upright, and independent politician. He ha[s], in some way or another," Buckingham explained, "become unpopular in the federalist party" leadership.[33] Considering the growing political dissension and dissatisfaction within Boston, this was not wholly bad for Quincy.

As the depression plundered ordinary Bostonians' household economies while the Federalist leadership did nothing, being viewed as outside the Federalist "cabal" or "junto" could be exploited politically. Indeed, in March 1820 a coalition of dissident Federalists and Republicans temporarily formed in Boston to successfully challenge the Federalist Central Committee's slate for the town's Board of Selectmen. In October the same coalition, with the *Galaxy*'s support, came dangerously close to upsetting Boston Federalist stalwart Benjamin Gorham's run for Congress with its own Samuel A. Wells. Buckingham captured the antiestablishment mood of Boston in his *Galaxy:* "we would sooner vote for Beelzebub than for the greatest and wisest man in creation, who should be nominated by a secret cabal, a junto of purse-proud demagogues, who care no more for the interest or the welfare of the middling classes of society than the afore mentioned Beelzebub."[34] Having been purged from the "secret cabal's" nominating list, Quincy was viewed favorably in the eyes of those who supported the *Galaxy*'s position.

Much to the astonishment of the Central Committee, after his censure by the party, in April of 1820 Quincy showed up at the Federalist caucus in Faneuil Hall. According to his son, "His appearance there, which was . . . a great surprise, excited as general a curiosity to know what he was going to say . . . —a curiosity probably not unmixed with anxiety on the part of those who had engineered the dropping of his name from the lists of candidates." In particular, William Sullivan was there representing the Central Committee. When Quincy rose to speak before a packed audience of rank-and-file Federalists in Faneuil Hall, his daughter proposed the supposition that it was the "turning point in my father's political life."[35]

According to Edmund Quincy, his father addressed the caucus "in such a strain of humor [and] wit" that the "old walls shook with laughter and cheers." After sardonically explaining the "way in which he had been thrown overboard" by the Central Committee because of his stand on Maine separation, Quincy endorsed the same Federalist ticket that had spurned him. In so doing, according to one observer, he became "the most popular man in the town." As Quincy had predicted, opposition to Maine statehood throughout the state had grown by the time he gave his speech in April. Numerous editorials chastising individual, proseparation legislators demonstrated that many in Massachusetts were now having second thoughts about letting Maine go. Quincy's vocal opinion on the issue during the statehood debates clearly had not been forgotten. Positioning himself in between the Federalist leadership and the party's rank-and-file, Quincy in one speech endeared himself to ordinary Federalists. He had shown himself to be highly critical of the Central Committee yet, all the while, selflessly loyal to the party as a whole despite its treatment of him. At the April Federalist caucus and working within the functions of the party, Quincy was challenging the Central Committee for leadership of the party. After 1820 Quincy's political strength would no longer come from the Central Committee. Instead, he would garner political popularity from a Boston electorate that viewed him as an honest and independent leader who had successfully stood up to the "self-appointed Federal[ist] dictators" of the Central Committee.[36]

Quincy's daughter claimed that her father met head on "the desertion of the Federalist leaders" with a newfound "spirit." Also, he had gained the support of many upper-class Federalists who deemed the committee's harsh discipline of him unjust and were skeptical of the committee's position on Maine statehood. Many loyal Federalist elites rallied to Quincy's side in part because they, like him, did not like the direction in which the Central Committee was taking their party. As with Quincy, when he had warned the committee against Maine separation and had been squarely rebuffed, these Federalists felt as though they too were being locked out of Federalism's high council. These men occupied a similar position within the party as Quincy before he had been purged. Men like John Phillips, William Phillips, Benjamin Pollard, and William Sturgis were established Federalist politicians. Nonetheless, they remained excluded from the inner councils of the Federalist Central Committee dominated by Harrison Gray Otis, William Sullivan, and Thomas H. Perkins. It was this group of dissident Federalists who continued to support Quincy despite the Central Committee's order. With John Phillips's support and influence, Quincy ran successfully for a position in the lower house of the General Court. Federalists loyal to the Central Committee made his election difficult, and Quincy just barely won a seat in the less prestigious house.[37]

Understanding that he had lost the Central Committee's patronage and aware of the mounting popular criticism being leveled at the Federalist leadership, Representative Quincy amassed legislative support among both regular Federalists and Republicans. In one of his first acts in the lower house, Quincy angered the Central Committee by calling for a statewide convention to rewrite the Massachusetts Constitution. "At 10 took seat in house of Rep.," Quincy wrote in his diary. "[A]t meeting . . . on the subject of proposing to the people an opportunity of amending the constitution. Argued to pass such a resolution and appoint a committee to draft." With the Maine district gone, Quincy logically and persuasively argued that the old system of representation within Massachusetts was invalid and had to be revised. This caused an unforeseen dilemma for the Federalist leadership. The old constitution of 1780, according to one Massachusetts historian, "was the pride of the conservative men who led the Federalist party" from its strongholds like Hampshire, Essex, and Suffolk counties. Support for Quincy's motion came from Republicans and representatives from the backcountry districts like Berkshire and Worcester counties, as well as dissident legislators from Boston.[38] By successfully pushing through a motion for a convention to completely overhaul the constitution, Quincy pressed the Central Committee to face democratic reform impulses which it would rather have ignored.[39]

Employing the talents and influence of Governor John Brooks, the Central Committee lobbied tirelessly against a convention. Claiming the existing constitution had been "drawn by [the] masterly hands" of John Adams, Brooks spearheaded the committee's position, arguing that any changes to the constitution should be drafted in committee by the General Court and then presented to the electorate for ratification. If done within the General Court, undoubtedly, all reformist influence could easily be checked by the Federalist-dominated legislature. The Central Committee's Federalist press strongly bolstered the governor's recommendations in editorial after editorial, but to no avail.[40] Stating that "the feder-al[ist] dictators, especially in and about Boston," were up to no good, the *Independent Chronicle* attacked what it identified as Federalist subterfuge against the will of the people. Despite the Federalist leadership's best efforts, the overwhelming opinion of both rank-and-file Federalists and Republicans prevailed. In a statewide referendum the electorate voted by a margin of two to one in favor of a convention.[41]

With convention delegates to be elected in town meetings throughout the state on October 6 and a commencement date set on November 15, the Central Committee rushed to devise a new strategy to control the convention. Much was at stake. If the reformers had their way, the apportionment of the senate would no longer be based on regional property holdings but on population. Federalist strongholds like Suffolk and Essex counties would lose their overrepresentation in the upper house. As things stood under the constitution of 1780, the combined weight of these two counties sent a third of the senate's representatives to the legislature. Also, reformers demanded that the legislature have more control over Harvard College because it received state funding. Reformers wanted to end the state's support of Congregationalism, which they viewed as unfair and discriminatory. Thus the Congregational church's coffers were threatened by constitution reform. The independence of the state's judicial branch also fell under reformist attack. Because the independent court system unfairly upheld the interests of the elite, reformers demanded legislative authority over the courts. Also, they called for the codification of universal male suffrage though, practically, it already existed.[42] These reforms were only those proposed before the convention met, although there were implications that the militia and debtor issues would be forced into the convention's agenda. Who knew what would emerge at the convention once the delegates met on November 15? Republicans like Levi Lincoln Jr. from

Worcester, James T. Austin from Boston, and Henry Dearborn from Roxbury were unpredictable and publicly had vowed radically to amend the constitution. Making matters worse, the Central Committee believed delegates sympathetic to reform would hold the majority at the convention.[43]

Aware of its compromised position, the Central Committee quickly worked to consolidate its forces in an attempt to mitigate the potential damage constitutional reform could wreak on the status quo. Harrison Gray Otis dispatched orders to his operatives throughout the state to support conservative Republican delegates who would be sensitive to Federalist orthodoxy. In the Republican power broker and state Supreme Court justice, Joseph Story, the Central Committee found its most effective champion. Though a loyal Republican, Story was dismayed by his party's consistent attack on an independent judiciary. Republican and some Federalist reformers were calling for legislative authority over the judicial branch. Also, as the *Galaxy* charged, "[t]he little state of Massachusetts [with Maine gone] must still have as many judicial officers, and pay them as high saleries, as when she had three times her present territory, and a third more inhabitants." As the *Galaxy* further explained, during the depression "when the farmer and mechanic are compelled to submit to low prices," why should not they "expect . . . some method to reduce the expenses of government, . . . by reducing [judges'] salaries or the number of salaries?"[44] For Story, who since 1809 had lobbied in the legislature for higher salaries for judiciary members, such sentiments were repugnant and secured his alliance with the Central Committee against reform.[45] Being perceived as a Republican partisan, Story would use his influence to pacify the more radical reformist voices at the convention.[46]

Cognizant of the committee's tactics, Republican reformist P. F. Degrand seemed disgusted with the ineptitude of his fellow reformers during the elections for convention delegates. Writing to his friend John Quincy Adams, Degrand vented his frustration in trying "to move our political friends to a sense of importance of electing [to the convention] their own men."[47] In town meetings throughout the Commonwealth, as in the convention itself, Federalist and Republican delegates were both supported and denounced by the Central Committee regardless of party. Traditional party alignments verged on being thrown into chaos.

On November 14, a day before the convention opened, Story was summoned to Boston to meet with the Central Committee's newest rising star and Boston newcomer, Daniel Webster. The gathering, which included other Republicans recruited to the cause, focused mainly on a new and ingenious strategy to undercut the majority power of the reformers. Webster's plan was to divide the convention into ten select committees. Each would have the task of evaluating each knotty constitutional issue being addressed at the convention. By controlling and framing the convention agenda in this manner, the most controversial concerns could be ignored and the legitimacy or illegitimacy of the entire constitution of 1780, as a whole, would never come under question, let alone fall under attack. Instead, the delegates and the issues would be sliced up into ten detached pieces and buried in ten separate subcommittees.[48]

The first essential step for the Central Committee to engage their plan was to secure the president's seat at the convention. It was the president's responsibility to appoint the chairman of each of the ten committees. If the antireformists could place one of their own in key chairmanship positions, the reformers could easily be controlled. Covering all their bets, Webster and Story decided to propose Federalist stalwart and chief justice of the Massachusetts Supreme Court Isaac Parker and the Republican Story for the position of president. No matter who won, the Central Committee would have its man.[49]

The next day, with the opening of the convention, Webster and Story witnessed the fruition of their scheme. Parker won the presidency by sixty-five votes in a close election that pitted him against Story. (Interestingly, disgruntled Federalist and Quincy's first cousin John Phillips' had been listed on the ballot as a third-party candidate of sorts and received fifty votes.) Many of the delegates from the western part of the state had not yet arrived at the convention when the vote was taken. Noting that many delegates were still making the long journey to Boston, the *Pittsfield Sun* of the Berkshire region argued Parker would have been defeated if the vote had not been rushed through.[50]

Clearly disgusted by Federalist political subterfuge, Buckingham criticized Parker's election, stating, "this is the first time that a . . . judge of the Supreme Court of Massachusetts has put off the . . . unsullied robes of his office and entered undisguised and naked on the political arena, converting the hall of justice into a caucus room, and its bench into a forum for the promulgation of sectarian sentiments." Jettisoning any remains of honorable disinterestedness, Buckingham exposed Federalism's descent into the petty politics of self-preservation. The Republican *Patriot* also reprimanded Parker but went farther, charging that the convention was fraudulent to its core: "we very much disapprove [of] the design and complexion of the whole [convention]. We cannot but consider it an *injudeious* [*sic*] attempt to influence the *people,* whose business it alone is, to alter and amend that Constitution. . . . The people are competent to the task without the aid of Lawyers."[51]

In spite of such criticism, the convention was masterfully rigged and the reformers largely defeated before the debates even began. Josiah Quincy had been elected as a delegate despite opposition from the Central Committee. Wisely, Parker appeased Quincy by appointing him to chair a committee which the Federalist leadership knew would limit his potential to disrupt the convention. As chairman of the committee selected to review Harvard College's relationship to the state, Quincy found himself toeing an antireform line. On Harvard, Quincy's loyalties were known and distinctly conservative. After Maine separation had so badly damaged the rank of Massachusetts as a leading state in the nation, Quincy foresaw that the Commonwealth's only hope of regaining national authority was by maintaining and strengthening its cultural and educational foundations. Although the state may have become "second class in population, and of the lowest in extent of territory," it could emerge, despite its numerical inferiority, as a national beacon to steer the moral and intellectual course of the country. According to Quincy, the maintenance, support, and growth of Harvard was crucial for the Commonwealth to reacquire national authority.[52] Needless to say, he was also a loyal alumnus. Thus, he endorsed and supported the continuation of state support for the college, despite reformist cries that Harvard was an elitist institution that had been "built up by the State" but was wholly "above the control of the State government."[53]

The one reform Quincy adopted in his Harvard committee lay within the dogmatic qualifications required in the old constitution that any and all ministers on the Board of Overseers were required to be Congregationalists. With Quincy's support and endorsement, this provision was swept away, and the committee recommended that "the constitution . . . be amended as to make ministers of the gospel, of any denomination, eligible to the office of overseers."[54] On other matters, Quincy bucked the Federalist leadership at the convention. During the debates on suffrage rights, Quincy distinguished himself from the Central Committee's representatives who fought to maintain the traditional voting qualifications. Under the constitution of 1780, voting rights were restricted to those who owned sixty pounds of freehold property or earned an income of three pounds annually.[55] Because, in actual practice, this translated into universal manhood suffrage, the issue was largely inconsequential. Nonetheless, it took on significant symbolic value in helping to define the convention's opposing sides. Reformers, such as Levi Lincoln Jr., asked that suffrage be extended to all of-age men who paid a state or county tax. According to Edmund Foster, a delegate from Littleton, "Men who have no property are put in the situation of the slaves of Virginia; they ought to be saved from th[is] degrading feeling."[56] On this, everyone agreed.

On a closely related matter, Quincy presented a convincing case to restrict paupers from gaining the vote. Arguing that voting paupers damaged the status of the working poor, he presented an amendment to the convention floor. Quincy contended that his "provision is in favor of the poor, and against the pauper;—that is to say, in favor of those who have something, but very little."[57] Quincy's position was an old argument that distinguished between the worthy and unworthy poor.[58]

The provision appealed to the lower-to-middling classes and debtors because it distinguished them from propertyless paupers. More importantly, Quincy convincingly argued that to bestow voting rights on a class thoroughly dependent on wealthy benefactors for its very survival was fundamentally undemocratic. Without his amendment, Quincy explained, "the poor man has . . . lost his political all; he has no power of indemnifying himself. Where as the rich [man], by the influence resulting from his property over the class of paupers, has the power of indemnifying himself a hundred fold." Comparing the problems he predicted in pauper suffrage to his personal anxieties about the future industrial course Massachusetts was taking, Quincy asked what barriers existed "to prevent manufactures [mechanics and factory operatives] from being absolutely dependent upon their employers. . . . The whole body of every manufacturing establishment . . . are dead votes, counted by head, by their employers. Let the gentlem[e]n from the country consider, how it might effect their rights, liberties, and properties, if in every county of the Commonwealth there should arise . . . one, two, or three manufacturing establishments, each sending . . . from one to eight hundred votes to the polls depending on the will of one employer, one great capitalist."[59]

Quincy's arguments during the suffrage debates expose his great fear of an electorate susceptible to manipulation. Bribery of the weak could lead to a managed electorate. The implications, as Quincy viewed them, would be devastating to a free and independent electorate. Paupers would be forced into economic dependency by unscrupulous partisan operatives, robbing society's most vulnerable of their independence. The electorate would fall victim to the corrupting influence of calculating partisans who would subvert the electoral system. Powerful interests would seduce society's most vulnerable members to surrender the most revered emblem of citizenship—the freedom to vote one's mind. Under such circumstances, the key foundation of a democratic society—an independent and autonomous citizenry's right to vote—would be placed in jeopardy. Whether it be paupers so destitute that financial desperation drove them to sell their votes, or a future industrialized world where masses of worker-voters forfeit political autonomy to "one great capitalist," the result would be the same. The independent Massachusetts citizenry would be coerced into a state of dependence and thus surrender electoral freedom.

Quincy's overt attack on the state's manufacturing interests appalled industrialism's advocates like Daniel Webster. After Quincy's speech, one of the reformers' most vocal representatives, James T. Austin, referring to Quincy, remarked, "One gentleman [has forewarned of] our becoming a great manufacturing people. God forbid." In their general opinion of the potential problems growing industrialization would have on the democratic process, Quincy and men like Austin agreed. On suffrage rights, they did not. Austin and George Blake, Republican delegate from Boston, forcefully championed the pauper's right to suffrage; yet, finding they held more in common than they thought, Quincy's and Austin's forces worked out a compromise provision that excluded paupers from voting but gave the vote to all of-age men who paid taxes.[60] As mentioned earlier, the suffrage issue proved largely symbolic. The codification of new suffrage rights in the state's constitution did not increase voter participation in Massachusetts after 1821.[61]

Despite Quincy's unpredictable nature, he, along with the reformers, had fallen victim to the Central Committee's covert scheme. All the significant issues raised during the convention were muted and the constitution that emerged upheld the status quo. Interestingly, militia reform secured a spot on the convention's agenda, but all hopes for any significant changes in the law were quickly put to rest when Joseph Varnum of Dracut was appointed chairman of the militia committee. Varnum, a Republican, was the major general of the Boston Brigade and, in 1820, had fallen under severe criticism by the Boston press for misappropriation of militia funds. Specifically, "A Friend to the Militia," accused Varnum in the *Galaxy* of syphoning off militia funds by giving them to his brigade quarter-master, who happened to be the major general's son. Clearly, General Varnum was highly invested in the maintenance of the existing militia laws. Chairman Varnum silenced the reformist voices in his charge, and the committee did little more than insert a clause into the new constitution that allowed under-age militiamen to vote for their officers.[62]

In many ways, the militia committee symbolized the whole convention process. Despite the great potential for reform that the constitutional convention offered the people of Massachusetts, in the end the reformers found themselves outclassed and overpowered by a Federalist machine that had employed the services of various antireform Republicans. As an exasperated Republican reform delegate, Nathan Martin of Marblehead, somewhat naively pleaded, "[We] know what's right, and what's wrong, . . . but it is not to be expected that we can express ourselves so politely; [we] who have not had the education" of the antireform forces.[63]

After the convention, Daniel Webster proudly wrote to his confidant, Jeremiah Mason, that "[w]e have got out as well as we expected. . . . It was a great body, in numbers . . . tho' . . . there was a good deal of inflammable matter, & some *radicalisms* in it. We are exceedingly fortunate, in finding a considerable number of Gentlemen well disposed, who might otherwise have occasioned much trouble." Webster's and Otis's strategy to control the convention had worked brilliantly. Writing to Mason, Joseph Story explained: "There was a pretty strong body of Radicals, who seemed well disposed to get rid of all the great fundamental barriers of the Constitution. Another class still more efficient, and by no means small in numbers was that of the 'lovers of the people, alias the lovers of popularity.' The combination of the two classes sometimes defeated us, and always posed us with difficulties. . . . It was no small thing to prevent sad mischiefs to the Constitution. The struggle for our part was not victory, but for the preservation of our institution. We were for the most part on the defensive: and . . . we have repelled the *most popular attacks*."[64]

Although Story did not declare total victory, the Central Committee's ability to stave off popular challenges to the constitution amounted to a significant triumph. The Central Committee successfully reached all its goals. It had purged the state of Maine Republicans and maintained a state constitution that benefited its interests. Even more significantly, the committee could claim that neither maneuver had been undemocratic or partisan—no one, that is, except Joseph Buckingham.

In a series of articles, the *Galaxy* attacked the convention for ignoring the economic devastation the depression inflicted on the ordinary citizens of Massachusetts.[65] "What has the convention done?" Buckingham asked. "Nothing—absolutely nothing." Explaining that the convention, in refusing to "lessen the state's expenses," had failed to address the depression-ravaged state of the Massachusetts economy, Buckingham accurately accused the "rich" of rigging the constitutional process. "Every article of produce has fallen from 20 to 50 per cent with a few years. The farmer and the mechanic are compelled to submit to lower prices for their produce and manufactures, and to many deprivations . . . and had the right to expect that the convention would devise some method to reduce the expenses of government, either by reducing salaries or the number of salary-taking officers. The Convention itself," Buckingham figured, "will cost the state $70,000, at the lowest calculation—and who is to pay it? Not the judges—not the clergymen—for they are all of the privileged orders; not the stock-holders in banks—their tax goes to enrich the funds . . . to buy every man's vote. . . . But the farmers and mechanic—the labourer; and the shopkeeper—[on top of] taxes, rents, . . . bad debts, and though last not least, the whole burden of military duty," will be forced to pick up the bill.[66] With this, Buckingham fused the debtor movement, the antimilitia movement, and the economic crisis with the betrayal that occurred at the constitutional convention. From the *Galaxy* editor's point of view, all these problematic issues were linked and could be solved if Boston opened its eyes to its oppressors.

In the same edition of the *Galaxy,* Buckingham included a speech given by Quincy at the Massachusetts Peace Society and followed it up with a very favorable editorial that was succeeded the next week by an equally positive article on the same speech. According to the *Galaxy,* the Peace Society, despite its being "the subject of sarcasm," contained "a few gentlemen . . . who saw and deplored [the] military fanaticism . . . pervading the country." Although Quincy's speech did not directly illustrate his opinion on the growing popular opposition to forced militia service, clearly Buckingham discerned the connection when he ran the articles side by side.[67]

The bipartisan alliances made before and during the convention hastened and exposed the fragility of the two-party system in Massachusetts. Just as members of both parties fought for reform, so too did bipartisan, antireform forces campaign vigorously for the status quo. During the debates, party alignment and the posturing of delegates on a given issue rarely corresponded.

Having distanced himself from the Central Committee during the debates by not toeing the antireformist line, a day after the convention adjourned Quincy took advantage of the resulting partisan disorder and cultivated a new base of power. On January 10, 1821, disaffected Federalists and a remarkable number of Republican partisans elected Quincy Speaker of the Massachusetts house. According to leading Republican, Levi Lincoln Jr., "Mr. Quincy had never been so well understood as since the convention." Republicans like Lincoln and James T. Austin, as well as Federalists John Phillips and William Sturgis, threw their weight behind Quincy and achieved what Lincoln claimed "no one would have" thought possible. As Eliza confessed in her diary, "I knew that my father was a candidate for [Speaker], but I did not expect his election." Illustrating Quincy's Republican support, Eliza recounted a conversation she had with Levi Lincoln. Lincoln stated "that no one was more happy to see Mr. Quincy in the Speaker's chair than himself."[68] Considering their past partisan warfare, this union between Lincoln and Quincy clearly revealed the growing dissatisfaction and fragmentation occurring within the Federalist party.[69]

Since the beginning of his political career, Levi Lincoln Jr. consistently spoke out vigorously against the Federalist Central Committee. Charging the committee with "intolerance and oppressive violence in electioneering," Lincoln argued that "[i]ndividuals have been threatened with deprivation of employment and an instant exaction of debt to the last farthing as a consequence of withholding a federal[ist] vote, or rather of not giving one." Although their arguments differed slightly, both Quincy, the Federalist, and Lincoln, the Republican, held a common commitment to protecting the autonomy of the working-class electorate. During the convention, each voiced his concern for the employed voter whose partisanship could be controlled by his employer. In his advocacy to change the basis of representation in the state senate during the constitutional convention, Lincoln posed the most formidable obstacle to the Central Committee's goals. He emerged from the convention with the distinction of being reform Republicanism's most powerful and candid spokesman. Feared and respected by the Central Committee, during the convention Lincoln forced the issue of senate representation onto the convention floor in the midst of imposing opposition. "Our government," Lincoln declared, "is one of the people, not a government of property. . . . Property is incomplete to sustain a free government. . . . Were it not for a government of the people, the people would be without property. . . . It is only necessary that all who are taxed should be represented, and not that they should be represented in proportion to their tax."[70] Quincy saw that the support of Levi Lincoln—a spokesman for the central part of the state, an advocate for debt reform, a defender of an independent electorate, and the Central Committee's most influential critic—could be a great advantage.

Seventeen days after his election as Speaker, Quincy hosted fourteen of the state's preeminent Republicans and those Federalists who had supported him at a formal dinner in his home on Hamilton Place. "I never expected to see Mr. Lincoln & J. T. Austin dining here," wrote an astonished Eliza Quincy. Quincy charmed his dinner company that night. To Lincoln he stated, "I always told you,

Mr. Lincoln, that I was the most of a *republican,*" whereupon Lincoln responded that he "did not expect to find that [he] was *more aristocratic* than [Quincy]."[71] The dinner conversation, which, according to Eliza, was very jovial and "chiefly political," indicates the initial preparations for a future bipartisan front to be launched against the Central Committee.[72]

Austin, a Republican activist from Boston, was considered by both Harrison Gray Otis and Joseph Story to be a dangerous and influential troublemaker. Writing of Austin that same year, Story described his fellow Republican as "hostile & impolite; and [someone who] essentially lowers the dignity of the great department he occupies." Nevertheless, "[p]ublic opinion," Story warned Federalist Jeremiah Mason, "begins to manifest itself considerably as to the merits of J. T. Austin. . . . [T]he demagogues approve it; and the mob cries hurra."[73]

Yet, if future articles are any indication, the editor of the influential *Columbian Centinel,* Benjamin Russell, who also attended the dinner, could not be won over that night by Quincy or his little circle of cohorts. Despite an editorial by Russell that had voiced subtle criticism of Chief Justice Parker's nomination to the convention's presidency,[74] Russell's political positions were strictly restricted within the criteria set forth by the Central Committee, which had richly rewarded his loyalty in 1819 by admitting him into its inner circle. Unlike Harrison Gray Otis and Thomas H. Perkins, Russell was not rich, nor was he ever going to be. Indeed, by 1844 he was penniless, sick, and living in a boardinghouse. As a fellow Boston journalist explained, "Russell was proud of his character as a mechanic. To the mechanics, as a class, he was strongly and affectionately attached. [Having] associated with men of the highest rank . . . and even courted by some of the leaders of his party, he never forgot that he was a mechanic." Russell founded the Massachusetts Charitable Mechanics Association and served as its president between 1808 and 1817.[75] Also, Russell and Quincy enjoyed an old friendship. Quincy knew Russell from the Washington Benevolent Society, where both had served as high-ranking members and together represented the cross-class basis of that organization.[76] Their old association may have prompted Quincy to believe Russell would be sympathetic to him and openly critical of the Central Committee, but Russell's loyalties could not be shaken. Quincy would have to find the editorial support he needed elsewhere. By the end of 1821, Quincy found his man and organ in the fiercely independent Joseph T. Buckingham and his *New England Galaxy.*

In May of 1821, Quincy's popularity in the House was reaffirmed when he was reelected as Speaker. After reform's failure at the constitutional convention, Quincy's original position on Maine statehood became increasingly popular. With Maine's independence and the convention, many in the Commonwealth perceived a strengthened centralized political aristocracy in the form of the Central Committee that did, in fact, exist in the state and was, in fact, repressing the rights of the people. In such a light, Maine separation seemed a big mistake. "Since her separation from Massachusetts," explained the *Galaxy,* "Maine seems to be making rapid advances in improvements, while the parent state, clinging with ridiculous veneration to old, absurd, and anti-republican principles and customs, jogs on the beaten path; and if an attempt be made to reform an error, to dispense with a useless office, or to reduce an extravagant salary, the author of it is immediately selected as a mark for the displeasure of our political oracles and aristocratic demigods. . . . In Maine . . . people are allowed to vote for whom they please, without danger of oppression from the rich. . . . But in Massachusetts, and especially in Boston, all the candidates . . . for . . . chief magistrate of the state down to the *keeper of the town bull,* are selected by the 'Central Committee.'" "The deserving" have been "driven from your service," the *Galaxy* declared to Boston. Traditionally, the Central Committee so controlled the politics of Boston, the *Galaxy* argued, that voters "might as well stay at home. [We ask voters] to break from this ignoble vassalage and act with independence [and fight against the] mere tools of a party, the pandar of a cabal."[77]

A year earlier, the *Galaxy,* in similar fashion, had advocated third-party activism in Boston. The first challenge Buckingham posed to the people of Boston had been blunted by the Federalist machine. After the convention debacle legitimized popular fears of an oppressive aristocracy, expanding economic dissatisfaction, growing opposition to Maine statehood, and with the advent of dissident Federalists like Quincy, Boston would meet Buckingham's challenge in 1822. This political insurgency would take advantage of the bipartisanship that grew out of the failed reformist platform at the convention, the debtor's plight, the militia reform movement, the early call for a ward-voting system, and other local issues that would arise in the upcoming year. Most importantly, the coalition would be held together by a deep distrust and even a hatred of the Federalist Central Committee, and by a new reverence for a revitalized and reconfigured political leader, Josiah Quincy.

IV • BOSTON REBELS AGAIN

Local Challenges to the Federalist Order

the moon had come nearer the earth . . . and had made some men mad.
—Observation of Boston Town Meeting, Dec. 1821

The People . . . were determined. . . . It was in vain to contend.
—William Sullivan to Harrison Gray Otis, Jan. 1822

In the midst of depression and the shrinking local economy, many Bostonians struggled not only under burdensome state militia laws and fear of imprisonment for indebtedness but also under a corrupt and inefficient tax system. What proved truly irksome for all but a few was the realization that the town had no power to reform its own tax codes. Many had expected the state constitutional convention, as Joseph Buckingham put it, to "devise some method to reduce the expenses of the government."[1] But the convention had failed the task and achieved little to ease the heightened sense of economic insecurity felt by average Bostonians.

With popular enthusiasm in Boston for meaningful tax reform peaking in the spring of 1820, integral political realignments soon followed. By 1821 vocal, cohesive, and widespread third-party activism erupted, shaking Boston's traditional political status quo. Advocates for the militiamen, debtors, and ward voting consolidated their forces around the call for tax reform and used the issue to move Boston's political structure toward a much more democratic system. By the winter of 1821–22, this coalition directly challenged the town's Federalist order. Stemming from what first seemed a fairly benign impulse for moderate reform, a successful endeavor to dramatically alter Boston's traditional system of governance ushered in a new municipal structure.

Coinciding with the rise of this coalitional insurgency and its demand for the radical restructuring of municipal governance, Josiah Quincy's problems with the Federalist leadership intensified to the breaking point. His defiance during the Maine statehood question and at the constitutional convention placed him and the Central Committee at each other's throats. After being reelected as house

Speaker in spring 1821, Quincy escalated tensions when he began publicly to criticize the Federalist Central Committee. Reinforcing popular sentiments in Boston, he openly lashed out at the party leadership, charging that "the most prominent [fault of the Central Committee] was apathy." On April 1, 1821, he made a cutting speech enumerating the severe problems he detected with the Central Committee's command of the Federalist party. "[T]hey care nothing about offices," Quincy alleged, "[a]nd this is one of their greatest faults. . . . There is scarcely a man among them fit for an office. And this is the reason why they fish up every crooked stick that floats . . . and make a mast of it." Clearly still embittered by the committee's decision not to nominate him to the state senate the year before, Quincy explained in the third person that "he had liked the [senatorial] office, and had no objection to serving several years longer. He was snug in his birth," Quincy claimed, "when these gentlemen [the Central Committee], without saying, *with your leave,* or *by your leave,* turned him out—tumbled him overboard into the saltwater." Conceding that "[t]his gave him something of a shock," Quincy concluded that the committee was guilty "of turning their officers overboard and making shark's meat of them." He explained that since the Central Committee had behaved "rather uncivil to him," he had reached out to "*our good friends the democrats* [Republicans]." Quincy's speech conclusively attacked the Central Committee, further distancing him from the Federalist party leadership.[2]

The relationship between Quincy and the Central Committee had become irreconcilable and each knew it. For many in Boston, Quincy seemed a concerned and independent voice—one that understood the problems faced by the vast majority of Bostonians. The *Galaxy* carried the whole of Quincy's speech and lauded its message. "There are few of our statesmen," Joseph Buckingham proclaimed, who are "more entitled to the esteem of their fellow-citizens, than the Hon. Josiah Quincy."[3]

Less than three months after the ratification of the new constitution and two months after Quincy's speech, in June 1821 the tax revolt was ignited in Boston. Eventually this issue would dramatically change the governmental structure of the town, and Quincy would combine his voice with a host of other outraged Bostonians struggling to be heard above the Federalist clamor that habitually enveloped the people's injunctions.[4] The modus operandi for tax reform ironically developed out of one of the few new opportunities given to local communities within the Commonwealth by the new conservative constitution. Specifically, Bostonians employed section 11 of the 1821 constitution, which sanctioned the establishment of cities within the Commonwealth, to achieve some sense of equity within the town.

Before the convention convened, beginning in the summer of 1820, moderate proposals in Town Meeting aimed at reducing the average Bostonian's taxes were met with fierce opposition by the county bureaucracy charged with assessing, collecting, and dispensing Boston's tax revenues. This audacity on the part of the county authorities clearly demonstrated to most Bostonians the town's inability to oversee its own affairs.

In May of 1820, the Boston Town Meeting approved a plan that would, in the upcoming year, consolidate the town and county treasurers' offices into one department. The original petition modestly argued that such a merger would prove much more efficient and help reduce the tax burden.[5] Because the proposition overextended the designated authority of the town and expanded into Suffolk County's legal domain, the state legislature had to amend existing law before the merger of offices could occur. Secondly, the governor-appointed judicial body that controlled county tax moneys and was made up of the much hated justices of the peace, the Suffolk County Court of Sessions, also had to sanction the proposal before the reform could be enacted.[6]

Although it took a year, in May of 1821 both the General Court and the Court of Sessions approved the plan as "proper and expedient."[7] Then, unbeknownst to anyone in Boston, on June 11, 1821, the Court of Sessions reversed its decision. At Town Meeting on June 15, Boston's selectmen had gotten wind of the court's retraction and reported that the Court of Sessions had defied the town's request by appointing two treasurers "at an increased expense" to Boston's tax-paying citizens.[8] Bostonians were furious. "Curiosity is alive," the *Galaxy* sneered, "to know the reasons why the purposes of the town has been defeated; and a spirit of indignation seems to pervade all classes of citizens."[9]

Such "disrespect to the People, . . . utter disregard to [their] interests, [and] total want of respect to themselves in their official capacity" led to a Town Meeting resolution that stated the Court of Sessions was "unworthy of the public trust and confidence."[10] Also, tax-paying Bostonians became concerned when the Boston press reported that $9,763.40 in county tax revenues under the direct control of the Court of Sessions could not be accounted for. "How happens it," Buckingham asked in the *Galaxy,* "that the court of sessions gave a statement of the probable expenses of the county, $20,000, and yet drew upon the town treasury for $29,762.40?"[11]

A committee, appointed by the town and led by William Tudor, immediately formed to look into how the court spent county tax moneys. Tudor's committee was to conduct a thorough audit of the Court of Sessions and report back to the town. Furthermore, an angry Town Meeting on July 2 appointed a second committee, chaired by town selectman and Boston shopkeeper Lewis Tappan, to investigate widespread accusations that the whole tax system was thoroughly biased—favoring Boston's large property owners at Boston's more modest property holders' expense.[12]

For years ordinary Bostonians had grumbled over the tax code, claiming that it unfairly accommodated "certain rich men, who *magnanimously* retire to their county seats . . . in order to avoid the [Court of Session's] assessors." But not until the court had so blatantly gone against the will of Boston were concrete accusations of corruption leveled at the court. Without doubt, the militia exemption policy for all justices of the peace and their high incomes (averaging $3,000 a year)[13] added to the animosity.

By September many property owners with moderate holdings strengthened their indictments, claiming that the court's assessors accepted bribes from large property owners who were buying favorable assessments.[14] Assessments held particular monetary significance for Boston's property owners due to the nature of the tax codes. Bostonians who owned real estate faced triple taxation. State tax required each citizen above the age of sixteen to pay a minimum of fourteen cents annually, plus a percentage on assessed property; county tax was based on one's assessed property, as was the town tax. If tax evasion—through bribing assessors or escaping Boston during the assessment period—proved impossible for the struggling small property owner, he would be forced to pay three levels of taxes.[15]

At Town Meeting in September, Tappan's committee, in a carefully worded report, only hinted at corruption while boldly asserting endemic unfairness in the tax system. The committee found that "checks can and ought to be made on [the assessors'] ability to abate taxes [because] opulent citizens do not hesitate to exert persevering personal application to the Assessors until they obtain reductions of their taxes." Reaffirming what most ordinary Bostonians already knew, Tappan reported that indeed many of Boston's wealthy fled to their country estates during the April assessment period and those who stayed in town often threatened to leave if their property assessment outstripped their tastes. Less wealthy property owners faced with having to fight off bill collectors during the depression and who were desperately trying to maintain their modest holdings within the town deeply resented such obvious injustice. Such deceit and selfishness by wealthy Bostonians who could easily afford such taxes exacerbated the growing wedge between the lower-to-middling and the upper classes. This anger helped forge a unified middling-class sensibility that eventually expressed itself politically. As "Brutus" complained in the pages of the *Galaxy,* "the power of wealth has corrupted the virtue and subjugated the influence of the many, to the selfish purposes of the aristocratical few."[16] "Another complaint to a considerable degree well founded," Tappan charged, "is that the richer classes of inhabitants are not proportionally taxed with those of smaller property. [The small property owner] is unequally taxed in proportion to those who are as rich or richer."[17] This class-based perception of injustice would significantly help define insurgent activism.

After the Tappan report, Tudor rose to deliver the results of his committee's audit of the Court of Sessions expenditures of county tax moneys. He reminded Town Meeting that Suffolk County contained only two towns, Boston and Chelsea, and that, in 1820, Bostonians, as always, had paid the lion's share of county taxes at $25,332.25, while Chelsea contributed only $187.63 to the county coffers. Since Boston paid well over 95 percent of the county taxes, Tudor argued that the Hub was fully justified in its attempt to find out where its money went, especially when (referring to the missing $9,762.40), "[i]t would seem . . . obvious that there must be some waste in our expenditure."[18] According to Tudor, when the committee asked to inspect the court's expenditure records, the justices refused, arguing "that as the court was not appointed by the Town, it could not . . . render an account of its doings." Undeterred, Tudor's committee bypassed the court, went directly to the county treasurer's office, and demanded to see the records. The treasurer complied, but as Tudor explained, the committee "found themselves checked in the outset, by a want of the Schedules . . . all of which . . . have been taken out of the files." The committee, he confessed, still had "not been able to find them."[19]

Accusing the Court of Sessions of a cover-up, Tudor charged that "this inferior department of justice seems liable to many objections under its present system; that the immediate expense is perhaps the least of its evils." Because "of these circumstances," Tudor's committee recommended that the town institute yet another committee "to ascertain whether the Court of Sessions cannot be . . . abolished." After printing and distributing the Tudor report throughout Boston, Town Meeting on October 22 overwhelmingly voted in favor of such a committee.[20]

When this third committee, spearheaded by Stephen Codman, concluded that the best way to abolish the Court of Sessions was for Boston to become its own county, others in the press and in Town Meeting began urging that an even better solution might be found. "If we adopt a city," one Bostonian argued, "we shall have the same beautiful, definite and efficient system, which we admire so much in its operation in our state and national concerns. . . . [t]he whole authority . . . emanating from the people."[21] The move to make Boston a city would intensify conflict between the Federalist leadership and the aspiring forces of political insurgency.

Even before the tax revolt, Boston's town meeting system of government periodically had fallen under criticism. Many charged that it was fundamentally undemocratic. As early as 1820, "Brutus" matter-of-factly stated that "in Boston, . . . a monied aristocracy has absolutely more sway and is more adverse to our boasting republicanism, than a legalized aristocracy of birth."[22] Even Josiah Quincy, who was highly skeptical of abandoning the old town meeting system, recalled when writing his history of Boston that not only was there "no direct check or control; no pledge for fidelity" on the part of the "agents of the town," but also typical "town meetings were usually composed of the Selectmen, the town officers, and thirty or forty inhabitants" at best. Buckingham's assessment of Boston's traditional system was even more withering. "Sometime fifteen or twenty, seldom more . . . do all the business of a town that contains near seven thousand voters," he explained. Also, "[i]t is well known," continued the *Galaxy* editor, "that, in Town-Meetings, when a subject of great importance is to be referred to a committee, the moderator . . . nominates three, five, or more, of the citizens present to . . . select such a committee. . . . Now it hath chanced that these gentlemen . . . have been under the disagreeable and embarrassing necessity of *announcing themselves* as the fittest persons that could be found to form the committee. This is a terrible evil," Buckingham charged, "and to get rid of it no sacrifice can be too great."[23] "It is yet to be hoped," heralded "Brutus," "that the middle and lower classes of the community . . . will tread back the path of error and endeavor to rescue themselves" from such domination.[24]

Ironically, the direct democracy promised by the town meeting system was routinely subverted by a handful of prominent Bostonians who dictated policy by their control of Town Meeting procedures. Using the parliamentary rules and practices of the town meeting system, the policy course of Boston fell under the direction of a few men with specific economic interests. Disgusted with selfish upper-class rule, Boston's middling interests demanded more democracy while Josiah Quincy sought the means to recapture the power that had been denied to him by the Federalist hierarchy.

When the Federalist Central Committee's William Sullivan gained the appointment to chair the committee responsible for "remedy[ing] the present evils" of the town, Buckingham's assessment of the exclusivity inherent in the daily operations of Town Meetings was confirmed. Yet Brutus's appeal to ordinary Bostonians had not been forgotten. When the Sullivan committee returned to Town Meeting with a proposition that fell far short of establishing a city charter, a jam-packed and unruly Town Meeting overwhelmingly rejected Sullivan's proposal and demanded that the committee be enlarged to include one representative from each of Boston's twelve wards.[25] These independent men, it was thought, could sincerely forge the town into a city without being influenced by the Federalist Central Committee. Buckingham strongly praised the independent course taken by Boston's citizenry. "The Municipal Affairs of Boston," heralded the *Galaxy* on December 14, "are . . . to be set right at last. The *long* experience, the profound legal learning, the acute, penetrating mental powers, and the disinterested political views of some of the venerable young members of the new committee, to whom the report of the old one was recommitted, afford solid ground to hope the errors and prejudices of our . . . Sullivans, and . . . Jacksons, will be corrected. Old folks used to *think* young ones to be fools, but our young folk *know* the old ones to be so. There can be no doubt, . . . that a complete system of municipal government will be reported, and joyfully accepted by the citizens at the adjourned meeting . . . all our old abuses *corrected,* and the honors of the new system fairly *distributed.*"[26] By the end of 1821, a growing consensus in Boston demanded the termination of the traditional town meeting system and the drafting of a city charter as a means of challenging Federalist rule.

Four earlier attempts to abolish the town meeting system and institute a city government in 1784, 1792, 1804, and 1815 had drawn great numbers and faced popular opposition in Town Meeting. Each time the proposals were defeated. In the past, Bostonians fought off any dramatic alteration to the town meeting system for fear that a centralized city structure would weaken majoritarian rule. Before 1821, all attempts to change the traditional system were instigated by the Federalist elite to further consolidate its power within the town. On this issue, a normally inactive Boston electorate in Town Meeting had consistently become active. Clearly, Bostonians in the past seemed to have understood elite strategy and rallied to crush all earlier city proposals by saturating Faneuil Hall with vocal opponents to the postcharter plans. In response, Federalist elites changed strategy and abandoned their calls for a centralized city government. Instead, they successfully consolidated power in Boston by assuming leadership positions in Town Meeting which resulted in their domination of Boston's civic matters.[27]

By 1821 popular attitudes dramatically changed. Boston's newfound acceptance of municipal centralization was fostered initially by the town's disadvantaged position within Suffolk County, the corruption within the tax assessment process, and a distrust of the Court of Sessions. On top of this, a large voting bloc came to embrace municipal change as a means to firmly establish ward voting within Boston. Ward voting meant more power to the disaffected. Although minor town bureaucrats traditionally were elected by ward, town selectmen and all state and federal representatives were elected at-large in Faneuil Hall.[28]

Since the 1820 state elections, ward-voting proponents had forcefully advocated the setting up of decentralized polling stations throughout Boston. In that year, numerous articles and editorials in Buckingham's *Galaxy* ridiculed the at-large voting system as "absurd and ridiculous"—an outdated system, "manage[d] . . . to monopolize those offices" by the Federalist Central Committee "junto."[29] By the winter of 1821, the supporters of ward voting, some of whom had taken on the title of the "Middling Interest," viewed the chartering initiative as a prime opportunity to codify their aspirations for a more democratic voting system into a new municipal structure.

Ironically, the Federalist Central Committee also came to support a city system, but for very different reasons. Men like William Sullivan, Thomas H. Perkins, and Harrison Gray Otis agreed with the popular criticism of the power held by the Court of Sessions, but more importantly, they viewed a city structure in much the same light as Federalist elites had in earlier years. To the Federalist leadership in 1821, a city charter potentially could offer the means to strengthen its power within Boston, but only if it could control the charter's drafting.[30] Paradoxically, the two combative factions had hit upon the same strategy to achieve their opposing goals. For Harrison Gray Otis's individual political ambitions, a city structure meant even more.

Otis had served in the U.S. Senate since 1817. During much of his tenure in Washington he found himself discredited and ineffectual due to his villified participation in the Hartford Convention. In an attempt to rectify his political reputation in Congress, in 1817 and 1818 Otis spent much of his time collecting and organizing as much material on the convention as he could find. In 1819 he edited and drafted a public defense of the convention. Hoping his *Letters Developing the Character and Views of the Hartford Convention* would finally silence the constant badgering and criticism he faced on the Senate floor, Otis published his appeal in the Washington *National Intelligencer* under the pseudonym, "One of the Convention." When his defense collapsed, Otis began planning a hasty escape from Washington politics. As he wrote to Connecticut Federalist and the Hartford Convention's secretary, Theodore Dwight, in 1821, "a boundful allotment of the odium attached to the Hartford Convention has been heaped upon me." Claiming "'the hounds are all out,'" sniffing and baying at him, Otis plotted his next political move.[31]

Irritated and consistently checked in the Senate, Otis set his future ambition on the Massachusetts governor's seat. His friend and Federalist compatriot, John Brooks, let it be known that he would not seek reelection in 1823, opening the way for Otis to move in. Coinciding with Otis's decision to run for governor, the city chartering controversy raged in Boston. Seeing an opportunity in Boston's call for a city system, Otis devised a strategy to help ensure his ascent to the governor's mansion: he would become the first mayor in Massachusetts and use this highly visible position to launch his campaign for the governorship. As Eliza Quincy recalled, "Mr. Otis . . . was put up for Mayor, and it appeared that a plan had been formed by a number of politicians, that he should be the first Mayor, as a stepping stone to the Governor's Chair, & would then have the arrangement of the City offices & salaries & could then reward partisans who had proposed the City Charter through the Legislature for this purpose." In early January 1822, Sullivan assured the senator: "If you incline to live in 'the Mansion House,' I will mount the stamp for you,—as will many other who can do more than I."[32]

Driven by such ambition, by December of 1821 Otis became highly invested and deeply involved in the details of the Sullivan chartering committee. Sullivan pledged to do all he could for his old friend and ally, "whom," he "expect[ed] to see engaged at the labour of putting the [city] machinery in motion." Reassured by Sullivan's unswerving devotion, from December 1821 through January of 1822 Otis shot off a litany of firm instructions to his operatives in Boston from Washington, thus securing his influence in the town committee charged with forging the city charter. "It is easier to manage the town of Boston," he advised Sullivan, "by a Lancastrian system of political discipline than to institute numerous schools." "[G]ive [the Mayor] a *right,* without imposing an *obligation* to ask advise" from other city officials. The executive, according to Otis, must have the "veto upon . . . laws (such as relating to taxes and taking away private property). . . . [G]ive him the power to ride out the squalls." Although he had no intention of serving as mayor for more than one year, Otis directed Sullivan to ensure that the mayor "be appointed for more than one year at a time. . . . If you make your mayor respectable by giving him high authority you will give him auxiliaries to try the whores and rogues." Otis also strongly urged that the mayor should receive a "good salary."[33] On ward voting, Otis was most adamant. "If it is done in wards, the town will be revolutionized."[34]

Unfortunately for Otis and his operatives, Boston's insurgents who supported the charter viewed ward voting as an essential element of any acceptable proposal for a city structure. Indeed, the enlarged Sullivan committee, charged with drafting a city charter, contained twelve new members, two of whom were Boston's most vocal proponents of ward voting and were the founders of an embryonic third party in the form of the Middling Interest: a riding instructor from the sixth ward, Michael Roulstone, and the wealthy disaffected Federalist, William Sturgis of Ward 10.[35] Potentially, these committee members could obstruct Otis's specific designs for the new charter.

Applying tactics similar to those employed during the constitutional convention, Otis's forces seduced at least one of the "venerable young members of the new committee," Republican Gerry Fairbanks, into the fold. As a leading member of Boston's minority party, Fairbanks feared the politics of Roulstone and Sturgis perhaps even more than the Federalist Central Committee. If the third-party activism which these men advocated gained significant appeal in Boston, it would disproportionately damage the Republicans more than the Federalists, who traditionally enjoyed majority status in Boston. Republicanism's position in the town had always been tenuous, and its chronic vulnerability could be easily exploited by a third, coalition party that would address the grievances of Republicanism's traditional constituency. Fairbanks correctly surmised that rank-and-file Republicans would abandon his party for the Middling Interest. If this occurred, the Republican party would become even less of a force within Boston than it already was. For these reasons, Fairbanks helped shape and solidify Republican opinion on the new chartering committee while reporting his every move to Otis. Providing Otis with detailed analyses of Republican sentiments on the chartering issue, Fairbanks was a valuable source of information for Otis and his forces.[36]

On December 22 the Sullivan committee presented its proposal to Town Meeting. At first glance, the document seemed to be a compromise between Otis's operatives and the advocates for ward voting. But after the charter's publication and distribution throughout Boston, and the resulting Town Meeting debates of December 31 through January 2, 1822, most Bostonians clearly refused to view the document as a victory for ward voting in any way. Otis had feared such popular resistance, but Gerry Fairbanks assured him that the plan would have the full support of Boston's Republican leadership. Five days before the debates, on December 26, Fairbanks guaranteed that the Republican members of the Sullivan committee were thoroughly under control. "In fact," Fairbanks assured the senator, "the prospect for moving for a recommen[dation]" that excluded ward voting "came from a republican source." Despite recent articles in the *Boston Patriot* that suggested Republicans were making the charter a partisan issue, Fairbanks promised Otis that the *Patriot* did "not speak for the sentiments of the party."[37]

Although Fairbanks's report to Otis may have been sincere, Fairbanks seriously underestimated Boston's popular opposition to a chartering plan without an ironclad ward-voting component to it. This omission gave rise, according to one observer, to "Bedlam" in Town Meeting. It was as though "the 'moon had come nearer the earth . . . and had made *some* men mad.'" The stately and orderly decorum of the exclusive few who traditionally ran and quietly dominated Boston's town meetings was overwhelmed by a Faneuil Hall filled to capacity with an unruly Boston citizenry that consistently hissed and shouted them down. Federalist Francis J. Oliver, charged with the unfortunate task of moderating Town Meeting between December 31 and January 2, later described the debates as highly "arduous" and totally "perplexing."[38]

Much to the astonishment of Otis, Fairbanks, Sullivan, and other Boston "betters," the deferential character that had so characterized the traditional Boston Town Meeting was consumed in turmoil as ordinary working Bostonians like town crier Ebenezer Clough and rattrap maker Samuel Adams actively participated in the discussions by bellowing out objections to the Sullivan committee's proposed city plan.[39]

In spite of Otis's objections, Chairman Sullivan, in an unsuccessful attempt to appease ward-voting advocates, recommended that a city common council of fourteen members be elected in wards. No longer would Bostonians have to trek all the way to Faneuil Hall to elect this body of local representatives, he claimed. Committee members and ward-voting advocates Michael Roulstone and William Sturgis had battled hard for this arrangement. Yet, as Sullivan confessed, though Boston's electorate could vote for councilmen within their own districts, "it would not be expedient to have one Selectman [councilman] for each ward, as it would tend to divide the town too much into distinct portions." William Tudor, an original committee member, agreed that such an arrangement would "break up old associations, good feelings, [and] there [would be the] danger of [Boston] splitting into twelve little towns."[40] Thus, though city councilmen would be elected in each of Boston's twelve wards at twelve separate ward polling stations, each ward was not guaranteed a representative from their ward in the city council according to the proposed charter.

Having followed Otis's instructions on another matter, Sullivan, with Fairbanks's support, pushed through the committee a provision guaranteeing that all state and federal elections would be held at-large in Boston's traditional central polling station, Faneuil Hall. As Otis lectured Sullivan, "You should give no temptation to your Town Government to dabble in [state or federal] politicks, [because] if they [Bostonians] be democratic [Republican] which they will sometimes be—you may yet be safe in the State."[41]

Again following Otis's instructions to establish a "Lancastrian" system, the proposed charter held that the city's executive would be elected not by the people in wards or otherwise but by the common council.[42] In an attempt to justify this provision, Sullivan disingenuously argued before Town Meeting that though he "was always reluctant to take away privileges from the people . . . an executive officer will necessarily come in to contact with the inhabitants; many will be offended; if he does his duty he will not be reelected, or he will be so bending as to be unfit for reelection."[43]

If the response to and the fate of the Sullivan committee's proposal on the first day of the debates is any indication, this was not at all what the town wanted or expected. Some, like Ebenezer Clough and William Emmons, so despised the Sullivan report that they switched their positions and fought against any form of a city charter. Others, understanding the limitations of the single ward-voting provision in Sullivan's charter, revealed that in the past they had felt too intimidated to vote their conscience in an open meeting at Faneuil Hall. Addressing his statement to Sullivan and moderator Oliver, Samuel Adams explained: "For instance a journeyman who is in your employ. They feel so delicate in your employ, they are afraid of offending you." With voting in wards, Adams charged, "there would be no more coaxing mechanics, threatening them with loss of work. . . . We know each other [in our wards]. . . . Here [in Faneuil Hall]," Adams confessed, "we are strangers." Concluding his arguments, Adams threatened that "the whole will be lost if we don't agree to vote in wards."[44]

Adams spoke to the common fears of many Boston mechanics, journeymen, artisans, and laborers who were resentful that their financial well-being and security was often directly dependent upon how they voted at Faneuil Hall. This issue resonated and, much to the Federalist Central Committee's dismay, refused to dissipate as a key issue. Indeed, similar apprehensions about the autonomy of an electorate had been raised by representatives like Levi Lincoln and Josiah Quincy during the constitutional convention just one year earlier. At the convention, the issue was presented as a hypothetical potential problem to democracy. In the chartering debates, people like Adams were presenting it as a reality. After much angry debate on both sides, a compromise was reached. A townwide referendum would be held on January 8 to decide whether all federal and state elections would be held in ward polling stations or in Faneuil Hall.[45]

The next issue that quickly came under immediate and staggering attack was Sullivan's proposal for the election of mayor. Clough successfully argued that the mayor should be chosen in wards by the general electorate. According to Clough, if this was left to the city councilmen, the mayor would "be determined by the rich men . . . and the poorer people will have to pay for it."[46] The outcry against this proposal proved so prevalent, determined, and hostile that Sullivan and his allies quickly acquiesced.[47]

After the first Town Meeting debates on December 31, Sullivan and the Otis forces left Faneuil Hall astonished and bloodied. The customary reticence of Boston's electorate on such matters evolved into an articulate and potent defiance that firmly rejected Sullivan's motion for the election procedure for mayor. Also, though consensus was elusive, the proponents of ward voting had gained a significant victory with Town Meeting's overwhelming approval of a referendum to decide on voting in wards.

On January 8, 1822, both the revised charter and the question of ward voting were presented to Boston. By a vote of 1,805 to 1,006, Boston accepted the revised charter. Ward voting also passed by over 400 votes. Although the total of Bostonians who voted came to an impressive 2,811, close to double that number voted on the ward-voting issue. The fact that 4,806 cast ballots on this referendum question indicated that the ability to elect state and federal officers without the customary intimidation being dispensed by Federalist elites to control Boston's voting behavior in Faneuil Hall held significant meaning for the town's electorate.[48]

Upon hearing the news, eleven days after the referendum vote a dismayed Otis wrote to Sullivan: "If the provision respecting voting in wards for political affairs is irreversible, I am not about to cry for spilled milk—But I am hard of the conviction of the expediency of the measure, and am full of fears, (if the federalism of the town be worth an effort to preserve—which I may live long enough to question)." Then, on a more optimistic note, Otis added, "perhaps the organization of wards, may be available for political arrangements in favour of good men and measures—though I had wished to see them kept altogether distinct from each other."[49]

Sullivan one day earlier had shot off a long letter to Otis. "The People," he explained, "were determined. . . . It was in vain to contend against this determination." As if to hearten Otis, Sullivan placed a positive spin on the defeat in Town Meeting, assuring the senator that the victory of ward voting would not affect his ambition to be Boston's first mayor. Utilizing the same pragmatic logic as in Otis's letter, Sullivan suggested that, despite the town's decision that "[t]he mayor and aldermen [were] to be chosen by the citizens, voting in wards[,] . . . so long as the present majority in the town continues, the mayor and . . . aldermen, will be agreed on in Caucus. Proper measures will be taken," Sullivan promised Otis, "to have this agreement understood at the ward meetings." This would ensure the Federalist Central Committee's influence over ward meetings and guarantee Otis the Federalist party nomination for mayor. Although their original strategy had been stymied, Sullivan remained buoyantly optimistic. The wards could be controlled, he believed. The Republican party continued to be impotent in Boston and was not a serious threat. There seemed to be nothing to block Otis from becoming Boston's first mayor and, thereby, achieving the first phase in his overall design to become governor.[50]

Also, as both Sullivan and Otis understood, the charter first had to be approved by the General Court before it could become law, and Otis and the Central Committee still maintained significant power there. Having prepared for a worst-case scenario coming out of Town Meeting, Otis had instructed Sullivan to have the charter altered after it was sent up to the General Court for legislative approval.[51]

When the charter reached the senate on February 12, loyal Otis Federalists flexed their muscles in a successful attempt to suppress ward voting in Boston. In an act of utter audacity, the upper house quietly scrapped the provision in the charter. The senate's amendment "provid[ed] that the elections of State and United States officers shall be holden as heretofore in Faneuil Hall, instead of being holden in wards as proposed by the bill." The senate's actions did not go unnoticed by the town. When the charter arrived at the lower house, Otis's forces were not prepared for the opposition. On February 16 the much more independent lower house, by a close vote of 63 to 61, refused to accept the senate's revision concerning ward voting. This was a serious blow to the Central Committee, but Otis's operatives in the senate had added another amendment that slipped by the discriminating eyes of the Central Committee's opponents in the lower house. Section 30 of the revised charter stated that nothing in the charter "shall be so construed as to restrain or prevent the Legislature from amending or altering the same whenever they shall deem it expedient." Otis's opponents in the House had overlooked the implications of section 30.[52]

For his part, Otis had wisely predicted problems in the lower house. As early as January 8 he had instructed Sullivan to see to it that once the legislature got hold of the charter, the senate should "insert in the charter *some faculty of obtaining amendments.*—As this would *be a privilege,* it might be added without [the] instructions from the town." Following Otis's orders, Sullivan had recruited William Tudor to unobtrusively drive section 30 through the legislature. Tudor was a perfect candidate for the job. His nonpartisan role as the town's auditor of the Court of Sessions and his genuine outrage at the court's resistance and corruption made him seem trustworthy to members in the legislature who distrusted the Central Committee. More than anyone else, Tudor provoked and instigated Boston to move toward a city system in the name of reform. Nevertheless, as Sullivan fully understood, Tudor was no radical reformer but a loyal supporter of Harrison Gray Otis and would follow the Central Committee's directives to the letter. Though he strongly supported a city structure, Tudor had consistently opposed ward voting. Having reached no consensus on ward voting, the legislature sent a revised charter complete with section 30 and the ward-voting question back down to the people of Boston to decide on both issues in yet another town referendum on March 4.[53]

Josiah Quincy had served on the Sullivan committee, and as usual he had taken an independent stand on the chartering controversy, coming out against any form of city structure. Like many in Boston, he did not trust Sullivan. Only two short years before, it was Sullivan who had replaced him as the Federalist Central Committee's candidate for the state senate, and Quincy remained resentful. Also, since 1821 Quincy had chaired a Town Meeting committee to deal with the growing numbers of paupers who begged on Boston's streets. Just as he struggled to navigate through Boston's political transformation toward a popular democracy, he also struggled to maneuver through Boston's urban transformation. Proving himself to be an institution man, Quincy explained that "[t]he leading principle" of his pauper committee "was,—*the duty incumbent upon society of discriminating in its charitable provisions and arrangements, between the poor by reason of infancy, age or misfortune, and the poor by reason of idleness, or vice.*" Quincy's committee had successfully lobbied Town Meeting in 1821 for funds to establish a House of Industry in South Boston that would segregate the "idle and vicious poor" from the "worthy poor." By housing and employing the "deserving poor" in the healthier, pastoral atmosphere of rural South Boston, far away from the corruption of Boston's seedier neighborhoods, which naturally, according to Quincy, bred licentious behavior, they could rectify their lives.[54]

The town had approved the plan, and Quincy worried that his pet project would be stalled if a radical change in the town's government occurred just as the appropriations to build his House of Industry were being decided upon.[55] Adding to this, Quincy, according to the *Galaxy,* perceptively "saw mischief in the section [section 30] which gives the legislature unrestrained power over the charter."[56] Fearing "corruption and abuse," as his son remembered, Quincy "resisted" the charter "by speech and pen as long as there was any chance of defeating it."[57]

Quincy was not alone in his objection to section 30. "[I]f the Charter is accepted," with section 30, observed one Bostonian, "we may have as Mayor, possibly, some worthy gentleman from Berkshire." Buckingham predicted in the *Galaxy* that section 30 would provoke "many, who are in favour of incorporation as a city, [to] vote against the present bill—presuming that the legislature has the power essentially to alter the charter or constitution of government . . . without the concurrence of the citizens." Because of this and another provision, section 22, which granted authority to the city common council to decide the number of representatives to be sent from Boston to the General Court, Buckingham opposed the charter. He closed his arguments by reiterating Quincy's fears that the charter constituted nothing but a plot by the "central committee" to disarm the power of "the people."[58]

One day before the town vote, on March 3, William Emmons stood before Boston's citizenry at Faneuil Hall in a final attack against the city charter. "I am fully aware of the disadvantage, a humble citizen labours under, when addressing an assembly [at Town Meeting] composed of the powerful, and that power is their wealth," yet Emmons still believed that the old system was more democratic in the long run, if "the voice of the rich will no [longer] be raised higher than that of the poor." Stand with the "intelligent decisions of a Quincy, and the penetrating eye of an Austin," Emmons implored. Vote against the charter.[59]

Despite the apprehensions of Emmons, Austin, Buckingham, and Quincy, the day after Emmons's impassioned speech, on March 4, 1822, Boston accepted the charter by a vote of 2,797 to 1,881. On the ward-voting question, 2,813 Bostonians overwhelmingly came out in its favor, while only 1,887 had voted against it.[60]

After an agonizing year of heated debates, political maneuvering, and intrigue, Boston, with this vote, finally became a city, complete with polling stations in every ward. On April 8, 1822, the city would hold its first mayoral election, and, for the first time, Bostonians would independently cast their votes with a sense of security and safety in their own neighborhoods.

Despite the imposing influence of Harrison Gray Otis's Federalist machine working at high bore, the majority of Bostonians had earned the sort of charter they wanted. It had not been easy. Boston's "senators and representatives," railed one angry Bostonian, "not only opposed the wishes of their constituents, but joined in the votes which in one instance defeated the purpose of the large majority of the town. . . . We allude to the . . . provision in the city charter, for the election of State and United States officers in wards."[61]

In spite of their representatives' behavior in the General Court, a voting system that ensured more democracy to Boston's ordinary citizens carried the day with little support from their own legislators. Unlike the reformist impulse that was effectively quashed by clandestine political tactics during the constitutional convention, in the chartering controversy the Central Committee's machinations failed to quell the resolute voices of democratic reform.

During the controversy, and quite ironically, the town meeting system and its straightforwardly democratic structure worked in the interests of Boston's majority. The hated Court of Sessions had been abolished, and the mayor would be elected for one year by the people—not by councilmen; executive power would be limited by the City Council; and most importantly to the people of Boston, all city, state, and federal officers would be elected in wards. The 1821–22 debate over chartering was a milestone event for the forces of democratization in Boston. Not only had Boston's past deferential voting behavior been boldly addressed in a public forum, it had been squarely condemned as undemocratic. Boston's electorate then defiantly acted upon its own antideferential rhetoric, helping to shape a new municipal system that would better protect independent suffrage. Both practically and psychologically, the chartering battle broke down the traditional patterns of deference that had been instilled in the political life of Boston. Almost all of Otis's edicts for the structure of a new city government had been squarely checked by a politically charged citizenry empowered and inspired with growing confidence and a distinct municipal vision that offered Boston's lower-to-middling classes a voice in determining the new city's future.

This was new to Boston. What had begun as a minor tax revolt calling for modest reform in the tax codes resulted in a full-blown and successful popular challenge to the traditional deferential nature of Boston's political culture. With both ward voting established in the new city and a raging economic depression that spawned popular dissatisfaction with the militia, tax, and debtor's laws, political dissidents like William Sturgis, Michael Roulstone, and a Boston newcomer and Baptist minister, Francis Wayland, saw an obvious political opportunity to forge a powerful enough insurgent third party to cripple if not completely destroy the Federalist party in Boston. If Federalism fell in its stronghold, these men believed, the party would soon atrophy and wither away to nothing throughout the state. Carefully choosing an inoffensive name, the insurgents formally named their organization the Middling Interest and began preparing for its first challenge—the new city's first mayoral race.[62] In the course of this new endeavor, they had to seek out someone who would both champion their cause and be able to stand up to the Federalist machine and its leader, Harrison Gray Otis.

V • "POPULAR HALLUCINATIONS," "TEN-FOOTERS," AND "LORDLY NABOBS"

The Middling Interest Leadership and Coalitional Unity

These lordly nabobs['] . . . object is to keep the mechanics and labourers in eternal servitude.
—Joseph T. Buckingham, 1822

the people are not only the real but also the acknowledged fountain of all authority.
—Francis Wayland, 1825

a band of murmurers . . . a parcel of demagogues
—Ralph Waldo Emerson, 1822

Less than one month before the city charter reached the General Court for approval, on January 16, 1822, Josiah Quincy resigned his position in the Massachusetts House of Representatives. "I relinquish this chair," Quincy announced, "with a reluctance, which I cannot conceal and yet, which I cannot express." He assured his colleagues that his experience as Speaker of the House had been "a source of unqualified delight and satisfaction." Speaker Quincy proudly acknowledged that he had earned bipartisan support which he deeply valued, and he congratulated both sides of the lower house for their nonpartisan allegiance to him. "From every gentleman of every party, I have, at all times, received and reciprocated the greeting of a friend and a brother." Reinforcing this position, Quincy endorsed Republican Levi Lincoln Jr. as his replacement as House Speaker.[1]

"On the motives of my resignation," Quincy cryptically stated, "it is not suitable for me, in this place to speak. I may be permitted, however to assert, that it has proceeded from a sense of duty, distinct and unequivocal; and in the existing relations of my mind—irresistible." Providing no specific designs for his future plans, Quincy, nevertheless, proclaimed his expectation that the bipartisanship he had cultivated in the legislature would continue and grow once he established himself "in another sphere." In the foreseeable future, Quincy challenged Federalists and

Republicans "to join my labours with yours, in promoting the interests of the people of this great Commonwealth."[2]

As the tone of Quincy's mysterious resignation speech suggests, and as his daughter confirms, the "irresistible" motive that persuaded Quincy to relinquish his influential seat as House Speaker lay in his ambitions for higher office. Specifically, Quincy had set his sights on the governorship of Massachusetts. His daughter Eliza recalled that Quincy "thought that some of the Federalists of that day were on a wrong track." His opposition to Maine separation and his consistent defiance of the Federalist party leadership, Eliza argued, made him "generally known & justly appreciated throughout the State & his new friends [wanted to] run him for Governor."[3] Such lofty aspirations would pit him against Harrison Gray Otis, and the bipartisan support Quincy earned in the General Court had the potential to seriously divide and disrupt Massachusetts Federalism. Also, the likelihood of controversy in the upcoming legislative session made Quincy's resignation in January highly pragmatic, timely, and politically advantageous. By absenting himself from the General Court one month before the proposed city charter reached the legislature, Quincy avoided having to take a legislative stand on the most divisive issue the General Court faced that year. When the Middling Interest publicly attacked Boston's representatives, "who not only opposed the wishes of their constituents, but joined in the votes which . . . defeated the purposes of the large majority of the town" over the ward-voting issue, Quincy could not be castigated for "utterly disregard[ing] . . . the people of Boston."[4]

Instead, Quincy evaded the controversy and lobbied to obtain an appointment as a municipal court judge in Boston—a position he received and accepted later that month. Ironically, Quincy's adversary, Governor John Brooks, awarded him the judgeship. Why is not clear. Perhaps, from the governor's point of view, Quincy would be less troublesome to him and the Central Committee as a municipal judge than as House Speaker. During Quincy's tenure as a municipal judge, he would consolidate power within what was rapidly becoming a divided town in the midst of a dramatic struggle to upset Federalist political hegemony in Boston.[5]

The news of Quincy's resignation from the General Court baffled Harrison Gray Otis. "Mr. Quincy's movement does indeed surprise me," he admitted to William Sullivan on January 19, 1822, from Washington. "It is a sort of practical bathos, to jump from the speaker's chair into that of the Boston old Bailey." Concluding that Quincy's "zeal for his friends and party have hurt his popularity, he probably expects the reward of neglect, which his friends and party first or last are apt to show towards those who are too zealous . . . —and as he gets nothing by being a great man amoung gentlemen, he will try his hand by showing himself a good one amoung whores and rogues—Good luck to him say I."[6] Otis clearly was unaware of Quincy's more ambitious intentions and had all too quickly written him off as an insignificant force within the state, let alone a serious political adversary within Boston. As future events would show, Otis's swift dismissal of Quincy was short-sighted.

Despite the optimism of his sponsors, Quincy's bipartisan power base did not have much endurance beyond the boundaries of Boston—and for good reason. By 1822 the Republican party's power had grown throughout the state. Although Federalism commanded Suffolk, Essex, and Hampshire counties, the party of "good men and good measures" faced decisive and growing opposition elsewhere in the state. The treasonous legacy of the Hartford Convention continued to haunt Massachusetts Federalism, providing Republican candidates with an easy, effective, and engaging line of attack in many parts of the state. The rural interests of town's like Plymouth, Bristol, Barnstable, and counties such as Norfolk, Berkshire, Hampden, and Worcester voiced opposition toward the mercantile and manufacturing interests so endemic to the Federalist party platform. In the fishing communities of Cape Cod, Martha's Vineyard, and Nantucket, Republicanism consistently was the party of choice.[7]

Led by a popular and articulate leadership, men like Levi Lincoln Jr. of Worcester, David Henshaw of Leicester, and William Eustis of Boston scrupulously sowed the seeds of Republicanism throughout the state. Although Federalist Governor John Brooks won seven consecutive elections, often by wide margins, his Republican challengers, Henry Dearborn, Jacob Crowninshield, and William Eustis still captured significant numbers throughout the state, demonstrating that Republicanism held substantial appeal. Clearly, the Republican party of Massachusetts represented a viable opposition, perfectly capable of challenging Federalism on the state level.[8]

Indeed, the key to John Brooks's political success within the Commonwealth was his moderate, nonpartisan stance. Since his first victory in 1816, Brooks had disingenuously praised Republican leadership in Washington while masking his predisposition to Federalism's most elitist doctrines. So pronounced was Brooks's nonpartisan image that President James Monroe, while visiting the Bay State, reciprocated the governor's flattery of the "Virginia Dynasty" by applauding Brooks's seemingly nonpartisan leadership of Massachusetts. As the Federalist organ, the *Palladium,* confessed, Brooks publicly restrained his excessive Federalism and followed a much less offensive course of "moderation and candour towards his opponents." Most importantly, Brooks took great care to avoid being identified as a member of the Federalist Central Committee. This was never more apparent than when, upon Brooks's first gubernatorial victory, the Massachusetts House of Representatives greeted him by proclaiming that the new governor came from "the same school" as former Republican governor, Caleb Strong. Brooks swiftly appeased his Republican critics by appointing them to public office. According to one student of Federalism, Brooks "beat back successive Republican challenges with a policy of moderation," which according to another exemplified "his artful dodging [that] belied a carefully contrived electioneering image of a simple-soldier-in politics."[9]

After the Hartford Convention, even in Massachusetts, campaigning as a staunch advocate of traditional Federalist principles would be political suicide. Understanding this, Brooks adopted the image of a sincere patriot who exemplified the nonpartisan tranquility of the Era of Good Feelings. His "artful dodging" consistently quelled Republican challenges to his administration and helped maintain Federalist dominance in the state. His reelection numbers steadily rose between 1816 and 1821.[10]

If the Federalist party nominated a candidate less bipartisan than Brooks, the Republican party could offer numerous creditable candidates who could run, perhaps even successfully. For Quincy, competing in a state that held a Republican party that, given the chance, could strongly dispute the dictatorial character of Federalism's backroom leadership in Massachusetts, a viable bid coming from an independent third party like the Middling Interest for the governor's seat was unrealistic. If reform in the manifestation of an antielite, anti-Federalist platform was to successfully evolve and break Federalism's traditional, yet increasingly tenuous stranglehold on Massachusetts, the Republican party could do the job.

By the early spring of 1822, Quincy abandoned his plans to run for governor and set his sights on the more reasonable goal of becoming Boston's first mayor. In this quest, the bipartisan support Quincy had garnered and was known for in the legislature and his reputation as a highly independent politician and staunch foe of the Federalist Central Committee would serve him well. Unlike its deteriorating political situation in the state, party organization in Boston soundly favored Federalism. Despite increasing hostility toward Federalist elitism, because of tradition and the party's highly organized machine Federalism remained the only viable party in town. The Republican party continued to be weak in Boston while Federalism remained ascendant. Thus, unlike reformers elsewhere in the state, Boston reformers could not look toward Republicanism as their savior. Any significant challenges to Federalist hegemony in Boston necessarily had to develop from a third party with the ability to woo regular Federalists into insurgent political activism.

By the beginning of 1822, such an insurgency was refined into a polished and highly defined third party that gained clarity from a controversial local issue that spoke to the direct concerns of many of Boston's lower-to-middle class voters. Beginning in 1821, many Bostonians were growing upset with an old 1803 fire law that restricted the building of wooden structures higher than ten feet within the town's limits. The anger that middling and lower orders first expressed over state issues such as the militia laws, the debtor's laws, and oppressive tax codes was reinforced and heightened due to the inability of many Bostonians to build affordable decent housing. The town's restrictive building codes severely confined the expansion of low-income housing in Boston and forced many poor-to-middling Bostonians to become dependent on landlords who easily sustained high rent rates by exploiting Boston's tight housing market. Also, the wooden building law limited work for many Boston master carpenters and journeymen, as well as profits for emerging entrepreneurs interested in raising cheap row housing. The 1803 fire law forced Boston's poor to search for inexpensive housing in Boston's poorer, more decrepit neighborhoods like the notorious North and West Ends. For the "respectable" mechanic or master carpenter, the law greatly obstructed his ability to erect a home or a lodging house that was affordable. This seemingly innocuous issue localized antielite, anti-Federalist sentiments for many disgruntled Bostonians whose backs were already bent and whose pocketbooks were empty—or close to it—because of the depressed economy.[11]

Boston's popular classes experienced a meaningful victory over the town's "betters" during the city chartering dispute while also sustaining a struggling embryonic, yet vocal, oppositional third party called the Middling Interest. Seasoned by past political action, they developed a unified group identity of sorts that clearly and forcefully would exhibit its class interests in the once forbidden realm of local politics. As insignificant as the wooden building issue perhaps seems, it functioned as the first test case in public policy for a newly energized Boston electorate—one freed from the bonds and obligations so inherent in Boston's past deferential political structure. The wooden building issue served to clarify insurgent third party activism by grounding earlier, somewhat inexplicit calls for reform to a precise local public policy concern within the specific confines of Boston.

In 1821 South Boston resident Lot Wheelright petitioned Boston Town Meeting to exempt South Boston for five years from the town ordinance that restricted the building of wooden structures higher than ten feet. In May, Town Meeting voted to grant Wheelright his request, stating "It was Voted, That the Town consent that the Laws, restricting buildings of Wood, more than ten feet high, may be suspended for the term of five years, so far as it relates to that Section of the Town."[12] Taking advantage of Wheelright's successful petition, Boston resident Josiah Jones presented his own petition asking Town Meeting to make an appeal to "the Legislature to alter or repeal the Law prohibiting the erection of Wooden buildings . . . more than ten feet high" throughout the whole town. Unlike Wheelright's, Jones's request covered all of Boston and demanded the total abolition of the 1803 law.[13]

On June 6, the town committee charged with considering Jones's petition presented its recommendation to Town Meeting. Committee chairman and reformer Stephen Codman explained that "it is the opinion of the Committee, that the existing Law may now be modified without any injury [to the town]; and inasmuch as it appears to be the general wish so to modify the Law, as to meet the wants and means of a large portion of respectable citizens, who have not the ability to erect buildings entirely of Brick or Stone[,] . . . [t]he Committee . . . recommend[s] . . . that the Legislature should be requested . . . to modify the existing

Law."[14] Codman's proposal overwhelmingly passed Town Meeting by "a majority [vote] of four to one," and the town's petition moved to the General Court for final approval.[15]

The legislature responded to Boston's petition by granting South Boston the right to raise wooden buildings above ten feet but denied the same privilege to the whole of Boston.[16] Bostonians responded with immediate disdain. "Mill Creek Wharf" wrote to his fellow "mechanics of Boston": "how astonished were the petitioners, to hear, when the bill was brought in, that it was entirely contrary to the expectations and wishes of a great majority of the town. This astonishment was not diminished when it was found that the greater part of the representatives from Boston chose to be absent on this occasion." "Mill Creek Wharf" explained that, "after the bill had received the signature of the . . . Speaker of the House [Josiah Quincy]," further qualifications were imposed by Boston representative Nathan Hale that basically neutralized any changes distinguishing the 1821 bill from the original 1803 fire law. "It is difficult to conceive," reiterated the editorialist, "why, after the petition had been approved by the town, any of our representatives should have been so much interested as to object." "MECHANICKS," heralded "Mill Creek Wharf," "keep your eyes well to the right—and steady—and at the next election of representatives, send such men to the general court as will do their duty without fear and trembling."[17]

Less than a month later, on July 13, a fire broke out in a wooden boardinghouse on Union Street destroying at least eleven buildings after spreading to Salt Lane and Creek Square. One week earlier, another fire ravaged Charlestown, incinerating at least $20,000 worth of property before being extinguished.[18] Such outbreaks seriously diluted, at least momentarily, Boston's outrage. Any significant reform in Boston's fire laws would have to wait until the summer fires in and around the town faded from public memory. This would not take long.

In January 1822, while the chartering controversy simultaneously raged in Town Meeting, John H. Wheeler raised the wooden building issue once again. This time, not only did the petition reiterate earlier demands for reform in the fire laws, it also directly charged that Boston's "Senators & Representatives be directed to use their influence in procuring the passage of a Bill by the Hon. Legislature conformable to the . . . vote [on wooden buildings] of the Town."[19] As had the Jones' petition, Wheeler's easily passed Town Meeting and was sent to the General Court for approval. As the petition's addendum ordering Boston legislators to follow the town's instructions suggests, the reformers, this time, left nothing to chance. The petition would arrive at the State House supported by a town committee hoping to persuade Boston's legislators to vote in favor of the town's request. If Boston's representatives in General Court snubbed the town once again, there would be serious consequences.[20]

Upon hearing the news of the second petition's overwhelming support and passage, Harrison Gray Otis, from Washington, shot off orders to his operatives to block the petition. "I see with dismay, the vote for wooden buildings," Otis anxiously wrote William Sullivan on January 19, 1822. "It seems incredible—Cannot you check it in the legislature befor[e], 'Ucalegon burns next.'"[21] As a landlord with extensive land and property holdings in Boston, Otis knew that the abolition of the fire law would directly affect the value of his properties. With a greater risk for urban fires, insurance rates would soar while property values would decline. Also, if the rental market in Boston expanded due to the erection of cheap wooden apartment buildings, Otis would face new competition. His rent rates would decrease and his income would fall.[22]

Accommodating Otis's directive, Sullivan orchestrated an effective counterattack. By stacking Town Meeting with antireform, established landlords, Sullivan forced through the passage of a formal grievance refuting the legitimacy of the Wheeler petition. According to Sullivan's remonstrance, Wheeler's proposal was invalid because it had not been presented in a referendum. As a result of Sullivan's parliamentary tactics in Town Meeting, the General Court would first have to rule against the grievance before it could even address the town petition. By employing such a strategy, the Central Committee crippled reform by complicating the wooden building issue once it reached the legislature.[23] For insurgent activists in Boston, Sullivan's conduct was all too familiar. His orchestrations represented all the problems with the town meeting system rolled into one. If Bostonians were not yet convinced that a Federalist "cabal" manipulated the system for its own political and personal interests against the will of the people, here was yet another blatant example of the Central Committee's shameless misconduct. The Federalist leadership seemed to be using its political influence to halt any competition to its economic interests in Boston. Although the wooden building issue held little interest in Boston when it first arose as a question, the way in which it was handled by the Central Committee seemed to many Bostonian to be a direct violation of the principles of democracy.

Buckingham was furious. "Certain people," he fumed in an editorial, "who never trouble themselves to attend town meeting,—thinking it rather beneath their *honorable* and *dignified* characters to meet in the same hall with mechanics and labouring men,—have presented a remonstrance against the petition." Attacking reform's opposition, Buckingham stated that "[i]t is, in short, a mere question of self-interest, in which the purse-proud landlord is arrayed against the mechanic. The remonstrance would never have existed, had not the large owners of real estates, seen in the success of the petition, a reduction of their already overgrown incomes from cruel and exorbitant rents. They would have no objection to wooden houses of two stories, provided they had the exclusive privilege of erecting and leasing them."[24] Without reform, Buckingham explained, the "present interest and future prospects of the middling and poorer classes" would remain bleak. "[T]here are mechanics, who, with the savings of a few years labour, might live in decent houses of their own, and look forward to a comfortable competency—perhaps to independence: and this is the reason, why the petition is so violently opposed. These lordly nabobs['] . . . object is to keep the mechanics and labourers in eternal servitude. . . . It remains," Buckingham challenged, "for the legislature of Massachusetts, to say whether the mechanics and labouring people of Boston shall be allowed to participate in the rights of privileges, which any form of government professes to guarantee to all, or whether all the lands and houses shall eventually become the property of a few landlords—whether a mechanic may be a freeholder, or whether he must be a tenant."[25] Despite Buckingham's appeal, the General Court agreed with the Sullivan grievance committee and rejected the town's request. Otis's strategy had worked. Expansion of the housing market would, temporarily at least, be stopped and existing rental rates maintained.

The town was again outraged by the legislature's behavior. So vocal was the criticism that many of the town's representatives grasped for the first time the immense popular support the issue wielded within Boston. Fearing defeat in the next elections because of their antireformist stance, some Federalist representatives broke with the Central Committee's standing orders and scrambled to reposition themselves on the question. As one Boston newspaper reported, "a representative from Boston, who lately remonstrated against the petition for leave to erect wooden buildings has set his name at the head of the new petition for the same object. What can have operated so *potentially* on his mind, as to induce him now to advocate a measure which three weeks ago he considered fraught with mischief and destruction to the town? Is it possible," queried the editorial, "that the fear of losing his seat in the legislature at the approaching election can have wrought such a miracle, as unstopping the ears of the deaf, opening the eyes of the blind, unloosing the tongue of the dumb, and convincing the understanding of the dull and obstinate?"[26] By the end of February, the Central Committee's traditional authority in the legislature buckled under the weight of overwhelming popular support for reform in the fire laws. Even obedient and traditionally loyal Federalist operatives found themselves turning their backs on Otis and the Federalist leadership out of political necessity. A number of Boston legislators perceived that to block this particular popular reform would be an act of political suicide. For Boston's popular electorate, the wooden building issue came to represent much more than simply the freedom to raise more affordable housing or to reduce rents. By February, the issue came to embody all of common Bostonians' objections to their city's wealthy Federalist leaders. However modest the reformers' goals, the wooden building issue became the urban proletariat's symbolic stand against what the electorate viewed as an elite Federalist hierarchy.

With a petition signed by a staggering 4,500-plus Bostonians, on March 6 Asa Lewis reintroduced the issue at Town Meeting and, after written ballots were taken, the measure passed by an awesome majority of 2,263 out of 3,411 votes. This time not only would the town selectmen lobby Boston representatives, but

Town Meeting also granted that "the petitioners [themselves] be empowered to appear . . . on behalf of the Town or City, to advocate, and defend the petition before the Hon. Legislature."[27] Buckingham's *Galaxy* commended Lewis and the petitioners while scolding Sullivan for having blocked the provision. "This result," Buckingham snorted, "will stop the clamour which was made at the former meeting on the same subject, because the vote was not decided by ballot. It is incontestably proved," claimed Buckingham, "that a large majority of the voters (of those at least who care any thing about the business [of Boston]) are in favour of the present unreasonable, unjust, and oppressive restrictions being removed." Broadening his critique of the wooden building issue, Buckingham squarely fused reformist goals with the plight of "the poorer classes [who] are hungry and homeless."[28]

Fearing further defections, the Federalist press down-played the issue as trivial. According to Boston's leading Federalist organ, the *Columbian Centinel,* reform of the old fire laws was of "no great significance to either party."[29] By so misreading the salience of the wooden-building issue, the Federalist press and its masters, unlike dissident Federalist legislators who switched their position, were oblivious to the third-party activism that had been smoldering for so long within the town's less affluent wards. This third-party movement would finally coalesce and ignite over the wooden building issue. Also, the Federalist leadership's response revealed to the town's insurgents Federalism's vulnerability—its brazen arrogance.

The Federalist *Daily Advertiser* squarely illustrated the party's temerity when it smugly argued that Boston mechanics, struggling with high rents, should be happy with their prospects and stop complaining. "As to the rent paid by the mechanics," the *Advertiser* asked, "would it be better for them to have the price greatly reduced?" Of course not, answered the *Advertiser,* because "high rents are a mark of prosperity."[30] Such insolent and insensitive logic infuriated a Boston working class that continually struggled to put food on the table, pay rent, avoid militia duty, and stay out of debtor's prison. An incensed Joseph Buckingham responded to the editorial, stating that "[i]f '[h]igh rents are a mark of prosperity,' so are thefts and robberies. A pick-pocket steals your purse and justifies himself by this convenient logic—'It is a mark of your prosperity; for if you had not a purse, I could not have taken it.' Another rogue breaks into your house; and this too is a mark of your prosperity, because if you had no house, he could not have committed the burglary, and a third murders you—all for your good, . . . proof that you had life, and you might not have known it had you never swallowed his arsenic or felt his dagger." Making matters worse, the "writer in the Daily Advertiser," charged an incensed Buckingham, irreverently insulted all who had signed the petition. The *Advertiser,* Buckingham claimed, "intimates that many of the signatures to the petition were procured in grog-shops. This is altogether in *keeping* with the general tone of the writers in that vehicle of aristocracy. It is meat and drink to them to libel the mechanic, and middling interests."[31] Indeed, the *Centinel* claimed that the "ten-footers," as the wooden building reformers were called, had "designing intentions, or to say the least the intemperate zeal of a few, to create out of an honest difference of sentiment on this minor topic, a general feeling of hostility which may . . . divid[e] a party [Federalism]."[32]

Although this undoubtedly was the intention of the Middling Interest, the *Centinel* boldly underestimated the insurgency's broader foundations. Despite the insurgency's youth and disorganized state, it had not developed on a whim, as the Federalist press suggested. Nor was the movement predicated solely on the wooden building issue. Reforming Boston's fire laws only provided the Middling Interest with one highly charged and popular plank to be added to its overall reformist platform. As Buckingham explained, the insurgency's principal agenda was to wage a protracted battle against the aristocratic and elitist course Federalism had recently taken—to fight against those who "see none of [the poor's] miserable tenements, [and] bears none of their gleanings—for them, he [the greedy Federalist] has no sympathy, with them he has nothing in common, but [collecting from] them *rent*." According to Buckingham, unlike the Federalist party, the Middling Interest championed "[t]he mechanics of Boston as intelligent, and as respectable in every thing, except the *respectability of wealth*, as any body of men that ever gave strength, support and security to any city or nation on earth."[33]

For ordinary Bostonians, Federalism's covert and consistent opposition to the ten-footers seemed symptomatic of the party's larger intentions: to maintain a ruling political and economic aristocracy at their expense. Two earlier attempts to reform the wooden building laws by functioning within established political guidelines were crushed by the Central Committee. By the spring of 1822, there was little doubt among the majority of ordinary Bostonians that the political system was being manipulated to sustain elite hegemony against the ascension of the honest and respectable plebeians. By restricting the upward mobility of Boston's respectable laborers and mechanics while exploiting their labor, extracting excessively high rents, taxing them through the militia laws and inequitable property assessments, forcing hardworking Bostonians into debt while, simultaneously, demanding and pompously expecting deference, the party of "good men and measures" lost the respect of the majority in Boston. As Buckingham asked Boston's ordinary voters, "shall they [the mechanics and laborers] be forever *cowed* down and kept out of countenance by a contemptible minority of overgrown landlords, and speculators, who were originally as low—aye, and much lower,—in the world than themselves?" These "haughty lordling[s] and the princely nabob[s] . . . possess no feeling in common with other men and [their] sympathies are never awakened but by the jingling of dollars." Because the legislature had disbanded for an extended vacation, this question, according to Buckingham, would finally be decided in Boston's upcoming mayoral contest. The hostile sentiments of the town indicated that the Federalist nominee would not run unopposed.[34]

The prospect of having the wooden building issue define the city's first mayoral contest certainly did not appeal to the Federalist leadership. Harrison Gray Otis maintained a controlling interest in the Mount Vernon Proprietors, Broad Street Association, and Mill Pond Corporation which had resulted in his commanding a real estate empire. The prospect of loosening the town's fire codes clearly was not in his or his various corporations' interest. With the abolition of the fire laws, Otis's empire would be jeopardized by more affordable building.[35] Also, although Otis and his operatives underestimated the strength of the insurgency, by March he and his handlers came to understand that the populist rhetoric of the ten-footers potentially threatened the Otis mayoral campaign. Quickly responding to the Central Committee's new insights on the election, the Federalist press no longer totally dismissed the ten-footers as irrelevant but instead attempted to appease and quiet the dissident factions of the electorate by calling for party unity. "[I]t can hardly be thought good policy," wrote the *Columbian Centinel,* "to endanger the peace and harmony of our city" over the wooden building issue. "Let us not . . . in the name of common sense, permit the evil spirit of discord to preside at the first election of our city officers." "Let us not . . . create out of an honest difference of sentiment on this minor topic, a general feeling of hostility [which will] divid[e] a party who have hitherto acted with no less union than success."[36] But the call for party unity came too late.

Much to the astonishment of the Federalist leadership, the wooden building controversy so vividly illuminated Federalism's aristocratic intentions that the party had, in fact, suffered serious desertions as Boston mechanics and laborers broke for the Middling Interest. Even worse, Boston Republicans had been first to rally around the issue and were swelling the insurgency's ranks. Finding itself on the defensive, the Central Committee was forced to acquiesce on the wooden building question. In an attempt to preserve Otis's mayoral prospects and salvage Boston Federalism from the menace of popular insurgency, the Federalist leadership reversed its position. As he had done in the past, Harrison Gray Otis managed damage control from Washington. "From the signs of the times," he wrote Sullivan on March 21, "I infer that if you mean to prevent the triumph of the revolutionary movement manifested in the new city, you ought to let the advocates for wooden buildings or the Roulstone party or who ever they are, understand that your opposition will be withdrawn. . . . I go upon the supposition that the wooden project cannot be resisted for any length of time: and as in the case of other popular hallucinations, the mischief must be yielded to, or others will follow the train." Concluding that the insurgency must be halted or "the Devil will break loose," Otis arranged for Boston's leading Federalists to publicly support the ten-footer's agenda in the upcoming Federalist caucus. He believed such a preemptive strike would effectively absorb the political potency of Boston's recent third party activism. By coopting the insurgency's most dynamic issue, the Middling Interest would be crushed while the vitality the third party had garnered by pressing the wooden building issue could be exploited to reinvigorate Federalism among the Boston masses.[37]

Initially, Otis's strategy seemed to work. During the March Federalist caucuses for the state senate, loyal Otis Federalists who had recently switched their position on wooden buildings gained their party's nomination with little opposition. Yet, Otis's cunning did not go unnoticed by Joseph T. Buckingham, who saw through the Federalist strategy: "We had hoped," Buckingham observed in the *Galaxy,*

> that the good sense of the mechanics would have triumphed over the shallow schemes of those who pretend to be their friends, when, at heart, they are the most thorough-going aristocrats in the town. We did hope that the wholesale dealers in *soft-soap,* who harangued the people at the late caucus, and daubed the middling interest an inch thick with that slippery commodity; and those who acknowledged their sudden conversion to the expediency of the city charter, (when they found it getting into popular favor) would receive from the mechanics the neglect to which their unstable, vacillating, toad-eating policy so eminently entitles them. We still hope that those, who are in favour of wooden buildings, have not pledged themselves to support the election of these men, beyond the power of reconsideration. Anything is better than a weathercock senator—who signs petitions one day and remonstrances the next—who, to gain a vote, will undergo a miraculous conversion, to the will of the people—and who wheedles with the oily tongue of a republican, though every drop of blood in his veins curdles at the approach of anything that is *mechanical.*[38]

By the end of March, insurgent leaders seemed to have reached the same conclusion as Buckingham. In a "large and respectable meeting" held at the Warren Hotel in Boston, two veterans of the wooden building reform movement, Michael Roulstone and William W. Blake, presided over the Middling Interest's first formal caucus.[39] It was from this meeting that the Middling Interest first developed a skeletal program that, in the months to come, would evolve into a highly articulate, refined and popular manifesto capable of providing an alternative to Federalism.

The insurgents adopted three primary resolutions reflective of future Jacksonian dogma. In keeping with its antiaristocratic foundations, the Middling Interest attacked the Central Committee, resolving that "no man nor corporation or association of men are better than the community in deciding leadership in Boston." Then, squarely confronting the deferential nature of Boston's existing political culture, the insurgents decreed that "all men . . . are in danger of being led by party names to act contrary to their true interests" and that this practice must stop. Finally, the caucus challenged the Federalist nominees for the state senate with its own nominees. Six office seekers came from both Federalist and Republican ranks, yet what each held in common was a deep distrust of the Central Committee. Heading the insurgents' list was Josiah Quincy's first cousin, fellow Federalist dissident, and loyal friend, John Phillips.[40]

The *Galaxy* announced the alternative caucus as an important triumph over "the nomination by the [Federalist] Grand Caucus, in which every puppet moves as the grand council of dictators pulls the wires." The Middling Interest's nominations, Buckingham explained, were, "[a]ll of them[,] . . . men in whom the mechanics and Middling Interest men have confidence."[41] Although the third-party slate threatened Federalism, the insurgency could not muster enough support for its senatorial candidates. The roots of past deferential behavior, though weakened, remained deep. Despite having amassed notable support, the Middling Interest men lost to the Federalist slate.[42]

To some extent, the third party's loss was to be expected. Since the beginning of March, the Middling Interest primarily focused its efforts on Boston's first mayoral race. More than any one issue, the insurgent struggle for ward voting during the chartering controversy distilled and largely shaped popular antiaristocratic dissidence into a compelling deviant political force within Boston-proper but had inspired little activism beyond Suffolk county. Although anger over state laws concerning debt imprisonment and militia requirements fueled populist discord within the town, little could be done to reform these laws on the local level. Against significant opposition, the town had successfully forced ward voting through the General Court, demonstrating that the state could be moved toward limited reform, if only on the local municipal level. By mid-March and under siege, the State House seemed to be warming to the idea of significantly reforming the city's fire laws, but, again, this only applied within the parameters of Boston. To achieve sweeping statewide reform without an established political organization and a sophisticated network throughout Massachusetts would be impossible. At best, the insurgency could and did exploit these state issues and, more importantly, Bostonians' anger over them to solidify a local coalition of interests; but actually to change state policy with the limited authority given to municipal Boston was as unrealistic as Josiah Quincy becoming governor. Also, the initial leadership for the movement stemmed not from the state but from the local level. Michael Roulstone and William Blake had little influence or experience in state politics. Because their concerns were predominately municipal in nature, they limited their ambitions to winning the mayoralty.[43]

Others in the Middling Interest held more inspired goals. Francis Wayland arrived in Boston in August 1821 to head one of only three Baptist churches in the city—the North End's First Baptist. As cleric to one of Boston's poorest wards, Wayland rose to a leadership position within the Middling Interest party less than a year after his arrival in Boston. Wayland's activist proclamations expanded the insurgency's ideological foundations by illuminating what he believed was the inseparable relationship between Christian theological doctrine and American citizenship. Christian duty and democratic citizenship held tangible social responsibilities that were inseparable and required devout citizen-stewards to organize and act against anything that threatened democratic principles. The result was a doctrine that justified Middling Interest democratic and social reform by blending it with Christian doctrine. "[I]f the church is faithful to herself, and faithful to her God," Wayland preached, "what are now called the lower classes of society will cease to exist. . . . [The] middling and lower classes of society understand the nature of liberal institutions, and those who are groaning under the weight of civil and religious oppression. The question at issue is, whether a nation shall be governed by men of its choice, or by men whose only title to rule is derived from hereditary descent." As Wayland revealed to his North End working-class parishioners, "Whatever we would do for our country, must be done for THE PEOPLE [for] the people are not only the real but also the acknowledged fountain of all authority."[44] In Boston outsider Francis Wayland, the Middling Interest found a dynamic, intelligent, and independent voice that offered ordinary people the self-determination to confront and abandon their traditional deferential voting behavior. The health of American democracy, Wayland pronounced, depended on an independent electorate freely voting its conscience unencumbered, not one entangled in a web of class spun by an economic elite.

As a populist leader Wayland could be trusted. He had come from a poor mechanic's family and had pulled himself up by his own initiative. He was born in New York City and raised within a staunchly Republican working-class family. As a tanner and an itinerant Baptist preacher, Francis's father fell in and out of debt. During the War of 1812, the family went bankrupt. At age twenty, Francis was accepted to Andover Seminary as a "charity case" and was the school's only Baptist student. After graduating from Andover, he wanted to continue his education at Princeton but, because he could not afford tuition, was forced to serve as a tutor at Union College to make ends meet. In 1821 he secured the Boston parish at the age of twenty-five.[45]

When Wayland arrived in Boston he was poor, and the parish he shepherded was even poorer. Indeed, the North End of the early 1820s was second only to Boston's West End for its number of brothels and dance halls. The town's most infamous whorehouse, the "Beehive," stood only blocks from Wayland's church. The neighborhood also housed a large proportion of Boston's mechanics, small shopkeepers, laborers, and artisans, many of whom were distrustful of Baptist evangelicals. Unlike their counterparts in other American urban centers during the early 1800s, Boston artisans had generally rejected the evangelical tide that swept the country. Customarily, Boston's artisans were not Methodists, evangelical Presbyterians, or Baptists but remained either Congregationalists or Unitarians. Much like Boston's Unitarian elite, artisans in Boston tended to clearly differentiate between their secular and nonsecular lives. For Wayland—the new minister charged with bringing life to Boston's dying First Baptist Church—Baptist doctrine proved a hard sell; yet, if he could fuse his brand of Christianity with the economic and political struggles of the day (struggles that he could identify with), Wayland deemed his mission might be achieved. As with Boston's lower-to-middling class of all denominations during the early 1820s, Wayland's parishioners were hard-pressed during the depression. The young Baptist preacher soon became renowned for helping people struggling with debt. Plying his powers of persuasion to get credit extended or dispensing what little discretionary funds were available to him, Wayland aided North Enders threatened with debt imprisonment. His popularity grew within months of his arrival in Boston, and those who followed him became known as Waylandites. His followers were mostly young men who proved to be as politically defiant and zealous as Wayland himself. Following Wayland's teachings, they maintained that religiously defined aspects of social justice should direct secular social policy. Waylandites composed the core cell within the Middling Interest, while Wayland himself emerged as one of the insurgency's most charismatic leaders.[46]

Embracing the Middling Interest, Wayland distinguished himself from other insurgent leaders like Roulstone and Blake by carefully assembling a sophisticated three-pronged political program that appealed to a beleaguered working electorate that felt unfairly exploited by what it viewed as an uncaring and self-serving aristocracy. First, Wayland passionately believed that Christian duty demanded popular democracy. Without a government by the people, human progress could not evolve. According to Wayland, if the rich and wellborn continued to control the government, the democratic promise of universal freedom could never be reached. The future of the country "lay in the hands of 'the middling class of citizens, that portion of men who unite intelligence with muscular strength—the farmer, the mechanics,'" and not the wealthy, the connected, or the gentrified. In this sense, Wayland was a democratic idealist who, unlike Federalists of the Hamiltonian tradition, strongly believed that the voice of the people echoed the voice of God. Secondly, Wayland attacked both the Federalist and Republican parties, claiming that neither represented the true interests of their constituencies and served only the needs and desires of party officials.[47] As he wrote to his friend Mark Tucker, "[t]he longer I look and think, the more I am convinced that I am right. I will not be . . . the subject of a *party*."[48] By distinguishing the Middling Interest from both established parties, Wayland's antipartyism allowed the nonpartisan insurgency to draw membership from both Republican and Federalist rolls. And finally, like his insurgent colleagues, Wayland quickly came to despise what he identified and distinguished from the rank-and-file as Boston's oppressive Federalist aristocracy. This was an appealing political and social doctrine predicated on traditionally unpopular evangelical values.

While Joseph T. Buckingham persistently utilized the *Galaxy* to expose the impact of Federalist elitism on the ordinary citizens of Boston and the state, and consistently demanded specific reforms, Wayland simultaneously attacked the corrupting influence of the two-party system on the human soul. "The spirit of party," he reminisced in 1826, "pervaded all ranks of society, and mingled its bitter waters with all the relations of civil and domestic life. . . . [It] infused its hateful influence into the services and devotions of the sanctuary of God. . . . The salvation of the soul itself seems unimportant, in comparison with the all absorbing question, which of these two political parties should be uppermost."[49] Although publicly Wayland assaulted both parties equally, privately he confessed his rhetoric was designed to tear down Federalism.[50]

Traditionalist Federalists throughout Massachusetts balked at the insurgency's public pronouncements. Recent Harvard graduate and Otis supporter Ralph Waldo Emerson clearly illustrated his contempt for the insurgency. Writing to John Boynton Hill in March 1822, Emerson explained that the third party was "a band of murmurers . . . a parcel of demagogues, ambitious . . . of being known, [and] hoping for places as *partisans* which they could not achieve as citizens."[51] The Federalist Central Committee viewed Wayland's party and his diatribes in a similar light. How else could Federalism's leadership interpret such threatening statements being issued from the North End as "the great changes in a nation must always be commenced [by] the common people" or "[t]he question at issue is, whether a nation shall be governed by men of its choice, or by men whose only title to rule is . . . from hereditary descent"?[52] Wayland even went after the newly revised state constitution, stating that it was "utterly worthless" because it was not "written on the hearts of a people."[53] With Wayland's vital contributions to Middling Interest doctrine, Federalism faced an energized political force inspired by moral righteousness.

By the winter of 1822, the disparate and often fragmented voices of Boston discontent found a viable home in the Middling Interest party. Armed with a litany of meaningful state and municipal issues, a sympathetic organ, the *New England Galaxy,* from which to disseminate party ideology and positions, a leadership that held a distinctly democratic doctrine zealously fortified by Christian principles, and a disgruntled electorate eager for social and political reform, the Middling Interest party in Boston rapidly developed into a mature, viable alternative to Federalism. In March the insurgency leadership began searching for a suitable candidate to pit against the "aristocracy's" chieftain, Harrison Gray Otis.

VI • THE MAYORAL ELECTION OF 1822 AND THE TRIUMPH OF THE MIDDLING INTEREST

The wheels of revolution are in motion.
—Joseph T. Buckingham, 1822

It is the magic of the many that sets the world on fire.
—Harrison Gray Otis, 1822

By late spring 1822, a broad and fractious coalition came together under the Middling Interest's reformist banner. "Ten-footers" united with frustrated debtors and angry militiamen. Ward-voting advocates and tax reformers joined in as well. Boston's dissenting electorate concluded that neither the Federalist leadership nor the ineffectual Republicans could or would satisfy its demands for reform. Thus it looked elsewhere. Possessing a new political awareness, ordinary Bostonians moved beyond past partisan rancor and embraced the insurgent vision put forth by Francis Wayland and other Middling Interest spokesmen.

The depression of 1819 initiated a charged atmosphere of social and economic reform that gave rise to political unrest in Boston. As the reverberations of the depression spread throughout the city, popular resistance to the political status quo erupted. Under the weight of depression, required militia service seemed no longer an act of patriotism but an oppressive tax. Imprisonment for debt seemed excessive when so many Bostonians were unemployed, or working harder than before only to avoid the debtors' gaol. Boston's fire laws no longer seemed practical when they helped maintain high rents and stifled the "small man's" prospects of ever owning a modest home to ensure a secure retirement. Modest property owners condemned a tax code that taxed thrice over for no other reason, it seemed, than to fill the pockets of unscrupulous judges.

Even the 1780 state constitution had seemed stale and in need of change due to a myriad of new developments within the state and the people's consistent calls for reform. Adding to popular frustrations, once a constitutional convention met, the reformists were swiftly silenced. Slippery lawyers and unscrupulous judges had rigged the convention before it had even convened to quell reformist impulses within the state. On the local level, Boston's voting majority no longer revered the small band of Federalist elites who controlled Boston's traditional town meeting system of governance. Instead, the majority demanded a representational system where all could vote in the privacy and security of one's own neighborhood, far from the prying employer's or client's eyes.

These were the issues and battles—both won and lost—that helped bind the Middling Interest coalition together in 1822. The single most resonant chord among the variety of interests within the coalition was a unifying and impassioned hatred of a common enemy—the Massachusetts Federalist Central Committee. For many Bostonians, the Federalist leadership of Harrison Gray Otis, Thomas H. Perkins, William Sullivan, and their lackeys—those "purse-proud devils," as Joseph T. Buckingham called them—was viewed no longer with deference but, instead, with overt contempt.[1] The adherents of the Middling Interest viewed this leadership as having betrayed the people's trust. From the Central Committee's stubborn defense of the militia system to its hidden role in blocking any significant constitutional reforms in 1820–21, from its stand against ward voting to its neglect of the debtors' plight, the Central Committee faced an increasingly hostile citizenry. Voters began to detect a pattern in the Central Committee's actions. To Boston's insurgents and their followers, the Federalist establishment rigidly quashed any popular challenges to the deference it had for so long enjoyed.

The antideferential stance toward Boston's traditional economic, social, and political establishment (as represented by the Central Committee) led to a class confrontation in Boston. This political and cultural rebellion challenged the patterns of dominance traditionally exhibited by the established Federalist elite. Specifically, the insurgency exposed the Central Committee for what it had become: a prejudicial, closed fraternity that promoted and perpetuated, through political manipulation, its own power and class interests. At the same time, the committee continued to claim a disinterested and paternal devotion to all the people within the Commonwealth.

With the committee's cynical responses to popular demands for reform between 1819 and 1822, many disgruntled Bostonians became skeptical of the "honorable" intentions, if not the very honor, of Federalism's leadership. The deference ordinary Bostonians once voluntarily bestowed upon leaders like Harrison Gray Otis and William Sullivan turned sour in the wake of depression. With the Boston elite's paternal intent under fire, a political and cultural mutiny arose among the city's rank-and-file electorate.

As they had during the war years of 1812 through 1814, Bostonians in 1819 endured a depression. But, in that earlier period, the Federalist establishment's prompt political and economic response had attended to the needs of the public. Leveling all blame on the Republicans for the war and the resulting depression, the Federalist establishment had doled out patronage and employment to ease the region's economic burden. This was not the case in 1819, and ordinary Bostonians took matters into their own hands, calling for a variety of political reforms to ease spiraling economic hardships. Elite leadership replied to such grass-roots activism with obdurate resistance and an insensitive attitude of upper-class superiority. The result was the formation of an aggressive, coalitional insurgency, unified in its common resentment toward the upper class's behavior, which drew support from both Republican and Federalist ranks.

For the Central Committee and the interests and class it served, the development of such a dissident political body held profound implications for its dominance of Boston, if not the state. For Boston's "commoners" to so overtly defy the will of their "betters" demonstrated the fragility of elite-class political and cultural hegemony in Boston. In this sense, Harrison Gray Otis's fearful characterization of the Middling Interest as a "revolutionary movement" was not without foundation.[2]

In the spring of 1822, the insurgency formally introduced its populistic manifesto, reinforcing Otis's fears. In a widely distributed pamphlet, the Middling Interest declared: "We claim from our Constitutional agents *deference* to the known will of the majority." In a thinly veiled condemnation of the Central Committee, *An Exposition of the Principles and Views of the Middling Interest* announced, "we deprecate the secret influence of a FEW" who ignored the authority of the majority. Focusing its outrage on the committee's recent political intrigue in blocking various Boston reforms, the Middling Interest claimed that the people "have been denied in measures. They have been utterly disregarded by those, whom the people of Boston elected into the last Legislature. . . . Our senators and representatives not only opposed the wishes of their constituents, but joined in the votes which in one instance defeated the purpose of a large majority of the town. . . . We allude to the petition for wooden buildings, and the provision in the city charter, for election of State and United States officers in wards." Ward voting, the Middling Interest explained, was essential because "the majority are, and of right ought to be, sovereign; and that there is not, nor can be danger intrusting to the majority, when every voter in the Commonwealth is left free to form, [to] express and act upon his own opinion of men and measures." Holding that the majority "were treated with contempt," the *Exposition* assailed those class interests that the "FEW" represented and the specific business ventures which had helped make Otis, Perkins, and Sullivan wealthy and prominent men in Boston: "We hold it preposterous to admit that a high prize in a lottery, or *a successful speculation in land* or merchandize, confers knowledge and understanding, and still more admit that any man can or ought to have influence on any other qualification than the soundness of his judgement, the fairness of his mind, and his ability to be useful."[3]

Adding a touch of antipartyism to the Middling Interest platform, the *Exposition* stated that insurgents "pledge[d] themselves to nothing but the suppression of party spirit, and the violence and overbearing domination of those, who seek power for the gratification of possessing it, and use the influence it gives, to control freedom of opinion and independence of suffrage." Addressing the hypercritical and obviously threatened Federalist press, the pamphlet concluded: "It has been sneeringly said, that the Middling Interest is an array of the POOR against the RICH. On the contrary, the Middling Interest are as ready to admit the just influence of the rich as the few, who affect to enroll all of them in their ranks, . . . [yet] we know many rich men who have not a particle of political influence." These men, according to the *Exposition,* would be welcomed into the insurgency.[4]

If anyone in Massachusetts politics *seemed* to have "not a particle of political influence" and had rebuffed "enroll[ment]" into the "ranks" of the "FEW," it was Josiah Quincy. After twenty years in politics and at the age of fifty, Quincy's professional life seemed a profile in political decline. In just nine years, he had fallen from prominence as a nationally known figure in the U.S. Congress to an inconsequential municipal judge. Indeed, Harrison Gray Otis, in January 1822, had written Quincy off as a tired political has-been. Having fallen out of favor with the Central Committee, Quincy found a renegade urban constituency ready to welcome him. In his role as a municipal judge, Quincy first courted and then captivated this dissenting element in Boston's political landscape. The man on the outs with the Central Committee, was now the champion of the Middling Interest.

While "try[ing] his hand . . . amoung whores and rogues," as Otis disparagingly characterized Quincy's departure from the State House to the municipal court, the new justice promptly distinguished himself as an activist committed to reforming what he charged were obstacles to the "just distribution and wise execution of the principles of justice."[5] Quincy understood the enmity the populace felt toward the judiciary. As a judge he would use this animosity for his own purposes. From popular frustration over judicial exemptions from militia service to countless charges of judicial corruption, judges of all stripes bore vigorous popular attacks on their character. Since the depression's beginning, judges had been criticized for their excessively high salaries. Their attempt in Boston to maintain their taxing powers by preserving the Court of Sessions had raised the ire of most Bostonians. "The truth is," wrote Joseph Story to his fellow judge, Jeremiah Mason, in January 1822, "the Judiciary in our country is . . . open to attack from all quarters. . . . Its only support is the wise and the good and the elevated in society."[6] It was just this segment of society on which the Middling Interest had declared war. As a judge, Quincy quickly differentiated himself from the rest, who were routinely perceived as unscrupulous and money-grubbing.[7]

Within two months of his appointment and with an eye toward gaining the "mass of the community's" support, Judge Quincy launched a two-pronged attack on the same judicial system he had so recently joined. First, he criticized the practice of judicial sentencing. Because Boston maintained only one jail, all convicted of a crime within the municipality, no matter the severity, were confined to the Leverett Street Jail. There was little, if any, segregation of inmates. Women, children, and men—the violent, the deviant, and the disturbed—all who were convicted, ended up on Leverett Street; violent criminals freely commingled with debtors and poverty-stricken children guilty of petty theft. Such integration outraged Quincy, for, as he stated before the Suffolk County grand jury within a month of Boston's first mayoral contest, "society itself does little else [under such a system] than plot the ruin of every juvenile offender, and every novice in crime, when it provides no other alternative for punishment, than confinement in gaol." "Why," Quincy asked, "should not a power be invested in the judges" to separate criminals on the basis of "age, or sex, or degree of offense?"[8] Joseph Buckingham's *New England Galaxy* concluded that by "degree of offense" Judge Quincy was referring to debtors and their imprisonment. Having consistently criticized the treatment of debtors, the *Galaxy* heralded Quincy as "entertaining such rational and philanthropic views [as] to produce a reformation" in judicial sentencing. The *Boston Recorder*, a nonpartisan Congregationalist magazine, praised Quincy's charge, asserting, "we have long felt, doubtless in common with the mass of our fellow citizens, that there are great defects either in the laws themselves or in their execution."[9]

Quincy's second salvo revitalized long-standing popular grievances stemming back to the constitutional convention that accused the judiciary with inefficiency and corruption. In his March directive, Quincy denounced his judicial brethren for making "gain from their [the people's] vices: as making profit by their [the people's] passions; and as interested to enhance their [the people's] losses and miseries, by multiplying, or lengthening out their [the people's] controversies [trials]," while steadily accumulating excessively high court fees. Echoing complaints first issued by reformers during the 1820–21 Convention, Quincy charged the judiciary with serving its own selfish interests at the taxpayer's expense. After scolding his fellow judges for their blatant economic opportunism, if not outright corruption, Quincy declared that "everywhere the robe of justice should be spotless," for it was the poor who suffered most under a fraudulent judiciary.[10]

Quincy's widely publicized demands for judicial reform undeniably added to his popularity. As Boston editorialist "LABEO" commented, Judge Quincy, in his argument before the grand jury, "enlarge[d] with much force and eloquence upon the manner in which justice is administered to the lower classes of society by the inferior judicial tribunals. And he very properly adverts to that disgrace of the Statute Book, the act by which the compensation of Justices is made to depend upon the number of cases they decide; an act that gives them direct interest in the stirring up of petty suits, and embroiling the whole mass of society." This same criticism of the judiciary's compensation had been raised by Stephen Codman in Town Meeting one year earlier.[11]

As the Codman committee reported to the town, $1,366.45 was paid "to *one* Justice between February and October," while, that same year, three more had divided the tidy sum of $3,100.63 among themselves.[12] Justice Joseph Story estimated that the average salary of a state judge stood at $2,400, not including fees rendered in court.[13] When the average wage of a common laborer rested at 80 cents a day, a carpenter's at 89 cents a day, a printer's at $1.22 at day, and a blacksmith's at under $1.00 a day, the justices' base salaries of $7.00 a day (not including their fees) seemed excessive.[14] Considering that in 1822 a gallon of Jamaican rum cost $1.25, a cord of wood went for $3.86, and a gallon of lamp oil sold for $1.00, the high cost for life's most basic necessities combined with a modest income placed great financial burdens on the average working Bostonian.[15] Popular resentment toward the judicial branch's lucrative earnings remained high in 1822 and probably grew as the lingering depression undermined the average Bostonian's ability to pay debts, rents, and taxes. Once in the court system, the common debtor all too often watched as lawyers, judges, and plaintiffs walked away with his hard-earned money, leaving him deeper in debt and facing jail time.[16]

Certainly, concerns about debt imprisonment weighed heavily on the minds of many Bostonians who would vote in the April mayoral election. The call for the abolition of the debtor's law was as vigorous and incendiary as ever. In the spring of 1822, Middling Interest spokesmen seized the issue, stressing it as an essential component in the upcoming mayoral contest. Days before the mayoral election, the *Galaxy,* now fully committed to the insurgency, joined the outcry against the law. "[I]t is much to be deplored," wrote Joseph T. Buckingham, "that some kind of law cannot be made to give relief to a very numerous and very respectable class of people" who, in unprecedented numbers, were being sent to prison for indebtedness. "[A]bolishing imprisonment for debt . . . is demanded on every principle of justice and humanity."[17] Other insurgent partisans concentrated their wrath on the hypocrisy that Josiah Quincy had identified in judicial sentencing. As Middling Interest spokesman William Emmons asked, "how long shall we inflict a cruel, unholy, and unconstitutional punishment on the unfortunate of our land, while we treat the felon with less severity than we now treat poor unfortunate Debtors!"[18]

Although Quincy had not directly championed the debtor's movement, his condemnation of sentencing "respectable" offenders to the same "gaol" as "vicious" criminals, combined with his assault on the integrity of the bench, earned him the support of the debtor's wing of the Middling Interest. This support only intensified when, one month before the election, he proposed a solution for minor crime such as debt delinquency, which he claimed society was responsible for: How "strange" it was, Quincy declared "to prosecute and punish crime, [when] there is little . . . in our public institutions of the character of prevention."[19] According to Quincy, crime—though endemic to humankind—could be curbed if all of society faced itself and took responsibility for its uglier sides. Quincy believed in the organic nature of community. Therefore, to stop crime, all citizens held a moral obligation to work toward its prevention through social reform.[20]

Quincy's successful promotion in Town Meeting for the House of Industry in

1821 was predicated upon this conviction. It was the duty of the organic whole to distinguish between the "vicious" and the "virtuous" poor.[21] Potentially, both could be reformed, Quincy believed, but each required dramatically different types of disciplinary instruction. In 1821, despite criticisms leveled upon the exorbitant cost of the House of Industry, Quincy argued that segregation of the "vicious" and the "virtuous" was a "moral duty . . . in a republican form of government, . . . connected intimately with the very principle, on which its preservation depends. In such a form of government, the great object of attention is the character and condition of the mass of the community. What ever tends to contaminate, to corrupt, or to demoralize the mass, has a direct effect, not only on the happiness and prosperity of the state, but also its safety; on the security of property, of life, and of liberty; all of which are . . . directly dependent upon the moral character and condition of the people. [This responsibility] cannot be tested by any narrow scale of pecuniary expense and saving."[22] As a municipal court judge, this philosophy informed Quincy's decisions in sentencing criminals he faced in his courtroom.

Faced with what he viewed as an unreasonable dilemma of having to sentence both "honorable" debtors and "dishonorable" thieves to the same prison, Judge Quincy distinguished himself from his judicial brethren by publicly lashing out at the prison system. According to Quincy, the "moral character and condition of the people"—the very foundation of "a republican form of government"—depended upon the benevolent role of an activist state, which held the power and duty to prevent the demoralization of the masses which would lead to social chaos. Such an essential obligation of the government outweighed any private concerns over the cost because both social order and democracy hinged on "the character and condition of the mass of the community." The mixing of the "virtuous" debtor with the "vicious" criminal amounted to a dangerous betrayal of the people by the state. Such integration, according to Quincy, would naturally lead to the contamination and corruption of society. Remaining true to his convictions, Judge Quincy served uncharacteristically light sentences to those whose only crime was their poverty.[23] Furthermore, Quincy's March pronouncement on the judicial system adequately distanced the potential mayoral candidate from the entrenched judicial establishment, helping him forge an independent base from which to run for mayor.

When, in the spring of 1822, the Middling Interest deliberated the choice of a viable candidate to stand against Harrison Gray Otis and the Central Committee, Josiah Quincy seemed an exemplary prospect. First, he desired the position. Secondly, Quincy had a long political association with some of the insurgent leadership going back to his involvement in the Washington Benevolent Society. One of the Middling Interest's founders, Michael Roulstone, had served on the same 1812 standing committee that had asked Quincy to join the WBS and function as its first vice-president. Also, while in the Massachusetts House of Representatives, Quincy earned the Republican minority's respect, especially from those representatives from Boston who had become recent converts to the insurgency like Francis Wayland's deacon, the representative of Boston's Ward 1, Heman Lincoln. Lincoln had been a loyal Republican before shifting to the Middling Interest cause and, like Wayland, advocated a Quincy mayoralty.[24]

Middling Interest men who had stood against city chartering like Joseph T. Buckingham, a dissident Federalist, and William Emmons, a converted Republican, supported Quincy as well. This faction within the Middling Interest remained leery of the charter due to the excessive authority over the city that section 30 surrendered to the General Court.[25] Accurately regarding section 30 as a Federalist Central Committee ploy to control its interests in Boston, the anticharter bloc still viewed the charter with great suspicion. Because Quincy shared precisely the same misgivings, this wing of the insurgency believed that if anyone could be trusted as mayor it was Quincy. As Buckingham explained, "Mr. Quincy's opposition to the charter may, with some persons, be an objection to his eligibility to the Mayoralty. We think otherwise. He opposed it because he saw . . . mischief in the section which gives the legislature unrestrained power over the charter. He is . . . still of the same opinion; and . . . will be still on the watch to see that we are not made the foot-ball of a foolish legislature, and [he will] be ready to repeal the danger when it approaches." Emmons agreed. Also, it was remembered that in one of his last acts as Speaker of the House, Quincy had endorsed the original bill to reform Boston's restrictive fire laws. Although the Federalist legislature overwhelmingly struck down the reform bill, Quincy had supported the Middling Interest's well-publicized policy stand against the "haughty lordling[s] and . . . princely nabobs." The prominence of the wooden building issue in the insurgency's laundry list of policy reforms equaled ward voting in defining the movement. It was a reform that would have a consequential impact on hundreds of carpenters, renters, and ascendant entrepreneurs.[26]

Although Quincy's position on the divisive issue of the militia laws remained ambiguous, his speech before the Massachusetts Peace Society in late December 1820, attacking the "military fanaticism which was pervading the country," indicated Quincy's sympathy for militia reform. Quincy believed war resulted from the two-pronged evil of an unreformed society where poverty and entrenched military establishments necessitated war. Why would the poor choose peace over battle when they "go . . . to war beggars, [and] return from it nabobs," their pockets filled with "plunder," Quincy asked. With the maintenance of organized military establishments, "fighting and killing one another," Quincy argued, "is, no longer . . . a matter of blood, but a matter of business." Though he did not directly vilify the militia laws, clearly he viewed them as barriers toward "improving [the] moral and intellectual condition of mankind," which, according to Quincy, was the only course society could take to achieve ordered peacefulness.[27]

In many ways, the connection Quincy had made among poverty, military organizations, and the creation of a peaceful society harmonized well with the anti-militia movement's message. The movement had never been based on pacifist principles; rather, it stemmed from the growing economic insecurities of ordinary militiamen who regarded mandatory service as yet another oppressive tax being heaped upon them by the elite to protect the moneyed interests. Forced militia service drove them into poverty. Thus the movement's rhetoric emphasized class inequity within the unreformed militia laws. As with the debt reformers, after the militiamen's petitions to the legislature were ignored or voted down and their voices in the constitutional convention silenced, they rejected past partisan loyalty and united with the Middling Interest.[28] Like the tax reformers, the debtors, and the ten-footers, the militiamen searched for a candidate who hated the manipulations and political intrigue so often employed by the Central Committee. In Josiah Quincy they found their man.

Indeed, as early as April 1821 Quincy had accepted his ostracism from the committee and began publicly distancing himself from the Federalist establishment as a whole. His speech chastising the committee for "turning [him] overboard [in the state senate] and making shark's meat of [him]" clearly was a well-timed jab at the party leadership meant to help redefine his political image.[29] A year later, with his independent stand as a municipal judge, Quincy had completed his personal process of political transformation. To the delight of Middling Interest men, not only did Quincy seem perfectly content with his ostracism from the Central Committee, but he seemed to relish in it. Freed from the committee, Quincy thrived, putting forth his own reformist vision that served as a distinct political alternative for dissident factions in Boston's electorate.

In early March 1822, according to Eliza Quincy, "a number of Citizens . . . sent a Committee to his [Quincy's] house in Hamilton Place, headed by a Master Carpenter to ask him to stand [as] their candidate for the Mayoralty." Because of Quincy's highly publicized opposition to the Boston city charter he hesitated, stating that "it would be like choosing Guy Faulkes [*sic*] for mayor, for he had done all he could to blow up the city." Nevertheless, now that the governor's office seemed beyond his grasp, Quincy undertook a personal campaign to reposition himself in his race against Otis for the mayoralty. Despite his false modesty, Quincy immediately accepted the delegation's offer to lead the insurgency.[30]

Having found a candidate, Middling Interest strategists formed a scheme to capture the mayoralty. The insurgents planned to raise a floor fight at the Federalist nominating caucus and thus replace the Central Committee's candidate, Otis, with Quincy. On April 4 the caucus met at the Boston Exchange Coffee House. William Sullivan served as both caucus moderator and Otis's emissary. Many men were nominated for mayor, but after a number of ballots were taken, the contest came down to Quincy and Otis. The Middling Interest strategy seemed to be working. However, in the final balloting, moderator Sullivan ensured that Otis received the majority by allowing some Otis supporters to cast their votes after the balloting had officially ended. Holding only five more votes than Quincy, Otis was declared the Federalist mayoral candidate.[31]

Middling Interest delegates immediately rejected the decision, charging that the caucus had been rigged. The insurgent delegates, according to the Boston press, "contend[ed] that persons [Otis supporters] had been permitted to mark after the vote had passed for the closing of the marking." The insurgency's charges were valid. As early as January 18, William Sullivan had guaranteed Otis the Federalist nomination. He assured the senator: "Proper measures will be taken [during the caucus]" to secure the ticket. Indeed, as the *Galaxy* later exposed, the caucus had been controlled by "the exclusive and one-sided policy [of the Central Committee]." In an attack on Sullivan, the *Galaxy* went on to explain that "[t]he moderator of [the] caucus has *convenient ears;* he never hears the name of an independent man; but he can hear *whispers* from the well known, tried and faithful servants of the aristocracy, or he can, upon an emergency, take *nods* and *winks* for a nomination."[32] For the insurgent reformers, the Central Committee's conduct in caucus recalled past unscrupulous indiscretions experienced during the constitutional convention and the Town Meeting debates over the charter.

Even before the caucus, the Middling Interest forces were at a distinct disadvantage. Sullivan had been hard at work consolidating Otis loyalists. Beginning in March, the full weight of the Federalist machine had been set in motion to promote the Otis ticket and crush any challengers. On March 19, 1822, the "fanatical" Federalist editor (as Joseph Buckingham described him) John Russell heartily endorsed Otis for mayor in his *Evening Gazette.* The *Daily Advertiser,* which Buckingham declared existed solely to "support a monied aristocracy," followed suit as did the "irritable in the extreme" Benjamin Russell in his *Columbian Centinel.* Not only did every Federalist organ in Boston predictably sponsor Otis, but the entire Federalist press in Boston refused even to acknowledge Quincy as a candidate. Only on Election Day did John Russell's *Gazette* grudgingly recognize the Quincy candidacy. Though declining to even identify the Middling Interest nominee by name, Russell, in one short and dismissive sentence, unequivocally opposed Quincy's bid for the mayoralty. As "citizens and federalists," Russell wrote, "we feel impelled to resist the nomination of *this* gentleman."[33]

Only Joseph Buckingham's *Galaxy* supported Quincy against the machine. On March 29 the *Galaxy* formally endorsed the Middling Interest–Quincy ticket, stating: "Our mayor should be a man who will consider himself the chief officer of a large and respectable republic—not the favored child of [the] junto—a man, who, in executing the laws, will not know a Tyrian from a Trojan; and who in nominating candidates for subordinate offices, will be free from the shackles of favoritism. Such a man is the Hon. Josiah Quincy. . . . [I]f a course of honest and *independent* conduct through evil report and good report—if experience in the deliberative assemblies of State and nation—if courtesy to political opponents, and the exercise of gentlemanly deportment to all, whether high or low, *rich or poor*, are to be of any avail, Mr. Quincy is pre-eminently entitled to be the first Mayor of the City of Boston"[34] Despite the *Galaxy* endorsement, Quincy and the Middling Interest still faced overwhelming odds.

What the Middling Interest proposed was a grass-roots challenge to a hostile Federalist leadership that viewed Otis's ascendancy to the mayoralty as the first crucial step in its ultimate goal of placing the committee chieftain in the governor's mansion. As the Federalist caucus indicated, the Central Committee proved willing to go to extreme lengths to achieve its final objective. In this sense, the committee wagered that the bonds of deference that had maintained the party's rank-and-file in the past would hold, despite its conniving behavior in the caucus.

It was within this context that the Middling Interest delegates broke with the Federalist caucus on the night of April 4, 1822. Furious and embittered by the blatant scheming of Sullivan and the Central Committee, the insurgents stormed out of the Boston Exchange Coffee House to hold their own independent caucus the next evening in Justice Quincy's own courtroom. On April 5 the "Middling Political Interest" caucus unanimously nominated Quincy as its candidate. Quincy, in turn, heartily accepted the nomination.[35]

"Of course," Eliza Quincy recalled, "the nomination of Mr. Quincy was a great surprise to [the Central Committee]. . . . Boston it was said had never been thrown into such a state of excitement."[36] To be more accurate, Quincy's acceptance of the Middling Interest nomination sent a chilling shiver throughout the Massachusetts Federalist establishment that proved to have devastating political, personal, and cultural implications.

Having been notified of Quincy's betrayal just hours after the Middling Interest caucus disbanded, Thomas H. Perkins dashed off an agitated letter to Otis, who was still in Washington. "Quincy has thrown himself into the 'Midling or Medling Interest' and has suffered himself to be put up as Mayor. . . . As I gave him my mind very freely on the subject, we are of course at Swords points. . . . [H]e will have the high gratification of having split up the federal party. . . . Wm Sturgis has been his great 'slang wanger,' and he carries with him the 'ten footers,' and a portion of the Democracy [Republicans] which is always the most opposed to the most conspicuous of the federal party—Webster, Lowell, Tudor, all the Judges and those whom I know you to feel a high respect for, are ardent in the expression of the wish that your name should not be taken from the list. . . . But for this most improper conduct of Quincy, the Election of the Mayor would have been unanimous."[37]

From faraway Salem, the Federalist chieftain of Essex County, Leverett Saltonstall, frantically wrote to his Boston friend and fellow Federalist, William Minot: "What are we coming to—or rather what are you coming to in Boston? Quincy v. Otis! This is too bad. There must be something in this business of which we at a distance are wholly ignorant. . . . [T]hat Quincy should swell the triumph of a wooden building faction—and of a party who have abused him these past 20 years. . . . Is he fascinated," Saltonstall asked, "by the miserable vapor—popularity? . . . Good Lord deliver us! . . . There must be extensive jealousies among you." Explaining to Minot that the insurgent tide was spreading into his own county, he wrote: "I found yesterday master Chander deeply infected—he thought Otis unfairly nominated—talked of intrigues, &c. . . . I am glad, I do not live in Boston. It would not do for my temperament," confessed Saltonstall.[38] Daniel Webster was no less frantic. The day after the Middling Interest caucus, he anxiously informed Joseph Story of the news from Boston: "We are in a deplorable state here. . . . Mr. Q[uincy] has opposed the City from the beginning! He now wraps himself up in mystery, & importance—none of his old friends can get [an] *audience* with him—tho I have no doubt a very active communication exists between him, & a certain other quarter."[39]

Clearly, the Federalist hierarchy felt politically threatened by Quincy's stand. As Leverett Saltonstall, somewhat hysterically, pronounced on the eve of the election, "the Federalists are all dead—dead—dead! I hope the first election of the City of Boston will not portend its fall."[40] But, as these letters also suggest, the betrayal affected Federalism's leadership on a personal level. For Quincy to have so publicly betrayed the Central Committee not only proved a political embarrassment but held profound cultural meaning for men like Otis, Saltonstall, Perkins, and Sullivan, as well as for those, like Daniel Webster, who worked so hard for them.

Partisanship, class affiliation, and, thus, cultural identity were all tightly wrapped up together in the minds of Boston's nineteenth-century elites. To be a Federalist was to distinguish oneself culturally from others. In a letter to William Sullivan on January 19, 1822, Harrison Gray Otis summed up this sentiment when he wrote that one of the major reasons for his coming home to govern Boston was "to train the young leaders of my own breed." As one historian of Boston explains, "Office holding elevated Brahmin status [in the first decades of the nineteenth century] through the highly visible symbols and rituals of the political process. . . . [T]he Boston political and economic elites merged and government service advanced class power as well as class . . . honor." Another explains that to be a Federalist meant one "was expected to adhere to the Federal[ist] standard and acceptable conservative creed. To renounce one's [party] was tantamount to admitting a serious character flaw." Thus, when the Federalist *Portsmouth Journal of Literature and Politics* offered an explanation to its New Hampshire Federalist readership for the "unhappy division of parties [that] prevails in Boston," it concluded Quincy's betrayal must have been motivated by "personal considerations."[41]

Quincy's conversion to the Middling Interest discredited patrician honor and, by extension, weakened the class's cultural power, which the Federalist establishment reinforced and championed. His political alliance with those whom Ralph Waldo Emerson disparaged as "a band of murmurers . . . a parcel of demagogues . . . hoping for places as *partisans* which they could not achieve as citizens" demonstrated Quincy's political inclusiveness and illustrated his disagreement with Otis's reliance on the Lancastrian system of governance and the deference it demanded. In other words, for many ordinary Bostonians, Quincy's actions delegitimized the structure of political dominance used by the political and economic elite of the region. In this sense, Quincy challenged the legitimacy of elite-class rule by undermining its manifestations in politics.

Also, this act of political heresy exposed a fissure within elite-class solidarity. Pierced not by the dreaded mob of the masses, as the Federalist establishment had always feared, but by one of its own, the Boston aristocracy was taken by complete surprise. Its reaction to such apostasy was one of disbelief. Indeed, most Otis loyalists believed Quincy, at the last minute, would withdraw from the race rather than "be made the 'instrument of disunion and disorganization of the Federal[ist] party,'" which would condemn him to the peripheries of Boston's elite-class society. As Thomas H. Perkins proclaimed to Otis, "Quincy has done himself up by the course he has pursued. . . . [H]e will have the high gratification of having soiled up the federal[ist] party and if he succeeds in his object will lose the place to which he has pretended so much devotion." Let the election "turn as it may," Perkins explained, because there would be cultural retribution. "[T]here is no doubt," he concluded, "that Quincy loses, tho he may gain the majority." Saltonstall was utterly confused when he wrote to William Minot: "I have *had*, as you know, a great regard for Mr. Quincy, and regret that he should do anything injurious to himself," but "that he should be willing to disappoint friends who have stood by him firmly, . . . is truly mortifying."[42]

The Middling Interest challenge and Quincy's betrayal shocked loyal Federalists up and down the eastern seaboard. Philadelphia's leading Federalist organ, the *National Gazette and Literary Register*, reported on the severity of Quincy's dissidence. "A new division of parties has taken place in the good city of Boston, which threatens to destroy the political supremacy of the old 'federalists of the Boston stamp.' [The insurgency's] object [is] to show that they have the power of making a selection. It is probable that they aim at taking the nomination and choice of public officers, from the particular circle to which it is alleged to have been hitherto confined." According to Daniel Webster, the world seemed upside-down "when [one] sees Mr. Quincy the very darling of the Boston Democracy!" Harrison Gray Otis judged Quincy and the insurgent party in apocalyptic terms. "They cry out, desert your old friends and leaders & come into our tabernacks! Sir, . . . desert your friends! [It] is the same which since the world began[,] corruption speaks to weakness and treachery—which seduction holds to virtue. [It] caused sin into the world and death by sin. . . . It is the magic of the many that sets the world on fire."[43]

For his part, Quincy seemed to thoroughly enjoy the stir he was causing among Boston's Federalist hierarchy. When Thomas H. Perkins scolded him for leading the Middling Interest out of the Federalist caucus, Quincy, according to a shocked Perkins, simply responded with "a formal bow, and a stately 'good morning,'" having totally dismissed him and his censure. The day before the election, Quincy and his daughter Eliza were walking down Summer Street after church when they observed Harrison Gray Otis's son Harry, "hurrying along." According to Eliza, "Mr. Quincy called after him saying, 'Where are you going so fast, Otis?'" A red-faced Harry replied, "'working against you Sir, as hard as I can.'" Quincy laughed and waved him on, saying, "'Very well, only take care you don't work *too hard.*'"[44] According to Eliza, while "Mr. Otis's partisans were very angry [about Quincy's] interference," and Otis's "sons and sons in law distributed voters" throughout the city in "every effort" to get the crusty old senator elected, Quincy remained very relaxed and satisfied about the upcoming election results.[45]

Not only had Quincy infuriated his old colleagues, as Webster fumed, by wrapping "himself up in mystery, & importance [so that] none of his old friends c[ould] get [an] *audience* with him," but he seemed to be rubbing their noses in it. Worse, he did not seem to acknowledge or care about the disruption he was causing. According to Webster, "the dirty squabble of local politics" was subverting "her [New England's] proper character and consequence. . . . I feel," he confessed, "the hand of fate upon us, and to struggle is in vain. We are doomed to be hewers of wood and drawers of water. . . . What has sickened me beyond remedy is the tone and temper of these disputes. We are disgraced beyond help or hope."[46] Middling Interest founder Francis Wayland viewed the situation quite differently. Writing to his friend Alonzo Potter on the day of the election, Wayland optimistically explained: "In all probability there will be a revolution in politics. . . . Boston it is thought will be democratic shortly, and this will give a strong impulse to the state[;] this will produce a mighty stir in the [country]."[47]

Realizing that its candidate, George Blake, had little chance in Boston because the Middling Interest coalition drew significant support from Republican as well as Federalist ranks, Republican party strategists took the only course open to them. They tried to coopt the antiaristocratic platform of the insurgency for themselves by claiming Quincy was a charter member of the "aristocracy." Characterizing Quincy and Otis as elitist brothers, the Republican press argued: "Upon what *American* principles, upon what *American* feeling can such men be worthy of the suffrages of American citizens? In the memory of many a Bostonian such men would not be tolerated in Boston. They would, like the Tea, be thrown into the bay, by a parcel of Indians, or they would be habited in such suits of domestic manufacture, that their dearest friends would shrink from their embraces."[48]

The glaring problem with this strategy was that Quincy, since 1820, had established strong connections within the Republican party. Some of the state's most prominent Republicans, men like Levi Lincoln Jr., had graciously accepted Quincy's legislative help, friendship, and even his leadership during the Maine statehood debates in the General Court. Also, Quincy's involvement in the constitutional convention of 1820–21 further solidified his relationships with Republican leaders Lincoln and James T. Austin. Thus, likening the reformist Quincy to the chairman of the Massachusetts Federalist Central Committee seemed totally erroneous and only played into the antipartyist hands of the insurgency. Indeed, the Republican strategy proved a complete failure. Out of the 1,200 Republicans who voted in the mayoral election, only 157 marked their ballots for Blake. Josiah Quincy stole the vast majority of the Republican vote, seducing a remarkable 802 Republicans into the insurgent fold. Although the Republican party had always been ineffective in the Boston, with the city's first mayoral election Boston Republicanism reached a new low.[49]

But what loyal Otis Federalists wondered was whether their party too would meet the same fate. The Middling Interest could bank on 600 firm third-party partisans, but the number of regular Federalists and Republicans persuaded by insurgent precepts remained unknown. Two days before the election, Daniel Webster privately offered his gloomy prediction to Joseph Story, confessing that "[n]othing seems practicable but to go forward and support Mr. O[tis] & probably be beaten."[50] Undoubtedly, the Central Committee's behavior at the Federalist caucus had increased the insurgency's numbers. Other Otis Federalists rejected Webster's pessimism. Far too much was at stake.

Foreseeing a Middling Interest victory, in a last-minute ploy to ensure a third party defeat, the Central Committee threw another candidate's name into the race. According to Eliza Quincy, because "Mr. Quincy [clearly] was ahead," the committee hoped to fluster and confuse insurgent voters by placing the name of another Middling Interest man, Thomas L. Winthrop, on the ballot. As Eliza recalled, "Mr. Winthrop was put up without his knowledge, to divide the voters & at least defeat Mr. Quincy."[51] The sabotage succeeded.

Unbeknownst to him, this "other" Middling Interest candidate captured a total vote of 361, of which 92 came from disaffected Federalists, 90 from Middling Interest partisans, and 179 from converted Republicans. The vast majority of Winthrop's votes, presumably, would have gone to Quincy if the Central Committee had not added the second "insurgent" candidate to the race. Despite this, Quincy gained the majority, with a total of 1,736 votes. Remarkably, his strongest support came from traditional Republican partisans. Without doubt, Republicans identified Quincy as their candidate. As mentioned earlier, Quincy earned the lion's share of their votes, with 802 out of 1,200. Predictably, of the 600 Middling Interest voters, the vast majority of 510 went with Quincy. If there was any weakness in Quincy's popularity it came from the Federalist party. Out of the 1,900 Federalists who went to the polls, only 424 cast their votes for Quincy. The overwhelming majority of those who still identified themselves as Federalist in 1822 had remained loyal to Harrison Gray Otis. Nevertheless, in a political culture that maintained three parties, that proved insufficient. Otis appealed only to Federalist loyalists, garnering 1,384 votes. Not one Republican or Middling Interest man had cast a vote for the venerable senator. The remaining 62 votes went to a scattering of nominal candidates.[52]

Clearly, the extralegal manipulations and partisan zeal of the Central Committee spoiled any possibility for the Otis campaign to appeal to either the Republican or the Middling Interest rank-and-file. However, the Central Committee had offset the worst. Webster's ominous prophecy had been avoided. Winthrop drew just enough votes from Quincy to deny him a majority of all votes cast as the charter required. If the other insurgent candidate had not been brought into the race, Quincy would have received 361 more votes. Armed with a cumulative vote of 2,097 instead of his 1,736, the Middling Interest and Quincy would have easily captured the mayor's office, gaining the majority of all votes cast by 247. Yet, because of the election rules and the complicity of the Central Committee, the Middling Interest candidate would not ascend to the chief executive position.[53] Despite the loss, the insurgency found significant solace in the fact that it had successfully blocked the "servant of the aristocracy."[54]

Thus, after the initial balloting for Boston's first mayor on April 8, the Middling Interest and the Federalist Central Committee had reached a stalemate. Each had stymied the other, and both candidates withdrew from the race. For ordinary Bostonians, the visible difference between the two parties was clear. One had employed dirty tricks to check the opponent; in stark contrast, the other rejected such partisan scheming and adopted the honest campaign the insurgency had promised—one based on integrity and the authority of "the people." The contrast did not go unnoticed by the Boston electorate. In the second election on April 16, the Central Committee once again would find itself on the defensive, but this time it would have to acquiesce to the coalition's demands.

In the meantime, Buckingham viciously railed against the Central Committee. Outraged by the committee's recent clandestine behavior, the *Galaxy,* three days after the election, charged that

> [i]t is this kind of management which has produced a divisions in the ranks of federalism, and sown the seeds of a new party, which, like the fabled teeth of the giant, will soon spring up and become an army that will overpower it predecessor. The party is the middling interest, and comprises the men who are so far below a state of overgrown wealth, as not to be able [to] live without labour, and so far above mendicity [*sic*] as to be too proud or too honest, to live by *trimming* and *fawning.* It has been said that there is no such thing as a middling interest—that the rich have no interest separate from that of the labouring and poorer classes. This assertion is false. . . . The rich are in league to put down, and keep down, the mechanic and the tradesman. They have trampled upon the worm till it turns, and the mechanic and the tradesman would deserve still to be trampled to the dust, if they did not turn, and at least endeavor to curb these purse-proud devils of their will.[55]

The public outcry against the Central Committee's "management" before and during the election proved so overwhelming and hostile after Quincy dropped out of the race that Thomas H. Perkins was forced to deliver an "explanatory address" to the people of Boston. Perkins's address only roused them more by insulting the Middling Interest and Quincy. With this address, Perkins, who had maintained a low profile during the election, sealed his fate as, in Buckingham's words, one "of the crafty politicians." "It is not as . . . easy," Perkins explained, "to heal party dissensions, as to ferment . . . them—let the responsibility of the latter rest where it ought." "*Amen,*" Buckingham retorted, but "the question is, Where ought the responsibility . . . rest? Most undoubtedly on those [in the Central Committee] who, at the [Federalist] general caucus, after the marking for candidates was declared to be closed, persuaded others to come and mark for their favorite candidate, thus turning the scale against the candidate [Quincy] who had the majority of marks."[56] Buckingham then turned his wrath on the Federalist press which, he reminded his readers, had not even "deigned to mention that [Quincy] was a candidate." "Our ideas of duty and impartiality," Buckingham mocked, "may be very *unsound* and *absurd;* we know they are very *unfashionable* . . . ; but, such as they are, we feel 'impelled' to maintain them; and hope we shall never feel impelled to adopt that narrow-minded, exclusive sort of policy, which would seal up the press of this free and enlightened country, against the expression of the will and sentiments of a majority of citizens, and open it only at the will and pleasure of a cabal."[57]

In the interim between the first and second balloting for mayor, Boston's Federalist press tried to sort out what had happened. The *Daily Advertiser* explained that "the failure of Mr. Otis's election has arisen from the peculiar combination of the parties into which Boston is 'unhappily divided.'" Philadelphia's *National Gazette and Literary Register* accused Quincy of turning "democratic" and causing Otis's defeat: "The mechanics and other classes allied to [Quincy] formed an independent interest, *the Middling Interest.*" The *Portsmouth Journal of Literature and Politics* assessed the insurgency's social composition in more detail. Although the *Portsmouth Journal*'s editor seemed utterly confused by the specific "local . . . considerations" that had motivated such activist third-partyism in Boston, he concluded that "[i]t is well known that a party has for several years existed in Boston consisting of Insolvent Debtors and those who feel connected with them by interest, or feelings. . . . Federal[ist] and Democratic [Republican], and Wooden-building" partisans combining with "Insolvent Debtor[s] . . . constitutes a considerable portion of that which has lately assumed the name of Middling Interest."[58]

Considering the economic environment of Boston at the time, the *Portsmouth Journal*'s tentative identification of the specific interest groups that formed the insurgency's rank-and-file members seems highly accurate. The depression that first sparked popular political activism in Boston had not ended by the mayoral election and continued sending many poor and overextended middling citizens to Boston's debtor prison. Just weeks after the April 8 election—beginning in the middle of May and continuing into June—Boston faced a severe shortage in specie. Banks were "compelled . . . to demand immediate repayment of their debtors, for such notes have fallen due. In many case[s]," reported Boston's *Evening Gazette,* "such compulsion has been attended with extreme hardship, and has required numerous sacrifices."[59] The blighted economic atmosphere that originally fostered the insurgency was not getting better.

On April 12 the Middling Interest forced an open caucus to nominate an acceptable nonpartisan compromise candidate. Meeting once again in the Boston Exchange Coffee House and led, this time, by a humbled Thomas H. Perkins, insurgents, Republicans, and Federalists congregated to announce a nominee tolerable to all Bostonians. When John Phillips was chosen, clearly the Middling Interest held the upper hand at the meeting. Having been outraged when the Central Committee punished Quincy by taking his state senate seat away from him in 1820, Phillips, ever since, had proven a strong political supporter of Quincy. Personally their relationship was beyond question. They were first cousins, lifelong friends, and had suffered through Phillips Academy in Andover together. More significantly, John Phillips had stood as a Middling Interest candidate during the March state senatorial race despite his past Federalist partisanship. During that race, Joseph Buckingham bolstered the Phillips candidacy, stating that Phillips was the sort in "whom the mechanics and middling interest men have confidence." Since then he had served a term as the president of the senate and was described by Republicans there as a "moderate, intelligent, independent man." In the April 16 election, Phillips ran unopposed and overwhelmingly won by 2,467 votes out of the total 2,661 cast.[60]

With Phillips's election the Middling Interest declared victory. As Joseph Buckingham gleefully announced to Boston: "The cabal which has so long managed the federal[ist] party has received a blow from which it will not . . . recover, and will never again carry on its purpose with undisputed sovereignty."[61]

When Otis began the long journey home from Washington in May 1822, he must have been filled with despair. He had actively maintained a hand in local Boston politics since he had offered to sacrifice himself in the U.S. Senate as an "ambassador of peace and good will from Massachusetts," and now the senator could not even get elected mayor of his hometown. He had consistently attempted to manage damage control for his party from afar, but "Boston federalism of the old stamp" lay in shambles despite his best efforts. He had publicly offered to "yield to the wishes of his fellow citizens" and become the city's first executive because his "humble services," he thought, "might be useful in the organization of the new government," yet he had been attacked as an elitist, "purse-proud devil." Also, he had indulged in the luxury of envisioning himself seated in the governor's mansion, but now that too seemed out of reach.[62]

On May 12, when he rose to the floor of Faneuil Hall to address the city of Boston, his despair seemed to have turned to self-pitying rage. "I wish that every man of the middling interest was within reach of my voice, when I ask," bellowed Otis, "where are the tenants whom I have ejected—the Debtors I have sued—the Labourers whom I have pinched. . . . The poor whose faces I have ground." Providing Boston with his version of the trickle-down theory, Otis-style, he explained that "[i]f the stream of wealth sets in one channel it runs out by another, and the reservoir between both is connected with each other"; therefore, "there can be no permanent middling interest." Because of the flow of wealth from rich to middling and the rise and fall of personal fortunes, "[t]he people who a few years ago composed the middling interest now live in homes of brick" and have become rich. The "middling interest," Otis argued, was not a real party but a rabble of malcontents—"warm opposers to an *imaginary* privileged order"—"a mere name, calculated to break down [Federalism] and to build up its adversary." Arguing that "[t]hree parties can no more continue in a country, than three men can continue to fight in a single combat," Otis pleaded with his ex-Federalist brethren who had joined the insurgency to return home. Otis maintained that the interests of the insurgency and Federalism were "essentially the same." If he had sacrificed the mayoralty to bring this misunderstanding to the attention of all Bostonians, then so be it. "I ask not a return of popularity. I lament not its loss," Otis firmly explained. "But your esteem is a vested [right] I am entitled to . . . having earned it for good consideration—This you ought not withdraw without good cause—If you do so, you rob me [of honor]." Then in a quite melodramatic statement, which, according to the *Galaxy,* provoked muffled laughter from certain quarters of Faneuil Hall, Otis declared, "I feel it might be the last time in which I shall ever address you from this place—I am no longer a Candidate for any office—My race is run—I am delighted to give way to other com[er]s of higher, middle and better speeds."[63]

Otis's speech provoked the *Niles' Weekly Register* correspondent in Boston to report sardonically to his Washington office: "never . . . shall I meet with any assembly comprising so *much private worth* and *such elevated patriotism* and the HARTFORD CONVENTION!!??" Joseph Buckingham was astonished by the speech. "Mr. Otis," the *Galaxy* reported, "took leave of his fellow citizens . . . on Sunday evening." Explaining that the senator rose before the crowd "evidently embarrassed," Buckingham continued by addressing every point Otis had made and trouncing it. "When Mr. Otis pretends to see no cause for a disruption of the Federal[ist] party, he pretends to a degree of mental blindness. . . . His arguments against [the Middling Interest] were altogether inconclusive and absurd. . . . Why," Buckingham asked, "should the middling interest be forever chained to the car of the monied interest? . . . Why should not the middling interest do everything they can do, to overthrow the power, or at least, to neutralize the operations of a monied aristocracy, whos[e] patriotism is nothing but selfishness and the love of power, and whose public spirit is deposited, for safe-keeping, in the vaults of the bank?" Addressing Otis's appeal for Middling Interest men who had once been Federalists to come back into the fold, Buckingham predicted that this would never happen because "[t]he materials are [now] too discordant to amalgamate." "[T]he wheels of revolution are in motion," Buckingham declared, and nothing could now stop it.[64]

VII • "THE *SIEGE OF BOSTON* IS ONCE *MORE RAISED*"

The Betrayal of the Insurgency's Mayor and Federalist Death Spasms

[The] aristocratic band has been abolished, but a more oppressive and more horrible, and more odious one . . . has arisen to fill its place.
—"Agricola," 1822

Before an overflow audience in Faneuil Hall on May 1, 1822, Chief Justice of the Massachusetts Supreme Court Isaac Parker swore into office Boston's first mayor, John Phillips. Resting on a table before the speaker's platform sat the newly written Boston city charter enshrined in a silver case. After taking his oath of office, Phillips rose to deliver Boston's first mayoral inaugural address. The speech took less than ten minutes and foreshadowed the naive and placid course that the Phillips administration would take in guiding Boston through its first year as a city.[1]

Like his cousin Josiah Quincy, Phillips had serious misgivings about the charter. But, unlike Quincy, Phillips lacked the will and the political dexterity to remedy any piece of it. John Phillips had served Massachusetts Federalism for twenty-five years, first as Suffolk County's state senator and then as a "fair-minded" public prosecutor in Boston. After observing the Federalist Central Committee's treatment of his cousin Quincy, Phillips had become highly suspicious of the Federalist leadership and, by 1822, was a Middling Interest insurgent. Despite his alliance with Boston's insurgency, the Phillips administration proved to be extremely conservative and timid. "Prudence, caution, and conservatism," according to Josiah Quincy, "were [his cousin's] predominating characteristics."[2]

Employing a literal interpretation of the charter, the new mayor proved powerless to mend its deficiencies. Although Phillips happily had accepted the mayoralty to placate both the Middling Interest and the Federalist parties, he had neither the inclination nor the apparent legal power as mayor to engage in a municipal administration of activism. The insurgents who elected him expected a mayor who would proceed aggressively to fulfill their aims. Less than three months into his term, Phillips faced severe criticism for his lackadaisical and ineffective approach to his new position, and his administration fell under fierce criticism from his former followers. "For what was our *town* government exchanged for that of *city,* but to break the bonds of an aristocracy, and relieve the oppressed?" asked a thoroughly disappointed Middling Interest man who had supported Phillips's candidacy. "[W]e protest against [the city's] arbitrary laws by which the free born citizen is oppressed and his rights wrestled from him." Reflecting back on Phillips's tenure, another argued that Boston's first mayor had done little except "slept on his post," while receiving a salary of $2,500.[3] Clearly, this was not what the insurgency wanted or expected in its first mayor.

Phillips faced two principal barriers in fulfilling the activist role that Boston's insurgents expected of him. The first was personal. Phillips had entered the mayor's office severely ill and weary of politics. After serving on the General Court for twenty-five years, the fifty-two-year-old statesman mistakenly viewed the mayoralty as a nonconfrontational, nonpartisan position of honorable retirement. He assumed the city would largely run itself—turning to its executive only for benevolent facilitation during occasional minor squabbles.

Phillips had contracted a mysterious disease that would kill him one month after he left office, exhausted, in 1823. As the course of his administration would show and as his inaugural speech suggested, Phillips trusted in an archaic notion of Boston's Christian character and benevolence. Afflicted with a terminal illness, Phillips, because of these factors and the compromise that put him in power, was not inclined to foment significant changes in Boston. Besides, extensive restrictions in the city charter impeded the new mayor's ability to employ executive power even if he had wanted to. In his inaugural address, Phillips explained that order and welfare would be maintained under his administration through the "[p]urity of manners, [the] general diffusion of knowledge, [and] above all," he added, "a firm, practical belief [in] Divine revelation." Harkening back to Winthrop's Puritan "city upon the hill," Phillips believed that "love of order, benevolent affections, and Christian piety distinguish . . . the inhabitants of this city." And thus the city government, according to Phillips, held few, if any, new responsibilities.[4]

Instead, Phillips extolled the virtues and memorialized the old town meetings as "testimon[ies] to the wisdom [of] our ancestors." Deeply troubled by the changes represented in Boston's abandonment of the town meeting system, Phillips placed Boston in stark contrast to "[m]ost of the towns in this Commonwealth [who] may . . . continue to enjoy the benefit[s] of those salutary regulations" inherent in town meetings. Only because of "the great increase of population in the town of Boston," Phillips sighed, was it forced to become a city. In this new city, Phillips explained, "[d]ifference of opinion must be expected, and mutual concessions made, in . . . the interests of a large community," but the new mayor made it explicitly clear that he would take no responsibility over how those "concessions" would be mediated. "I will not encumber you with unnecessary forms," Phillips promised the City Council, "or encroach on your time. . . . . [B]revity will be carefully studied." With this statement and after placing the overseeing of Boston in the hands of the "Holy Spirit," the mayor of Boston stepped down from the podium and abandoned any leadership role in the new City Council.[5]

Adding to Phillips's passive approach toward his new job, the charter also restrained executive powers. During the charter debates, Middling Interest spokesmen on the chartering committee had feared a strong executive largely because of democratic sentiments and because their opponents on the Federalist Central Committee had pushed so hard for one. Indeed, Harrison Gray Otis, on December 17, 1821, instructed his operative in the chartering committee, William Sullivan, to give the mayor the "veto upon some of the . . . laws (such as relating to taxes and taking away private property)" and then followed up a month later with a letter demanding that the mayor be "give[n] . . . a *right* [to widespread executive authority], without imposing [on him] an *obligation* to ask advise" of other city representatives.[6] Insurgent leaders Michael Roulstone, Isaac Winslow, and William Sturgis, who served on the committee, balked at such demands and crushed the Sullivan–Otis initiative in Town Meeting. Although, at the time, the Middling Interest counted this as a victory, by so limiting the authority of the executive in the revised charter, the insurgents had gutted from the document any practical function for the mayor's office. Even after a charter change in 1854 and various subsequent amendments in 1885, Boston's mayor during the early 1890s, Nathan Matthews Jr., still bitterly complained that "the mayor was little more than a figure head" due to limitations imposed on the executive that were left over from the original 1822 charter.[7]

Mayor Phillips could neither appoint city officials nor fire them; he had no power to veto city legislation or control the finances of the city. The only direct powers solely allocated to the mayor consisted of summoning meetings of the eight-member, elected at-large, Board of Aldermen, and the Common Council, a group of forty-eight elected officials who represented Boston's twelve wards. After 1822, these two municipal branches had taken over the responsibilities of the town selectmen and town meetings. The mayor could appoint committees that would report their findings to the City Council (the Board of Aldermen and the Common Council in conference), and he served as chairman of the Board of Aldermen but received no special veto or voting powers over it. In January 1822 Sullivan had assured Otis that the aldermen would be "nothing more than . . . an advisory council to the executive," but this too had not come to pass as hostile insurgents ensured that the popularly elected aldermen would have significantly more power than the mayor. Making matters worse, five independent town government boards, the Board of Health, the Surveyors of the Highways, the School Committee, the Overseers of the Poor, and the Board of Firewards, had survived the chartering process and stood as autonomous municipal agencies that zealously protected their traditional municipal domains. Because these were elected boards, the City Council held little authority over them. The council could cut off their funding but had no prerogative under the charter to then fulfill the municipal functions of these agencies. Almost immediately after the establishment of the new government, the City Council found itself hopelessly dependent on these independent municipal boards to oversee many of the basic functions of the city.[8]

Despite the weakness of his office and the decentralized, dysfunctional nature of the city's organization, the mayor remained the symbolic leader of the new city government. In the people's eyes, responsibility for the city's legislation and how it effected them rested with him. They had fought hard for a city charter and wanted significant results from their first mayor. Far from being a tranquil position from which to retire honorably from an active political life, as Phillips had hoped, the mayoralty left him exposed to levels of popular criticism that he had never before experienced. Worse, because of the limitations of his office there was little the chief executive could do about it. Unfortunately for Phillips, during his tenure the mayor's office essentially functioned as a sounding board for numerous gripes and complaints made by the city's citizens. By July 1822 Boston's first mayor began to discover the true nature of his job.

The small and ordered Puritan Christian community that Phillips had referred to in his inaugural address clearly no longer existed. As Josiah Quincy understood, Boston had become a city, and not just by legal title. Not only had Boston grown to over 44,000 people by 1822, but it contained a socially and economically diverse population, most of whom were hard-pressed by economic depression. By the late teens, many English Protestant and Irish Catholic farmers, financially ravaged in their native land by Parliament's passage of the Corn Laws and the Acts of Enclosure, escaped to Boston. According to historian Thomas H. O'Connor, by 1820 Boston held some 2,000 poor Irish Catholics, and by 1825 the number had risen to exceed 5,000. Historian Peter Knights estimates that newcomers to Boston composed the majority of the city's growing population of poor during the early nineteenth century. Most in-migrants to the Hub came from the countryside unskilled and "drifted into and out of a variety of low-level jobs."[9]

The demographic changes that occurred in Boston during the first two decades of the nineteenth century shocked shoemaker George Robert Twelves Hewes when he returned to his hometown an old man in 1821. "The place where I drew my first breath and formed my most endearing attachment," Hewes reported, "had to me become a land of strangers. Not only had my former companions and friends disappeared, but the places of their habitations were occupied by those who could give no account of them." In their place had come mostly young men from the hinterlands of New England like Moses Adams from Ellsworth, Maine. In 1816 Adams arrived in Boston to seek his fortune. After apprenticing for a merchant and a blacksmith, he worked on the docks and eventually signed on as a common seaman to the merchant ship *Atlas* in 1820. Upon his arrival in Boston as an outsider, Adams quickly forged alliances of comradeship and fraternity with other outlanders who held similar menial jobs and were also new to the city.[10]

Within such an evolving urbanized world that was growing in size and complexity from year to year, Phillips's approach to the mayoralty must have seemed archaic to most ordinary Bostonians. The Middling Interest had expected him to curb the unbridled power of Harrison Gray Otis and the Central Committee. Less a decision based on Phillips's qualifications as an insurgent and more a reactive move, the insurgency had not anticipated Phillips's antiquated vision of Boston and municipal governance. Although sympathetic to insurgent charges of an uncaring and selfish political and economic aristocracy that bastardized Boston's character, the new mayor clearly would not provide strong leadership in the struggle against the "FEW."

One of his first acts as executive foretold his skewed attitude toward his new job. Immediately after his inauguration, Phillips met with the city aldermen to work out future procedure and decide on various minor municipal appointments. One of the few significant powers the charter bestowed exclusively on the mayor and aldermen was the replacement of the town's elected Board of Health with a less autonomous commission that would be answerable to the mayor and aldermen. The old town Board of Health had fallen under such severe criticism for corruption and inefficiency that the General Court had added a provision to the charter abolishing the board. During the Town Meeting winter debates over the charter, as we have seen, most state legislative alterations to the charter were met by Bostonians with intense suspicion and meticulously scrutinized. The Board of Health amendment received no discussion. Clearly, on this matter Bostonians agreed that the corrupt board should be terminated. On the day of his inauguration, Phillips inexplicably reappointed the same members to the Board of Health. Without delay the board successfully reestablished sovereignty over its municipal realm. Having been given a reprieve from extinction, the board immediately consolidated itself and directly challenged the authority of the mayor and aldermen.[11]

On June 4, 1822, the mayor and aldermen received a stern order from the board's secretary, John Winslow, summoning them to stand before the Board of Health and explain why the city had not cleaned up "a quantity of filthy, putrid, and nauseous substances on the premises belonging to you, and under your direction. You will, therefore," the summons read, "appear before this Board on Monday . . . and show cause, if any exist, why the City of Boston should not remove" the garbage. Although exactly whose obligation it was to extricate the garbage remained unclear, the board laid down the gauntlet and challenged the jurisdictional authority of the Phillips administration and the new city government. The predicament the new mayor and his administration faced was whether they could engage one of the few powerful mechanisms the charter gave them and assert municipal authority over the board or shrink from the challenge. Would the mayor's office and aldermen claim municipal supremacy or succumb to a subordinate board and thus set a dangerous precedent of yielding under pressure to an inferior municipal division?[12]

Phillips held the letter for a few days before sharing it with the aldermen. Eventually he delivered the summons, and the aldermen acquiesced to the authority of the Board of Health. Although the city refused to clean up the garbage, Phillips had not claimed executive jurisdiction over the matter, thereby abdicating the authority expressly given to him and the aldermen in the charter. Garbage continued to rot "on the westerly side of [wharf] T," and the rectified Board of Health affirmed its municipal dominance over the executive and aldermen of the city.[13]

Because the garbage incident received little, if any, coverage in the city press, Boston's insurgents were kept in the dark about Phillips's bungling. Despite his less than awe-inspiring inaugural, Middling Interest men remained optimistic about their mayor. And, in fact, early in the Phillips administration there seemed to be reason for them to be hopeful—though it had little to do with the mayor's leadership. In late July, Phillips and the aldermen were briefly heralded by the Middling Interest organ, the *Independent Bostonian,* for supporting a piece of city legislation that dealt with one of the insurgency's most pressing grievances.[14]

In July the Board of Aldermen, headed by Phillips, approved a plan to extend prison limits for debtors. Although abolishing debt imprisonment, which Middling Interest partisans had advocated since 1820, clearly fell within the General Court's jurisdiction, the city aldermen and mayor claimed the authority to decide upon the areas within Boston where debtor prisoners on temporary leave could and could not go. The Overseers of the Poor traditionally allowed almshouse inmates a certain number of hours during the day to seek employment, visit their families, and pick up odd jobs in specified areas around the city. These areas, in the past, were designated by the town selectmen or the courts and were highly restrictive. Inmates on leave were usually restricted to Boston's docks and poorer neighborhoods. Often, imprisoned debtors were not allowed to enter the location of their shops or place of employment. With the aldermen's initiative, the whole city was opened to the debtor inmates, who could now move freely throughout Boston seeking work or plying their trade by day and return to the prison at night. Insurgent advocates for debtor's rights had been demanding this reform since 1820. The Middling Interest's *Independent Bostonian* supported the mayor and aldermen, arguing: "*we feel assured* that more debts will be honestly paid [this way], than by any system heretofore adopted—at least 'tis worth a trail."[15]

According to the *Bostonian,* the vast majority in Boston viewed the extension of prison bounds as sensible. Simply put, more debtors could pay off their debts under such a system, which pleased creditors as well. Others, however, opposed the ordinance, and the city law immediately fell under severe attack. "The extension of the prison limits has caused great excitement amoung a class of people commonly styled pettifogging lawyers," reported the *Bostonian.* "After having experienced a severe relaxation in business [due to] the late humane provision of the oppressed, they have resorted to the last and only means to place the system in a way most congenial to their own feelings, viz. by remonstrating to, and petitioning the honorable Mayor and Aldermen, to reconsider their vote by which the limits have been extended, and to confine them [debtors] within . . . Tremont and School streets."[16]

Until 1807 colonial custom dictated that insolvents in prison had the prerogative to practice their trade during the day to help pay off their debts. In 1807 Massachusetts Chief Justice Theophilus Parsons struck down this liberal policy as more sophisticated methods of debt collection became pervasive in the early nineteenth century and significantly restricted the bounds of debtors.[17] Despite the new city government's claiming authority over the Supreme Court and ignoring the "pettifogging lawyers'" petitions, editorialist "D" explained that he had "full faith in the integrity, intelligence and humanity of the honorable Board [of Aldermen]" to uphold its recent extension of prison limits. The aldermen had been approved by the Middling Interest and would not acquiesce to hostile lawyers, those "enemies of humanity [who] ruled" in the past by the "afflicting rod while accumulating high fees for their services." With the depression of 1819 gutting the Boston economy and more and more respectable middle-class voters falling deep into debt and filling debtor's jail, the mayor and aldermen had unilaterally overruled the Supreme Court's 1807 decision and returned to traditional custom. The only group that raised any objections were the lawyers. Thus, when the lawyers' petition reached the aldermen, it was summarily scrapped.[18]

With this defiant act, the new municipal government and, by extension, Mayor Phillips seemed to have adopted the activist role that the insurgents had so desperately wanted. The aldermen had flexed their muscles and professed supremacy over "trading judges" and "pettifogging lawyers." But there proved another side to prison extensions unrecognized by those who praised the administration's extension policy. By extending the boundary limits of insolvent inmates, the alderman and mayor strengthened the powers of the Overseers of the Poor. Being exclusively in charge of the Leverett Street almshouse/jail, providing "outdoor relief" to the impoverished, controlling an operating fund of over $100,000 and a second discretionary fund of $28,000–30,000 that could be drawn from the City Treasury on a need basis without having to account for it, the Overseers already held commanding power in the city of Boston.[19]

By extending prison limits, the Phillips administration only enhanced an already powerful independent municipal agency. As historian David Montgomery has suggested, during the early nineteenth century these guardians of the poor typically operated more like indentured labor brokers than benevolent stewards of the poor. Often they contracted out almshouse inmates en masse as a cheap labor force to local manufacturers,[20] and restricting the geographic bounds of prison labor would undercut the Overseers' powers to dole out patronage. Thus, by extending prison limits the mayor and aldermen had inadvertently strengthened this already powerful municipl board.[21]

Reacting against the city's seizure of power, early in 1823 the General Court made overtures to employ section 30 of the city charter, which gave the legislature discretionary veto power over any or all city laws, to override the aldermen's prison extension ordinance. By February the legislature succeeded, claiming sole authority to set prison limits in the city of Boston. Rank-and-file Middling Interest men throughout the city were outraged. The legislature, charged the *Bostonian and Mechanics Journal,* "has thought proper to take the power from the Mayor and Aldermen of assigning the *Jail Limits,* and by this measure, have virtually annulled the humane decree of that body, passed last season, fixing them to the bounds of the county of Suffolk. . . . [T]his very state, in 1823, passed an act TO ABRIDGE THE RIGHTS OF THE POOR DEBTOR, HUMANELY GRANTED HIM BY THE MAYOR AND ALDERMEN OF THE CITY OF BOSTON." The editorial demanded the abolition of debt imprisonment throughout the state.[22]

The Society for the Relief of the Distressed, which had published the now defunct *Debtor's Journal* and represented the debtors' interests within the insurgency, took a proactive position on the recent legislative decision. Explaining that

> "[t]he society is composed of some of our most enterprising and respectable citizens, who have in many instances, done much towards ameliorating the condition of the poor but honest debtor, who has been subject to the persecutions of an unrelenting creditor. [Our] object is not to combine against the law and justice . . . but to use every honorable and justifiable way to get a repeal of those laws, or *abolishment of imprisonment for debt.* To . . . inform [our] fellow citizens on the subject, and to get such men elected to office in our national and state legislatures as are favorable to an amelioration. . . . The late act of the legislature respecting prison limits, has produced a general excitement and alarm, it is almost universally deemed oppressive and cruel, and has had a tendency to rouse our citizens to action.[23]

Although the Phillips administration had stood up to the "pettifogging lawyers," it refused to confront the legislature by petition or in the courts. Partly because Phillips continued to abdicate leadership to others on the City Council and partly because, throughout the spring of 1823, various members of the city government were in the midst of secret negotiations with state legislators on another matter, the mayor and aldermen backed off, accepting the authority section 30 gave the General Court to override this municipal ordinance—and for good reason. The cloaked negotiations that were held between the legislature and some in the city government depended upon the power section 30 gave the state.

Incredibly, and in direct violation of the wishes of Boston's citizenry, in the spring of 1823 city officials sent a secret proposal to the legislature asking it to engage section 30 to eliminate the ward-voting provision from the charter. Although Josiah Quincy had opposed the whole chartering proposal because of the "mischief" he foresaw in section 30, most Middling Interest men had not heeded Quincy's warnings and supported the city charter largely because it contained provisions for ward voting. As Boston's *Independent Chronicle* explained before the city chartering in March 1822, "The chief reason for our friendship towards the city bill . . . is that it will introduce into power the *Middling Interest,* an interest among our citizens, which if it had assumed to its due weight [through a fairer democratic system of voting], would long ago have swayed the government of our town." By the end of the Phillips mayoralty, rank-and-file Middling Interest men's eyes were opened. The ward-voting provision had been essential in gaining enough votes from ordinary Bostonians to pass the city charter. As rank-and-file insurgents saw it, the charter held no validity without the guarantee of ward voting. Without it, Boston would return to its old deferential patterns of politics and the "FEW" would continue to dominate the "many."[24] When the news of the proposal by the Phillips regime to abolish ward voting leaked, insurgents throughout the city rose against the mayor and his administration.

The *Bostonian and Mechanics Journal* exposed the scheme and first accused the Federalist Central Committee of being the true force behind the plot. "Among the pitiful shifts resorted to by the FEW, nothing is more contemptible," charged the *Bostonian* in an article written for "Mechanics," "than their threats to withdraw their custom from those who may differ from them in opinion. . . . The game has carried on so long in 'the head quarters of good principles' [the Federalist party], that the labouring classes are no longer content [to] submit to dictators."[25] "The old doctrine of *passive obedience and nonresistance,* has long since exploded," editorialist "Alfred" explained, "and we trust will not be revived by the citizens of Boston. . . . The *monied few* are yet to learn that wealth alone will not entitle them to honors or distinction in this republican government. The industrious mechanics and the virtuous tradesmen are entitled to equal privileges as the most wealthy, and they are possessed with a spirit that will prompt them to maintain their rights, not withstanding the growlings and complaints of a *paltry, self created nobility.* . . . We are not of that servile race," declared Alfred, "who bow in adoration to the proud aristocrat because he has money."[26]

The *Bostonian* and Alfred's commentary on the city government's attempted betrayal articulated the rank-and-file insurgents' continued fear of an oppressive, moneyed aristocracy dominating city politics. As had been the case since the insurgent coalition's inception, those most guilty of perpetuating the "old doctrine of *passive obedience and nonresistance,*" according to the Middling Interest, were the Federalist "junto"—the Federalist Central Committee. But this time others outside the hated "cabal" were at fault, too.

Turning on the mayor and his administration, the *Bostonian* attacked the city government's betrayal: "How far a change of Municipal officers of this city may be necessary, must be obvious to every elector who is not blind to his own welfare, and to the prosperity of the city charter. Aristocracy or the assumption of power never intended to be delegated to city officers, should be received with extreme jealousy by every Bostonian who is independent enough to think and vote according to dictates of his own reason."[27] The attempt by city representatives to outlaw ward voting vividly exposed the duplicitous nature of the Phillips administration.

Although the city government had won accolades from many in the Middling Interest for extending prison limits, Phillips and his administration already had weathered significant condemnation by many in Boston for other municipal actions. Even before the ward-voting debacle, Middling Interest men's ire had been raised. Specifically, rank-and-file insurgents had objected to a city ordinance brought forth in the early summer of 1822 that intended to clear the congestion of Boston's narrow streets. The ordinance severely limited truckmen from plying their trade within the city by restricting where they could and could not go. The truckmen of Boston not only carted products from the docks to retailers throughout the city but also sold products directly from their carts at deflated prices. Their role in Boston's local economy was essential to those who could not afford the higher prices imposed by established merchants. When the ordinance also outlawed truckmen from setting up their carts on Boston's sidewalks, it put many of these men out of business and dramatically affected a shadowy, yet vital local economy on which many poor Bostonians depended.[28] Where are they to go, asked editorialist "Agricola," if "they are to be driven from the stands which they have long occupied? . . . This is not only oppressing the *truckmen,* but the *merchants;* for they cannot *truck* as cheap when two or three miles from the wharf. . . . [W]e protest against arbitrary laws by which the free born citizen is oppressed and his rights wrestled from him."[29]

During a period of severe depression, the Phillips administration's action seemed, as the *Bostonian and Mechanics Journal* put it, "a bare-faced affrontery" created "to trample . . . the honest and industrious citizen." Not only did the law hurt truckmen, but it crippled both small merchants, whose costs would increase, and those consumers who depended on the truckmen to sell goods below retail. "Why not, before they are forced off," Agricola pleaded, "provide them a suitable place for their stand[s]?"[30]

The Phillips administration ignored Agricola's suggestion, and suspicion toward the mayor rose. Far from being viewed as the champion of the "industrious" workingman who would crush the "purse-proud devils," Phillips began to be seen by some as an enemy of the "honest" workingman and those small merchants who had elected him. From their point of view, he was taking food from their tables for no other reason than to clear Boston's streets. Both the *Bostonian and Mechanics Journal* and the *Castigator* ran articles and editorials opposing the new city law. The *Bostonian* argued, "we can see no reason why an industrious and hard-laboring man, in this country, and especially New England, which professes to make no distinction between the rich man and the poor . . . should be denied the common right of every citizen, that of walking or standing in the street.—Where is the justice of such a law?" The *Castigator* approached the issue differently by glorifying Boston truckmen as the backbone of American citizenry and exposing "gentlemen" who refused to pay for trucking services—all the while railing against the elitism of "the new City Authorities" who have "grappled . . . by degrees without [the people's] consent or knowledge" "the privileges [*sic*]" of citizenship.[31]

Adding fuel to the anti-Phillips fire, the passage of another ordinance by the city revoking a number of liquor licenses for long-established bars outraged the Middling Interest. As with the truckmen issue, this action was looked upon as a direct attack on the "respectful and worthy citizen," who was already hard-pressed due to the city's depressed economy. Unlike the arguments against the truckmen law, the licensing controversy introduced a surprising new element into the attack on the Phillips administration. "[T]o license foreigners," argued the *Independent Bostonian,* "and deprive the respectful and worthy citizen of his right, his only measure to support himself and his family, is tyrannical, worse than the arbitrary laws of monarchy."[32] Although personally Phillips detested the more cosmopolitan social composition of Boston and pined for the more homogeneous Boston of the past, his administration seemed to be issuing patronage in the form of liquor licenses in a much less xenophobic way than in the past.

Railing against the new restrictions, a frustrated Middling Interest man asked: "Would it be right to pass by the peaceable industrious native born citizen, whose character has ever been distinguished for integrity and uprightness, and patronize the *foreigner* who has not been with us a sufficient time to acquire a character? Shall we continue to support the ostentatious pretensions of adventurers from abroad at the expense and ruin of our citizens at home? . . . [W]e . . . hope and believe that our new constituted authorities will ever be guided by patriotism, justice, and *national partiality.*" Amazed that the proposal for the ordinance had even come up, the *Independent Bostonian* pleaded: "Where are the Middling Interest men?"[33]

In early August, the licensing restriction was passed by the mayor and aldermen and became law, reaffirming for many that they had made a grave mistake with Phillips and his administration. "Is this the harbinger of what our *city* rulers intend to do?" asked an angry insurgent. "[I]f it is, we may expect soon to see [in] Boston . . . complete anarchy."[34] The *Castigator* went so far as to charge the city aldermen with overt corruption. Its editors claimed that aldermen were threatening to close down bars in the city if these city officials were not given private rooms to gamble in. Another editorial noted that aldermen who owned retail shops were keeping their stores open past the ten o'clock curfew that the city imposed on retailers, thereby undercutting competing merchants who would have their retailing licenses pulled for breaking the curfew ordinance.[35]

Harsh criticism had been leveled against the Phillips administration before the ward-voting debacle, but most of the disgrace that might have destroyed Boston's first city government had been deflected by the city's seemingly heroic and selfless stand on prison limit extensions—an issue that had a strong legacy in the insurgent movement. In early April 1823, with the public disclosure of the Phillips administration's attempt to abolish ward voting, any remaining support for Boston's first city government and its first mayor quickly evaporated.[36] The secret proposal to the legislature only confirmed what many Bostonians had already suspected: that Phillips and his administration, the darlings of the Middling Interest in the spring of 1822, had by 1823 sold them out.

On April 5 the *Bostonian and Mechanics Journal* published a front-page spread that not only reiterated the insurgency's political philosophy and its abhorrence of the Federalist Central Committee but also articulated the broader consequences of the Phillips administration's betrayal:

> We . . . renounce the assumed guardianship of a self constituted *Few,* who have usurped and exercised our rights, only to abuse them. . . . We would transfer the sacred rights of political self-government, from the drawing rooms of Aristocracy, to the public assemblies of the Sovereign People. . . . He who . . . bows to the iron rod and unauthorized proscriptions of a dictatorial *Few,* we are compelled to regard as *our* enemy, and *hope* he may not prove the enemy of himself and the Commonwealth. . . . Intimately connected with the Aristocratic policy of the *Few* leading the *Many,* is the fundamental maxim of all Oligarchies, that the People are not capable of instructing, and should not possess the power of controlling their Representatives. It is to be deeply regretted that this anti-republican notion, which grew out of ignorance and [the] venality of the European mob, should be most injuriously applied to the virtuous and intelligent citizens of this country and boldly acted upon, as it has very recently been, in this our native city.[37]

Connecting the licensing dispute and the truckmen's issue to the recent ward-voting affair, in its next issue a *Bostonian* editorial demanded the Phillips administration's ouster. "The conduct of our city government the last year, with regard to many of the acts, has produced much excitement and claims the attention of the electors. Their conduct with regard to *licenses,* the *Truckmen* and the last, though not least, their unjustifiable exertions in procuring an act to be passed, by the legislature, to prohibit *the meeting in Wards*" dishonored, the editorialist argued, all who had supported Phillips in 1822. Another editorial told "Mechanics!" that "[c]omplaint has been made in this part of the country, against southern slaves being entitled to representation in the Congress of the U.S. at the whim of others, although it appears, in this enlightened age, that in Boston the boasted home of Adams, of Hancock, and of [James] Otis, the enemies of oppression and the promoters of the glorious result of the American Revolution, a new kind of slavery is struck out, by those who are ambitious to drive the labouring classes like task masters." "The *Siege of Boston* is once *more raised,*" proclaimed the *Bostonian.* "Not only the City, but the whole Commonwealth, will feel the happy consequences of a victory, which will do more to raise us in the estimation of our sister States, than any political occurrence among Bostonians since the revolution."[38]

For most of Phillips's tenure as mayor, Joseph T. Buckingham's *Galaxy,* a major Middling Interest paper, remained uncharacteristically restrained. On prison limits, Buckingham reserved judgment, stating only that "[w]hether this will be a measure conducive to the general good, time alone can determine." Concerned with the broad latitude the ordinance gave to the "rich rogue, who voluntarily becomes bankrupt, and refuses to make any satisfaction to his creditors, some of whom may be much poorer than himself," Buckingham concluded that he "ought never to have the advantage of any limits beyond the walls of prison." Also understanding that the ordinance "amounts to a virtual repeal of the [state] laws relating to imprisonment for debt," which clearly was not within the jurisdictional authority of the city government, Buckingham remained skeptical of municipal prison reform. On the truckman issue he was mute.[39]

Throughout the Phillips administration, the pages of the *Galaxy* indicate that Buckingham seemed more concerned with the Middling Interest forays into state issues and national elections than with the governance of the city. He continued his attacks against the state militia law and persisted in calling for the its abolishment.[40] Also, he devoted much time covering the 1822 Suffolk County congressional race for the U.S. House of Representatives. This particular race intrigued Buckingham because it exhibited both the great strides and the frailties of the Middling Interest movement.

In Boston's November 1822 congressional House race, the Federalist Central Committee mounted Daniel Webster as its candidate for Suffolk County, calculating that a fresh young face would change the damaging image the party had acquired in recent local battles. Understanding that it had to garner sizable numbers from the ranks of the Middling Interest in Boston to achieve victory, Federalist strategists seized on one of the insurgency's most dynamic issues—antipartyism—and exploited it as their own. Despite Webster's invaluable service to the Federalist party during the Massachusetts constitutional convention of 1820–21 and his consistent loyalty to the Central Committee's local agendas in Boston, the 1822 Federalist caucus presented its nominee as a disinterested civil servant who "would be above the littleness of party feeling." One caucus member portrayed Webster as a man who "has a *head* and . . . a *heart,*" who understood that "the safest place is in the middle;" and, in fact, such a portrayal of Webster was not altogether inaccurate. By 1822 Webster became alarmed by the narrow and provincial approach to politics the Central Committee had taken. In a private letter to Joseph Story, Webster confessed that "[w]e [Federalists] are disgraced beyond help or hope by these things. There is a Federal[ist] interest, a Democratic

[Republican] interest, a Bankrupt interest, and a Middling interest, but I see no national interest, nor any national feeling." To Jeremiah Mason, Webster went ever further, proposing that Massachusetts Federalism should drop its party name because it had fallen into such disrepute in the minds of so many. To maintain traditional Federalist economic and political interests, Webster argued, the party should change its name and its insular behavior.[41]

At their caucus in November, Federalists disassociated themselves and their candidate from the partisan carnage and the divisive course Boston politics had recently taken. It leveled all blame for stirring up Boston's traditional placid political atmosphere on insurgent agitators who had polarized and confused the electorate. Claiming Webster would restore political harmony to Boston, one caucus member explained that the Federalist candidate "would not represent the 'middling interest' *merely,* but the general interest of the whole." In his statement in favor of Webster, Benjamin Gorham reiterated this theme and expanded upon it. According to Gorham, Webster should be supported not only because he would be "firm and independent" in his decisions and would transcend "local prepossessions, and narrow views" of partisanship but because he would understand that his most important role would be to counter "the gigantic influence of the southern states, whose representatives act in concert on all national questions. . . . The south," Gorham argued, "would never consent to lose her influences by dividing it amoung a number of candidates," and, therefore, neither should the North. "We want," Gorham continued, "representatives from the north, who cannot be drawn from their purpose by persuasion, nor driven by fear, but who can be heard, and felt, and respected; who [will] be able to beard the southern members in their own way."[42] In its approach to the Webster nomination, the Federalist leadership resurrected a tried-and-true strategy of creating a monolithic southern monster ready to gobble up northern interests. What was new about its approach was that the Federalist leadership fused this message with the popular and local antiparty principles of the Middling Interest.

The Federalist party leadership realized that it had been exposed by insurgents as self-serving, elitist, corrupt, and essentially undemocratic. Attempts by the Federalist leadership to counter this popular perception through mind-numbing explanations and defensive partisan tactics that bordered on illegality had proven costly and embarrassing, and also had largely failed. The party could not run and win by allowing local issues to define the campaign. By 1822 Federalism's credibility as a party willing to confront municipal grievances was highly suspect. Therefore, Federalism, under severe popular censure for past partisan improprieties, turned to the only available course open to it—broadening the political debate to include national issues and thereby exclude the partisan hazards of localism. The Federalist caucus's portrayal of Webster as a nonpartisan defender of regional duty undercut insurgent fervor over local grievances and temporarily weakened Middling Interest dissent and insurgent unity.

The Middling Interest party quickly responded to the Federalist tactic by hammering away at Webster as a Federalist tool who served elitist interests. To portray Webster as an antiparty man was absurd, the insurgency claimed. Middling Interest operatives reminded Bostonians of Webster's connections to the Central Committee and his history of avid Federalism. "You have already witnessed," stated the *Bostonian and Mechanics Journal* in early November, "the commotions excited by measures that are calculated to lull into repose the privileges of the MIDDLING CLASSES [of this city]—measures that are likely to advance into power and eminence, the *champion,* the *idol,* in fact, the *leader* of an aristocratic party—a man [Webster] who has ever opposed your interests—who would have the basis of your liberties founded on *wealth,* and who, in the late Convention for the revision of the Constitution, called to action all his eloquence, his rhetoric, and his logic, to promote the ascendancy of the *monied aristocracy* over *intelligence and virtue.* This gentleman . . . would have prostrated the liberties of your State, which may have placed you in the power of a class of beings, who pant to extinguish the spark you hold next to life itself," suffrage.[43] From the Middling Interest leadership's point of view, Webster's recent nonpartisan pose was utterly disingenuous. After all, he had been nominated in the Federalist caucus and enjoyed the backing of the Central Committee. Nevertheless, Webster's recent adoption of the insurgency's antiparty message potentially threatened Middling Interest solidarity. Ex-Federalists who had recently joined the insurgent cause out of disgust with the Central Committee's partisan trickery in local issues and its egregious self-interest might find Webster's nonpartisan and regional message attractive. Here seemed a very different type of Federalist from what Bostonians were used to.[44]

When the Republican caucus made a remarkably unprecedented and pragmatic move to capture the congressional election by disbanding its own caucus to join the Middling Interest's, ex-Federalist insurgents abandoned the Middling Interest en masse. Although a last-ditch effort was made by moderate George Sullivan to salvage Federalist support for the insurgency by proposing Webster as the Middling Interest candidate, he was shouted down by the Republican contingent at the caucus. After numerous flattering speeches, Republican stalwart Jesse Putnam "unanimously" received the Middling Interest nomination. When the speeches were over and the votes taken, the Republican party proved it had successfully coopted the insurgency caucus when it placed its man to head the insurgency ticket.[45]

The Middling Interest *Bostonian and Mechanics Journal* supported the caucus's choice of Putnam, claiming he was a "thorough-going *Middling Interest* man," "a friend of the MIDDLE CLASSES . . . who is not biased by ambitious and aristocratic views." Vilifying Webster as a many-faced "hydra that has now reared his head against your lawful rights and privileges," the *Bostonian* condemned the Federalist nominee as a tool of the "aristocracy."[46] Despite the *Bostonian*'s prediction that Jesse Putnam would "unite the whole strength of the MIDDLING INTER-

EST, in his support," the Middling Interest–Republican nomination had done just the opposite. When Webster thrashed Putnam by a solid 1,081 votes, it was clear that the insurgency's nomination of Republican Jesse Putman had alienated a large number of Middling Interest voters who temporarily returned to Federalism to vote for Webster. Even Joseph Buckingham was surprised. "Mr. Webster's majority over the opposing candidate, Mr. Putnam, was . . . a majority much larger than was expected by his most sanguine friends."[47]

Buckingham had reported extensively on Boston's congressional race, but uncharacteristically he offered neither candidate the *Galaxy*'s endorsement. Although the "electioneering contest was warm and spirited," the election was "not acrimonious," Buckingham stated with approval. Buckingham praised both Webster and Putnam supporters for not "resort[ing] to the aid of personal abuse to attain their objects."[48]

With the coming of Boston's second mayoral race, the *Galaxy* editor reengaged in municipal politics and once again became a unifying voice for Boston's insurgents. Perhaps writing more to himself than anyone else, Buckingham urged his readership to begin to "think on their municipal concerns, to see whether they have been managed the past-year with prudence and discretion, and whether the laws have been executed with the *promptness* and vigor that might have been expected under the new [city] organization." Reestablishing his editorial link with the Middling Interest, Buckingham renewed his attack on the Federalist Central Committee and pronounced the continued need for third-party activism in Boston. "While King Log [the Republican party] is despised," Buckingham explained, "let it not be forgotten that King Serpent [the Federalist party] is to be feared [most]. A wise people," Buckingham concluded, "will not invest either with power and supremacy."[49]

On the Phillips administration, Buckingham aligned himself with the *Bostonian and Mechanics Journal,* arguing that "the general tenor of the measures pursued by the city council has been . . . —oppressive in many cases to individuals, and in most cases injurious to the public." According to Buckingham, a dramatic shift in the mayor's office and on the City Council was needed to save the city from what he perceived as the prevailing "corruption" of the Phillips administration—"twelve separate, petty oligarchies, in each of which there is enough intrigue as there formerly was in the whole town." Buckingham saved his most scathing criticisms for the City Council; "[A]s a body, we know nothing they have done to entitle them even to such a poor reward as a vote of thanks for their services. That the genius of intrigue has been busy is evident from a variety of circumstances—witness the famous bill [suspension of ward voting] which was smuggled through the legislature for amending the city-charter." What was needed, Buckingham theorized, was a strong, independent executive who would curb warring partisans and municipal corruption so endemic to the Phillips administration.[50]

Under such decisive condemnation from those who had supported his election only a year earlier, the Phillips administration's scheme to alter the charter and abolish ward voting failed. Feeling the heat and recognizing that the urban insurgency's message potentially would translate just as well in rural Massachusetts as in the city of Boston, the legislature let the ward-voting proposal die. The times had changed, and the metamorphosis of Boston's political culture would not sustain such overt oppressive action. Although he probably was not personally involved in his administration's complicity with the General Court, Phillips faced most of the blame for the ward-voting affair. Exhausted, disgraced, and disillusioned, he decided not to run for reelection in 1823, citing ill health. The man who inspired the Middling Interest to declare victory over the "dictatorial FEW" in the Federalist Central Committee left office viewed as a traitor to the insurgent cause whose followers had elected him. Sadly, he would die just weeks after he stepped down from office, a broken man.[51]

Although the Federalist Central Committee's congressional candidate, Daniel Webster, managed to convince enough Bostonians to win a seat in the House, this election would be the last significant victory for the Central Committee. As Middling Interest leader Francis Wayland predicted early in 1822, the defiance first expressed by Bostonians toward the Federalist party in the 1822 mayoral contest quickly spread throughout the state. Feeding on Boston's defiance of 1822 and starved by economic depression, the people of Massachusetts in a resounding mandate finally abandoned the Federalist party, leaving it behind to atrophy and die.

Despite Harrison Gray Otis's 1822 declaration that he would never again run for any public office, in 1823 he decided to stick to his original scheme and campaign for governor. Not understanding the depth of popular hatred toward Otis within the state, arch-Federalist John Lowell thought Otis a fine choice and encouraged the senator. Lowell believed the average Massachusetts Federalist would have no choice but to vote the Otis ticket rather than defect to Republicanism. Indeed, it had worked for Webster. Only if a third-party candidate emerged like the "memorable treachery of [Quincy's alliance with the Middling Interest] March last," Lowell wrote to the ex-senator, would he have trouble carrying the state. Lowell calculated that "the 'oi Polloi' must follow us, because they have *no one else* to follow." After Webster's victory in the congressional race, Lowell's logic certainly seemed reasonable, especially to the ambitious Otis. "[T]he *washy* Federalist *must* act with us, *unless* a *third* Candidate shall be run," Lowell counseled Otis less than two months before the election. Even dissident Federalists like Quincy and Phillips would come around, Lowell predicted, for "[w]hat would Q [Quincy] & P [Phillips] & all the P's & Q's become, if Democracy [Republicanism] gets . . . well seated in the saddle?" Besides "we have *one* hold of them in *this* Election which appears to me too strong to break. *They* know, that on ye *power* of the *party* their very existence as publick men depends. . . . They will never again be heard of [if they once again betray the party]. They will eat no more Corporation dinners, nor be regaled any longer with the odoriferous praises upon which they have subsisted heretofore."[52]

Where Lowell's analysis proves shortsighted is in its assumption that the old party system could not mutate into something new—that the Quincys of the world had to be either Republicans or Federalist of the "old stamp." Unbeknownst to Federalist strategists, the political culture of Boston and Massachusetts had changed. The "oi Polloi" no longer blindly followed the old men of the Federalist party, whom they now viewed as, at best, out of touch with their needs or, worse, as self-serving and corrupt members of an oppressive elite regime. Nor did many of the "higher class," as Lowell called them, care about being "regaled" at "Corporation dinners." The "*power* of the *party*" was highly vulnerable in the 1822 mayoral elections and could do little but damage the political ambitions of politicians like Quincy. Indeed, Webster had won his seat in Congress not because of the Central Committee's support but despite it. As Webster understood, his victory had depended on playing the peacemaker among warring local partisan factions, on presenting himself as a candidate above the narrowness of partisan squabbles—in other words, adapting himself to Middling Interest principles. By redefining the issues from local to national, Webster discovered a viable vehicle with which to ascend to Congress, even while running under the Federalist party name. Portrayed as the nonpartisan defender of the region's survival, the Boston electorate overlooked Webster's affiliation with central committeemen like Otis, Sullivan, and Perkins. Otis would not have this luxury. By 1823, as Otis would learn, being a Federalist had become a grave political liability.

After 1822 the Federalist party existed only in name and in the stubborn imaginations of the upper-echelon members of the Federalist hierarchy, who were late in perceiving what had happened to them and their party. The realization that the times and rules had changed and that their proud party, in the end, had been undercut by its own rank-and-file membership's alliance with the Middling Interest men and the Republicans was a medicine that, at first, refused to go down easily. The final death blow to the Massachusetts Federalist party was hastened, ironically, by the party leadership's own insecurity and stupidity.

Scrambling to salvage the Otis campaign, the Federalist Central Committee botched a covert attempt to undercut the opposition late into the race. With this, most loyal Massachusetts Federalists abandoned the party out of disgust. In the spring of 1823, Boston's Middling Interest leadership made significant headway spreading the insurgent message to other parts of the state. Provoked by the Federalist's nomination of Otis, insurgent committees began popping up in communities outside of Boston to stop the Central Committee's candidate. Statewide Middling Interest organization was exactly what Lowell and other well-connected Federalists had feared, and the Central Committee aggressively responded to the challenge. From Worcester, an Otis operative reported to the Central Committee in Boston that "[s]pies have been [successfully] placed in several of [the Middling Interest] committees so that almost everything they have undertaken has failed in consequence of the information they have given to our veteran leaders." Unfortunately for the Central Committee, this letter had fallen from its operative's pocket and been retrieved by a Middling Interest man in Worcester who immediately sent it to the editors of the *Bostonian and Mechanics Journal.*[53]

The public disclosure of the letter in the *Bostonian* horrified the city. "We perceive in th[is] electioneering campaign [of the Central Committee] the last mad struggle of Aristocracy," explained one infuriated Boston insurgent. "They [the Federalist leadership] call upon us in the most pathetic manner to vote for *their candidate—their party.* How long is it since they tried to lull us to sleep by singing to us 'there is no party'—this is the 'era of good feelings'. . . . When will the mad ambition of these men cease?" Then, articulating the ultimate goal of the Central Committee, the editorialist condemned the antirepublican political perspective of the Federalist party. "They are striving to perpetuate in a few families their connections and dependents [for] all the 'high places.'" After the 1823 gubernatorial race, men like Lowell were forced to absorb new political realities. No longer would the "people" follow the "FEW." By 1823 the Federalist elite of Massachusetts had lost any remaining political legitimacy still associated with it.[54]

Otis suffered a devastating loss to Republican William Eustis. For the first time in the party's history, it lost the Federalist strongholds of Hampshire and Essex counties. In Boston, things were no better. With the hackneyed Federalist machine at its breaking point, Otis achieved what he could not the year before and carried Boston, but even in this traditional Federalist stronghold, the once well-oiled party machinery clogged with age and rust within the fresh and fertile democratic troposphere of the new urban realities. Otis won Boston by a meager 108 votes. Out of a total of 5,564 active voters in Boston, Eustis gained 2,728 votes to Otis's 2,836, indicating that the Republicans captured all the Middling Interest and Republican votes and, perhaps now not so surprisingly, a good number of rank-and-file Federalists. Equally significant, over 2,000 more people participated in the 1823 gubernatorial race than had voted in the mayoral race of 1822. According to Samuel Eliot Morison, an Otis descendant, "[w]ith the defeat of Otis, the Federal[ist] party lost its last state."[55]

Although Morison laments his ancestor's defeat, a Middling Interest man in the *Bostonian and Mechanics Journal* heralded the Republican victory, claiming it for himself and his party:

> Certain great men of the city, have asserted, that there is no such thing in existence among us as a *Middling Interest.* This may be very true, when affirmed of those wretched countries where nothing meets the eye but Palaces and the Mud-Cottages. But that this assertion is not true of Massachusetts, a thousand arguments might be adduced to prove; and the best argument of all is the success of EUSTIS. Had the people been blindly devoted to party, Mr. Otis would have been elected, for the Aris-

> tocrats had previously carried a majority. . . . But Mr. Otis was no sooner proposed than the people excersized [*sic*] *their Reason* instead of their Leader's. They saw *their* interest and that of the *Aristocracy,* led different ways. Otis recommended by his subserviency to his Party, but the people preferred a man subservient to *their own Interest.* And they chose *plain sense* in a *good cause,* in preference to *splendid talents* in *a bad one.*"[56]

Calling himself "A friend to Political Equality," another Bostonian proclaimed Otis's defeat a triumph for the Middling Interest but explained that the battle would not be fully won until the "Aristocrats" were driven from the City Council. "The ranks of Aristocracy are broken, and with one effort more," "A friend" predicted, "we shall destroy that dictatorial power which has so long bound us to service."[57]

Ironically, the mayoral candidate that the majority of the Middling Interest supported would turn out to be one of Boston's most dictatorial mayors of all time. Nevertheless, Josiah Quincy would govern Boston in a different way than Boston's past leadership. He did not expect the people to be bound to his "service" per se; instead they would be bound to the corporate good of Boston as he saw it. Unlike the dominant political order before the Middling Interest movement, the people's support and even the people's deference to Quincy and his administration would be earned through active municipal policy and not expected because of his status in society. The course of the city no longer could be determined simply by a select number of elites with mutual interests in a unilateral manner. Instead, municipal policy would have to meet with the approval of a highly critical and politically empowered electorate. Also, despite the future mayor's autocratic approach to municipal governance, insurgent rank-and-file Bostonians would demand an independent leadership that favored no one particular set of interests, least of all those set forth by the Central Committee. Instead, Quincy would court the collective interests of the majority in Boston.[58]

The Phillips administration had been a disaster. Absent of any executive leadership or direction, the city was left to the bidding of Boston's independent municipal boards and a City Council determined to gut the people of their democratic rights. In one year, the majority of Bostonians had gone from extolling the chartering and the Phillips mayoralty as a clear triumph for the "many" over the "FEW" to condemning the administration as a corrupt agency ruled by the few. By the mayoral election of 1823, the Phillips betrayal seemed as sinister as any of the Federalist Central Committee's past actions. Indeed, the duplicity of the ward-voting affair struck many insurgents as extraordinarily familiar. As one Middling Interest man put it, the Federalist Central Committee, "[t]hat aristocratic band[,] has been abolished, but a more oppressive and more horrible, and more odious one . . . has arisen to fill its place."[59] In the city's second mayoral contest, Boston's insurgents would purge this new "more horrible and . . . odious" band and place their confidence once again in Josiah Quincy.

VIII • PERSONAL PARTISANSHIP, POLITICAL FRAGMENTATION, AND THE POLITICS OF PUBLIC PERSONA

ICHABOD, the Glory is Departed.
—Joseph T. Buckingham, 1823

The success of the Middling Interest coalition during the gubernatorial race of 1823 marked the final demise of the Federalist party in Massachusetts. As Joseph T. Buckingham explained, "the federalist party of Boston, signed its death-warrant" by choosing Harrison Gray Otis as its candidate. "Boston federalism," Buckingham declared, might as well now "'hang out its banners on the outerwalls,' and inscribe thereon, 'ICHABOD, the Glory is Departed.'"[1] Daniel Webster agreed. He had predicted the ruin of Otis would seal the fate of Massachusetts Federalism. Writing to Joseph Story after the election, Webster criticized the "miserable, dirty squabble of local politics" that surrounded the gubernatorial race and confessed that he was "not disappointed at the result of the election. . . . My 'agony,'" he revealed, "was over before the election took place, for I never doubted the result. Indeed," admitted Webster, "I could have enjoyed the triumph of neither party."[2]

Webster's foresight notwithstanding, Federalism's crushing loss to the Republican party in the 1823 gubernatorial race baffled the city's pundits. No one in the Bay State had anticipated Federalism's disaster in 1823. Even Buckingham described the election's outcome as being "as unexpected as it was mortifying to the federalist party." "That [Otis] should fall so far behind his adversary in the political race could never have been believed till the fact had been proven."[3]

Scrambling to make sense out of it all, the Boston press attributed the upset to what the Republican *Boston Patriot* identified as "Sir Harry" Otis's past "treason" at the Hartford Convention. The equally Republican Boston *Statesman* agreed but also suggested that Otis's defeat could be better explained within the context of a religious controversy that had been brewing for two decades.[4]

As early as 1800 the state's Congregationalist establishment experienced an irreparable fissure between traditional orthodox Trinitarians and dissenting Unitarians. Although Unitarians were a minority, their largest concentration was in the economically dominant eastern part of the state. By 1805 Boston's elite Unitarians had seized Harvard University from the old Orthodoxy and used it to disseminate both liberal theology and conservative Federalism. Politically, the schism had not affected Federalist strongholds in the state. In these regions, Congregationalist and Unitarian Federalists traditionally buried their theological differences and unified on the Federalist ticket. Yet, in 1823, the denominational dispute spilled over into the governor's race and was effectively exploited by Republican–Middling Interest forces to help confirm Otis's alliance with the "money power" in Boston.[5]

The dispute centered around Amherst College, which had been founded by conservative orthodox Congregationalists in the traditionally Federalist stronghold of the Pioneer Valley. Although the college had been operating since 1821, it had not received a charter from the General Court and thus could not legally grant legitimate college diplomas to its graduating students. In the winter of 1822–23, the legislature rejected the town of Amherst's petition for a charter. The General Court justified its decision by arguing that the chartering of Amherst would unduly handicap the established colleges of Harvard and Williams. Outraged Congregationalists cried foul, claiming a Harvard–Unitarian conspiracy against them, while Republican–Middling Interest partisans scrambled to spin the action into a condemnation of Otis. Although Otis probably had nothing to do with the legislature's action and had never considered himself a religious man, he was a Unitarian and served on Harvard's Board of Overseers and its corporation. Because of this, Otis was vulnerable. In the wake of the political upheaval caused by the Middling Interest revolt, the Republican–Middling Interest press exploited Otis's affiliation with Unitarianism and Harvard to great advantage.[6]

Using the class-based rhetoric of the Middling Interest, a "Serious Federalist" in a broadside that circulated around Boston directly linked Otis with the General Court's seeming prejudice against the Orthodoxy, the rural western part of the state, and the college that would educate the people of that region. Otis was portrayed as a Unitarian zealot, a Harvard elitist, and an undemocratic snob who had applied political influence to sway the legislature in preserving Boston's predominance as the political, financial, educational, and ecclesiastical authority in the Commonwealth. Serious Federalist "refuse[d] to support Mr. Otis" because "we object to Mr. Otis, as christian patriots, on account of his *immoral character.*" Claiming that a certain cabal of self-serving Boston patricians were responsible for Amherst's failure to gain a charter and then condemning Otis, Serious Federalist situated the Amherst incident within the language and context of the Middling Interest's most effective indictment against Otis's Federalism. Otis was one of "the Boston and Cambridge junto," Serious Federalist charged, "connected with a Boston and Harvard College Aristocracy, who have for several years manifested a disposition to have the disposal of all important offices in the State." After endorsing William Eustis for governor, Serious Federalist indicated the depth of his resentment toward his previous party: "Our old partialities would indeed lead us to prefer persons of the Federal[ist] Party," but due to the Central Committee's belligerent refusal to relinquish the party reins, "[w]e are disposed to support the Republicans candidates for the present year." Also outraged, the *Statesman* argued that Otis should be denied the governorship because he was "one of the corporation of Harvard University, which is well known to be devoted to the propagation of a particular creed, to have exerted an undue and highly prejudicial influence to depress other literary institutions."[7] Although the controversy over the incorporation of Amherst College certainly had its origins in the old denominational feud between the Orthodoxy and Unitarianism, the conflict became politicized by Republican–Middling Interest partisans out to exploit the episode. The charge of malicious elitism—which had proven so successful in the insurgency's past battles with the Federalist Central Committee—was applied to the Amherst controversy. Once Otis became inexorably linked to the "Boston and Harvard College [Unitarian] Aristocracy," the popular insurgency had discovered yet another nail that could be driven into the Federalist chieftain's coffin. Ironically, this time, the criticism Otis faced was probably unwarranted.[8]

Thus, barely beneath the surface of a religious dispute lay the same class-based political warfare that the city's elite and plebeians had been waging for the past four years. Concerned less with past Federalist indiscretions at the Hartford Convention or the party's supposed wholesale conversion to Unitarianism and Harvard and more with rejecting the "self created [Federalist] central committee of THREE [Otis, Sullivan, and Perkins]," 14,909 new Massachusetts voters turned out in the 1823 gubernatorial race to subdue the "Aristocracy," the "Cabal"—the "FEW." In Boston, increased voter turnout paralleled the general upsurge in the state. Nearly 2,000 new voters went to the polls in Boston, the vast majority of whom, the *Bostonian and Mechanics Journal* claimed, had voted Republican because there was no third-party candidate.[9] Clearly, such wide-scale Middling Interest and Republican voter participation could not be attributed simply to Otis's role in the Hartford Convention or to the fact that he went to a Unitarian church. As Buckingham explained just days after the election, "[w]e take no notice of the slang about . . . the Hartford Convention" as sufficient reason for Otis's loss; nor did Eustis's Congregationalism "gain . . . or los[e] him a single vote." Dismissing such suggestions as mere "electioneering tricks" which had had "very little effect," Buckingham advised his readers to look elsewhere for explanations for Federalism's humiliation.[10]

Buckingham attributed Federalism's decline to the vital role an angry new generation of voters played in the election. According to the *Galaxy,* young voters flocked to the Republican candidate because Federalism's leadership had barred them from any participation within the party. "We apprehend," Buckingham explained, "that [the young adopted the Republican candidate because of] the course of favoritism and exclusion which has been pursued by the federalists." The "great political questions affecting [the] state" had little to do with Harrison Gray Otis's defeat at the hands of this new generation of voters, Buckingham argued. Instead, they had chosen the Republican party over the Federalist because the Central Committee had contemptuously spurned them. "[W]hat prospect is there for the gratification of [the youthful and ambitious voter] by uniting with the federalist party of Massachusetts?" Buckingham queried. "Not the slightest. When has it been known, within the last ten years, that any young man, whatever may have been his intellectual talents . . . has attained to distinction in the federal[ist] ranks? The leading men in the federal[ist] party cling to the honours and offices in the gift of party with an affection stronger than death . . . *Wealth and parentage,* (we speak particularly in reference to the Boston federalists,) are the universal and exclusive passports to office and distinction [and are issued by] our old superannuated nabobs and their special favourites."[11] At least for the editor of the *Galaxy,* Otis's defeat could best be explained by the candidate's high-ranking role on the Central Committee. Although the religious dispute over Amherst and the Hartford Convention were factors in the 1823 election, these episodes were more symbolic and symptomatic of a much larger conflict—Boston's battle against the "aristocracy."[12]

After its editors mulled over the dramatic political realignment in the state, the Republican *Patriot* eventually reached the same conclusion, confirming that a new generation of young voters "who have attained manhood since the termination of the late war [of 1812]" had rejected the Federalist party en masse. Such young men, the *Patriot* posited, dismissed Federalism as archaic and had "ranged themselves beneath the banner of democracy [Republicanism]." Indeed, William M. Penniman's newly established, Middling Interest–leaning *Young Galaxy* catered to exactly this new bloc of Boston voters and had squarely endorsed the Republican ticket in 1823 over that of the "aristocracy." To these young voters Harrison Gray Otis seemed a haughty old Federalist silk-stocking—hardly someone who would address their growing economic insecurities. Before the election, the Federalist press inadvertently reinforced this perception of Otis by devoting most of its copy to defend his involvement in the Hartford Convention. Also, it endorsed the Senator's failed congressional efforts in getting the federal government to reimburse Massachusetts for costs incurred by state militias for defending the coastline in the War of 1812. For the first-time voter who only vaguely remembered them, these concerns seemed anachronistic and insignificant when compared to the more pressing issues the depression generated in 1823.[13]

For its part, the *Bostonian and Mechanics Journal* claimed that the Republican victory indicated the fruition of the insurgency's hard organizational work, the immediacy of the insurgent message, and ultimately evidenced the firm establishment of the Middling Interest party in the city of Boston. "It is asserted," the *Bostonian* reported after Otis carried Boston by a scant 108 votes, "that the results of the late election in this City [have] converted at least one thousand of the late predominant party. The ranks of the Middling Interest are filling up with unexampled rapidity. It is scarcely possible to find a man who claims any affinity with the crest fallen aristocracy. Yesterday all was party with them, today they belong to no party."[14]

Resting just below the service of this new political culture lay deep-seated bitterness predicated on obvious class distinctions between elites and everyone else. As Buckingham explained, "[t]he honour and emoluments of office are fair objects for competition amoung *all* classes and professions, and it is right and proper that it should be so."[15] The artisans and petty merchants along with the laboring class of truckmen, stevedores, draymen, and peddlers had united with their employees against the common enemy. With these developments, Boston politics during 1820–23 established future patterns that would soon come to help categorize urban Jacksonian society and its aggressively confrontational political style.

Clearly, the political culture of Boston had changed enough to sustain realistic alternatives to Federalism. With no substantial disagreements on national issues being presented to define and distinguish the Federalist party from northern Republicans, local grievances relating to Boston's economy and management, generational differences, political persona, and partisan style (or lack thereof) became the predominating factors in determining whom Bostonians would support for governor. Local gripes and resentments were voiced through oppositional politics and took priority over traditional partisan voting behavior. Provincial, single issue, and highly volatile insurgent cells emerged out of past political complacency and partisan uniformity.

In Boston, the fulcrum that consolidated and moved this assortment of varied interests into action, the Middling Interest, had an ardent commitment to political independence and nonpartisanship which had struck a chord in an urban electorate. This coalition hankered to break away from the constraining partisan discipline the Federalist establishment expected and enforced. As the *Bostonian* explained, the fundamental purpose of the Middling Interest was to "check . . . the violent extremes of party bigotry and ambition." Part and parcel of the electorate's abandonment of Federalism was a popular commitment to antipartyism. "The present party designations," the Middling Interest declared, "have become . . . obsolete, as they are, in truth groundless and nugatory to ALL."[16]

Yet, the same antipartyism that had redeemed individual political freedom in Boston also opened an immense political void that created much political confusion and chaos. Having sacrificed their past loyalty to partisanship to achieve political autonomy and spurning all partyism as a corrupting influence, insurgent Bostonians found themselves in the spring of 1823 with little to hold on to except a politician's individual reputation. With party structures repudiated and partisanship scorned, Boston's insurgents looked to leaders who presented a proactive and independent persona—a leader unconstrained by party ties, yet some one who would prove dynamic enough to create change.

Although somewhat concerned by what he called the "distracted state of our politics at this unhappy period," Josiah Quincy enjoyed his independent status as a municipal judge and political pundit. His apostasy from the Federalist Central Committee made him one of Boston's most popular characters. At the Federalist caucus that nominated Otis for governor in the spring of 1823, the *Bostonian* reported that Quincy delivered "one of the merriest and most humorous speeches we have ever heard in the cradle of liberty." Quincy "harangue[d]" the caucus's choice for governor. Exploiting the popular image of Otis as a condescending aristocrat, Quincy sardonically claimed that exposing the gentle senator's constitution to the harsh rigors of the governorship would be unfair to the aristocrat's natural disposition. "[A] diamond necklace should not be converted into a drag-chain, or an Arabian courser turned into a dray-horse," Quincy declared, and neither should Otis be forced to undergo the bureaucratic rigors and drudgery required in serving as the governor. Humorously reminding the audience of "the failure of Mr. Otis in his struggle" for the mayoralty in 1822, Quincy argued that with Otis as the Federalist nominee the Republicans would easily win the election. He then shocked his audience by denouncing the Federalist party leadership. According to the *Bostonian,* "Judge [Quincy] concluded by hoping that the Federalists [at the caucus] would [choose] Mr. Otis and thereby give the Democrats [Republicans]" the governor's mansion. Although some Federalists listened to Quincy's speech with outrage, the "harangue" was conveyed in such an amusing manner that the *Bostonian* concluded "[t]he learned Judge, was, as usual, inveterately *popular*" when he left the hall.[17] Clearly, this was Quincy's intent.

Ever since becoming a municipal judge, Quincy had consolidated power around himself—often testing the limits of his judicial authority to reach this aim. The activism of the Quincy court was widely covered by the insurgent press. Hardly losing himself among "the whores and rogues," as Harrison Gray Otis had predicted, during his tenure as a judge Quincy remained prominently in the public spotlight. Never having given up hope of becoming mayor, Judge Quincy made decisions that, though often criticized by lawyers as dictatorial, were skillfully designed to lay the groundwork for a future campaign.[18] His brutal attack on Otis at the Federalist caucus proved a timely maneuver in a well-laid strategy to receive frustrated Federalist, Republican, and Middling Interest support.

In mid-December 1822, and after dropping out of Boston's first mayoral contest, Judge Quincy ruled on a highly visible case that assured him the continued support of Buckingham. His opinion outraged conservative lawyers throughout the state while it delighted the antilawyer sensibilities of many Republicans and Middling Interest men.

In the fall of 1822, the *Galaxy* published a number of scathing articles that arguably slandered itinerant Methodist preacher John Newland Maffitt. Maffitt was a highly popular evangelical whose flair attracted overflow audiences that often climbed through church windows just to hear him. In a series of articles, Buckingham presented the famous preacher as a con man and a lecher whose wanton behavior was "unbecoming a gentleman and a christian." Maffitt, it seemed, had a propensity for strong liquor and underage women, and the *Galaxy* had said so.[19]

After the *Galaxy*'s exposés, the Methodist preacher sued Buckingham for libel. The case ended up in Quincy's court. Maffitt's lawyer presented *Galaxy* articles that clearly tarnished the minister's character and argued that the case, therefore, was clear-cut. Quincy responded by boldly redefining the libel law. He would allow Buckingham and his lawyer to prove the truth of the *Galaxy*'s articles. If they withstood scrutiny, Quincy charged, they were not libelous and Buckingham would be acquitted. Quincy claimed that freedom of the press was at stake and that, under the Massachusetts constitution, the liberty of the press transcended an individual's right to privacy. On the other hand, Quincy decreed that, if Buckingham had fabricated the *Galaxy*'s stories, then they were written with malicious intent only to slander Maffitt and therefore Buckingham should be found guilty of libel. This interpretation of the Massachusetts constitution was highly unorthodox.[20]

According to Quincy's son, his father "argued that the common-law doctrine, that the truth could not be admitted in evidence under an indictment for libel,—or, as usually put that 'the greater the truth, the greater the libel,'—was overruled by the express provision of the Constitution of the State, which made a specific reservation for its citizens of the liberty of the press,—a liberty unknown . . . to the common law,—and declared that all parts of that law repugnant to that liberty are not to be considered law under the Constitution." After two days of hearings filled with witnesses and affidavits, Quincy ruled that Buckingham had written the truth and therefore was innocent. "This was the first time," Edmund Quincy explained, "that such a ruling had been made in the case of an ordinary indictment for a libel on a private individual, and it excited much discussion and no little censure at the time."[21] Having acquitted Joseph T. Buckingham by using such a radical interpretation of the law, Quincy ensured the *Galaxy*'s and its editor's loyal support in the future.

Quincy fully understood that maintaining Buckingham's support was even more essential to his 1823 campaign than it had been just a year earlier. Just as the Middling Interest fissured over the Webster–Putnam congressional contest, the insurgency would split over Quincy, just as he had expected. Much had changed in the past year, and the Middling Interest's *Bostonian and Mechanics Journal* refused to endorse Quincy for mayor. Instead, it went with the Republican candidate George Blake, and for good reason.[22]

After Otis's dismal showing in the gubernatorial contest, the Central Committee turned on its renowned chieftain in a desperate attempt to revitalize the party in Boston. To achieve this the Central Committee focused on winning the mayor's office. The dilemma for Federalist operative William Sullivan was how to appeal to Middling Interest men on local issues. Running a partisan Federalist within such a hostile political environment would clearly result in defeat. Considering the Middling Interest's effective campaign against partisanship—a campaign directed at the Federalist rank-and-file to undermine the authority of the Central Committee—and the growing appeal of antipartyism within Boston, Sullivan's task was tricky. The committee had to find a unique candidate whom the electorate trusted. It needed someone whose public persona reflected the new political values that were emerging within the city—someone who, above all else, seemed removed from the zealous partisanship of the committee's past.

Remarkably, and despite Harrison Gray Otis's vigorous objections, the committee decided to approach Josiah Quincy. As Eliza Quincy explained, Massachusetts "had become democratic [Republican], and Mr. Sullivan and other Federalists came and requested Mr. Quincy to consent to stand for Mayor as the last hope of [the Federalist] party," "as his popularity with the people gave [the Federalists] their only chance." To have, of all people, Quincy's archnemesis, William Sullivan, come, hat in hand, and beg him to save the Federalist party must have seemed to Quincy a just atonement for the party's past betrayals of him. Also, Quincy was clearly not a Republican, and the insurgency's recent shift toward that party made it difficult for him not to accept Sullivan's offer. However, Quincy remained highly skeptical of Sullivan's proposition. He hesitantly accepted the nomination, but on his own terms. He stipulated that all members of the Central Committee would take a back seat in the election. Like Webster, Quincy understood that the strong presence of committee members in his campaign would severely undermine his chances of victory. Instead, Quincy's campaign would be run by two of his most loyal Middling Interest supporters, insurgents Francis Wayland and Heman Lincoln. Instead of doing the bidding of the Central Committee, Quincy turned the tables and the committee lay utterly beholden to him as its party's only salvation. The combative insurgents whom the *Bostonian* spoke for viewed Quincy's "embrace" of Federalism with great suspicion, if not outrage, and sided with the Republican candidate.[23]

Harrison Gray Otis and his friends were also appalled and deeply offended by the committee's nomination of Quincy. How could the committee endorse the same apostate who had so seriously betrayed the party just a year earlier and had publicly disgraced the honor of Boston Federalism's most distinguished standard bearer, Harrison Gray Otis, just weeks earlier? For Otis's men the Central Committee's action was a betrayal too heinous to bear. Upon Quincy's nomination, Otis broke from the Central Committee and launched a campaign to destroy the unlikely Federalist candidate even if it meant putting a Republican in the mayor's office. A petty personal feud had caused an irreparable fissure within the already enfeebled Federalist leadership. Facing an internal reactionary rebellion within the ranks of its leadership, the beleaguered and besieged Federalist party could not withstand the pressure. Ironically, those who led the insurrection had been the party's most orthodox leader and its most loyal partisans. Just as the Federalist nominee for mayor splintered the insurgent coalition, Quincy's nomination cracked open the once impenetrable fortress of Boston Federalism—the Central Committee.[24]

Otis supporters began zealously searching for a specific issue to discredit and destroy Quincy. In *Maffitt* v. *Buckingham,* they found their cause and unsparingly exploited Quincy's unorthodox ruling to lead an assault on his intelligence, legal skill, and character. Before the election a pamphlet, rumored to have been written by Otis, circulated around Boston. The author, who identified himself only as "A Member of the Suffolk Bar," disingenuously claimed to have been a "busom friend [to Quincy], his 'council's consistory' in all bright and all dark periods of our nation's history for the last twenty-five years." But after the judge's ruling in the *Maffitt* case, "Member" explained he was now forced to betray his friendship and expose Quincy as dangerous to the sanctity of the Commonwealth's law. Charging Quincy with stupidity and "aggravat[ing] evil" while serving on the bench, "Member" claimed that the *Maffitt* decision was "evidence of [only] a superficial acquaintance with the law." Quincy was so driven by petty personal ambition that he overlooked the fact that his ruling was thoroughly "inadequate" and "illegal." "Determined to override . . . the supreme court" and make a name for himself, Quincy had not only botched the decision but broken the law, according to "Member," who portrayed the municipal judge as an ambitious amateur and a dangerous incompetent. The timing of the pamphlet's release makes it clear that Otis's supporters' intent was to discredit Quincy's mayoral campaign by attacking the judge's character. If it could be shown that Quincy was corrupt and inept—an utter failure as a lowly municipal judge—certainly Boston's electorate would not vote him into higher office.[25] After discovering corruption in the Phillips administration, Otis's partisans wagered that a similar indictment of Quincy's performance as a judge would tar his campaign.

The Federalist press took a neutral stance in the controversy. In a quandary over which faction to follow, Federalism's organs decided not to print or report the reproach, as Otis partisans presumably wanted. Realizing that the charges were as much an indictment of him as of Quincy, Joseph T. Buckingham rushed to his candidate's defense. The *Galaxy* addressed each of the pamphlet's points, squarely dismissing them as illogical and/or selfishly motivated by petty personal interest. Buckingham urged Bostonians to disregard the pamphlet as simply an "*ungentlemanly* attack of an anonymous writer . . . destitute of *good manners* . . . and quite derogatory to the character and official duty of Judge Q.," who had served the court admirably. He accused Otis of authoring the assault out of personal vengeance, and the dispute immediately became politicized. Catapulted from the realm of judicature, the *Maffitt* decision was thrown into Boston's vast political void, where only the slight remnants of party structures remained, thus helping to define the mayoral campaign of 1823.[26]

In his own pamphlet reprinted in the *Galaxy,* "Citizen" explained that the legal controversy was driven by personal partisanship and nothing else. Identifying Otis as the first pamphlet's author, "Citizen" revealed that "[w]hen the rancorous zeal of party shall have subsided, when the vindictive violence of personal enmity shall be spent, and when the voice of the false, insidious friend [Otis] shall be silent, [only] then will his title to applause be admitted." When they realized their ploy had backfired, Otis operatives vigorously denied that their leader authored the denunciation of Quincy, but few in Boston believed them. Although the anti-Quincy invective was, in fact, written by the old Federalist chieftain's impulsive son, Harrison Gray Otis was held accountable. The impact of the pamphlet wars only added to Quincy's popularity among wavering insurgents and rank-and-file Federalists, who were appalled by the hostile nature of the Otis pamphlet.[27] Otis's strategy was familiar to Boston, but his new motivation was not, and much of Boston was offended.[28]

Quincy's past record as a vocal Boston citizen and jurist also reinforced the sense that he was driven not by personal or elitist interests but by the insurgency coupled with a sincere desire for a better city. Though the provision (section 30) within the city charter endowing the General Court with power to unilaterally alter local Boston law and its municipal structure had not been a burning issue during the city's first mayoral contest, after the Phillips administration's attempt to repeal ward voting using section 30, middling Bostonians' fear of the provision was magnified in 1823. Bostonians had learned from the Phillips administration to dread the potential power over their lives section 30 gave to the legislature. At any time and for whatever reason, the General Court could usurp the autonomy of the Boston citizenry.

By the 1823 mayoral race, anxiety over section 30 proved one of the few remaining cohesive forces that bound insurgents together. Although the *Galaxy* and the *Bostonian and Mechanics Journal* represented the two opposing wings of the insurgency and could agree on little, both printed scathing attacks of section 30 before the election. Identifying section 30 as an undemocratic strategy implemented by the General Court to impose its mastery over the city, some Middling Interest pundits went so far as to recommend that the whole charter be revoked and replaced by the old town meeting system. Quincy had advocated this since 1821, and his spokesmen were sure to remind voters of their candidate's stand. Insurgent leader William Emmons referred to the "intelligent decisions of . . . Quincy" when he railed against the charter in a crowded Faneuil Hall. Indeed, as Joseph Buckingham explained, Quincy had consistently fought the charter because "he saw . . . mischief in the section which gives the legislature unrestrained power over the charter." As mayor, Buckingham posited, Quincy "will be still on the watch to see that we are not 'made the foot-ball of a foolish legislature.'"[29]

Between Quincy's 1822 and 1823 mayoral campaigns, he appealed to insurgent sensibilities on other matters as well as by using his position as a municipal judge to address pressing local concerns. As a judge, Quincy had shown sympathy for the truckmen's grievances. The case of *The Commonwealth* v. *Solomon M. Levengston* is representative of Quincy's regard for them. Levengston was arrested and charged with hawking his products directly to the public and shopkeepers below retail and established wholesale rates—something he did not have a city license to do. Also, because of the city's new truckman law passed by the Phillips administration, Levengston had broken the local ordinance by selling his products openly from his cart.[30]

Levengston's attorney, Republican partisan Andrew Dunlap, argued that, in his client's case, the local ordinance was unconstitutional because it restricted an individual's right to earn a respectable living and gave an unfair advantage to well-established retail merchants within the city. If "[a] man has a right to earn an honest livelihood by trade in his shop, fixed to a certain spot," why, Dunlap asked, should his client "not have this same right," even if his shop is his cart? Claiming that the licensing law did not apply to his client because Levengston's "case was not at all analogous to the restrictions upon innholders and retailers of liquor; for those restrictions are imposed and required from a regard to public morals; but no such grounds existed for the support of th[e] law" that Levengston was charged with breaking. All his client had done was sell nonalcoholic products to individuals and shops below competing retail and wholesale prices. Certainly, there could be no harm in that, Dunlap maintained.[31]

Summing up his plea, Dunlap placed the case squarely within the political context of the past four years. The law Levengston was charged with breaking "gives an exclusive advantage to one class of citizens, and imposes a partial burden then upon another; and, therefore, is unconstitutional." Judge Quincy agreed. "[T]he law," according to Quincy's ruling, "was certainly of a dubious character," and Levengston was acquitted. As the *Galaxy* explained, because the *Levengston* case "was the first case, which had arisen upon the law since its enactment," Quincy's charge authenticated him as a friend to the truckmen and petty merchant and, by extension, the insurgent movement.[32]

On the eve of Boston's second mayoral contest, the Federalist party was racked with factionalism. Joseph Buckingham had it right when he pronounved, in retrospect, that "the federalist party of Boston [died] when it voted for a city charter." Indeed, in the end, local municipal issues first introduced and then stubbornly pressed and doggedly pursued by the insurgent coalition incited feuding within the Federalist Central Committee. Under such extreme and mounting pressure, Boston's once united "lay priesthood," as Otis, Sullivan, and Perkins came to be described, divided into two opposing sects that devoured each other.[33]

Boston's electorate no longer could rely on any semblance of a cohesive party system to direct its voting behavior. The mayoral election of 1822 had been complicated enough with four candidates and three parties. In that election voters were asked to choose among Federalism's Otis, the Middling Interest's Quincy, and Republicanism's George Blake, with the mysterious fourth candidate, Thomas L. Winthrop, further snarling the process. Despite the clutter, each of the local parties in 1822 forged and articulated divergent agendas that represented substantial differences in popular opinion. On the surface, 1823 seemed much less complicated with only Republican and Federalist candidates making a bid. However, underneath what seemed to be a return to a simpler two-party competition lay only the broken hulls of past party structures and organizations.

Flailing about with no particular direction or command structure, and after a battle that bankrupted them both, the Federalist party and the Middling Interest coalitionalist insurgency discovered in 1823 that their fractured organizations no longer represented any meaningful programs for the future. Federalism descended into the petty politics of personal vengeance in the wake of its ruin, just as Webster had predicted. The Middling Interest's hatred of the "FEW" had been successfully exploited by the Republicans to force a schism within insurgent ranks that resulted in syphoning off enough numbers so that the Middling Interest had no chance to develop a viable party structure in the city, let alone the state. Although Republican accomplishment within the traditional Federalist stronghold of Boston seemed impressive, it was not enough to ensure Republican dominance in the city. So where would the majority of Boston's voters turn in 1823?

Acting as both a Federalist and a Middling Interest man, an independent Josiah Quincy invited them to come to him, and on Election Day the majority of Boston's electorate answered his call. A new coalition formed, this time around the persona of one of Boston's most independent citizens. With the *Galaxy*'s loyal support and the hard work of Francis Wayland and Heman Lincoln, a broad-based Quincy coalition narrowly defeated the Republican candidate, George Blake, by 325 votes. Quincy had snatched victory from the hands of the Republicans, who had been waiting breathlessly for the demise of Federalism. In the municipal elections for the Board of Aldermen and Common Council, Boston spoke even more forcefully. All eight of the Phillips administration's bipartisan aldermen were forced out of office. Of the forty-eight who served on the Common Council only eighteen survived the election. Significantly, William Sullivan, who represented Ward 6 during the Phillips administration as a city councilman, watched in horror as his ward turned Republican. In 1823 it had gone with William Eustis in the gubernatorial race and Blake in the mayoral contest. Adding insult to injury, in the municipal elections of 1823, Republican William Wright challenged Sullivan and won the old Federalist's seat on the council.[34]

Voter turnout in the 1823 mayoral race dramatically surpassed that of 1822, with 1,064 new voters going to the polls. Although voter participation in the mayoral race fell short of the 1823 gubernatorial race by 881, this was to Quincy's advantage.

According to Joseph Buckingham, the nonactive voters disproportionately represented "the *particular* friends of Mr. Otis [who] absented themselves from the polls" rather than cast their votes for the apostate Quincy or the "Jacobin," George Blake. Although Quincy easily won the traditionally Federalist eighth and ninth wards (gaining 63 percent of the vote in the eighth and 65 percent in the ninth), he had not carried them by the same margins Otis had earned just weeks before in the gubernatorial race (Otis carried the eighth with 65 percent of the vote, and the ninth by 72 percent). In those wards combined, Quincy lost nine percentage points, which presumably represented disgruntled Otis partisans who stayed away from the polls. But what Quincy had lost in the eighth and ninth, he gained by carrying one of Boston's poorest wards, the twelfth—a ward Otis had lost. Whereas Otis held six of Boston's twelve wards, three of which he had retained by very slim margins (Ward 10 by 48 votes; Ward 11 by 38 votes; and Ward 4 by only 15 votes), Quincy had won seven, and with significantly higher numbers (Ward 10 by 84 votes; Ward 11 by 98 votes; Ward 4 by 45 votes; and Ward 12 by 72 solid votes). On the whole, in the Republican-leaning wards that both Quincy and Otis lost, Quincy lost by less; and in wards both had won, Quincy had won by more. Throughout the city, Quincy captured 23 percentage points more than Otis.[35]

Although Quincy lost three of Boston's four poorest wards (1, 2, 3, and 12), he did manage to sway Ward 12 and did significantly better than Otis in these areas. In the wealthy wards (4, 7, 8, 9), Quincy easily carried the majority. In terms of Boston's middling-class wards (6, 10, and 11), Quincy won two out of the three, losing Ward 6 by 44 votes, but gaining the majority in Wards 10 and 11 with 84 votes over Blake in Ward 10 and 98 in Ward 11. The fact that Quincy lost the middling Ward 6 indicates the dilemma ordinary Middling Interest voters faced once Quincy accepted the Federalist party's endorsement. Also, it demonstrates the effectiveness of Republican strategy in coopting much of the insurgency's rhetoric and further confusing ordinary middling voters. Nevertheless, out of the 1,114 voters from the middling wards, Quincy gained the majority, holding 626 loyal partisans over Blake's 488. Clearly, the majority of middling Bostonians gave their votes to Quincy.[36]

Quincy's margin of victory significantly outstripped that of Otis's yet the new mayor's success over Blake remained ambiguous and certainly did not indicate a mandate. He had lost the gamble that the Middling Interest coalition would once again unify around him despite his acceptance of the Federalist party's endorsement. In a bizarre and hurried coalition formed from past bitter enemies, distrustful Middling Interest men and vengeful Otis supporters sided with the Republicans in an unsuccessful attempt to rout Quincy. For entirely different reasons, each group, by 1823, viewed Quincy as an apostate. After he agreed to run on the Federalist ticket, a minority of rank-and-file insurgents, led by the *Bosto-*

nian and Mechanics Journal, refused to consider Quincy a Middling Interest leader as they had in 1822. Supporting Blake, this Middling Interest–Republican bloc of voters demanded that Boston's next mayor be from the middling classes. Articulating this faction's position, the *Bostonian* stated, "the Mayor of London is a brewer, and the Mayor of Philadelphia is a hatter"; why could not the next mayor of Boston be from the middling sort?[37]

Having impulsively bolted from Federalism, Otis men also turned to the Republican party solely to deny Quincy political ascendancy. As Buckingham reported in the *Galaxy,* "Mr. Quincy was selected at the federal[ist] caucus, as the candidate for mayor; but instead of receiving the unanimous support [from] the federal[ist] part[y], the *particular* friends of Mr. Otis . . . gave their votes for the democratic [Republican] candidate!" Severely criticizing Otis's followers, Buckingham charged them with "imprudent stubbornness," having "sacrifice[d]" "patriotism" for "*private and personal views.*"[38]

Although the Quincy opposition was strong, his forces persevered with a coalition similar to the one he and Phillips forged in 1822. The Phillips administration's policies had alienated some Middling Interest men to such an extent that they refused to follow the nominee of their leadership, thereby forcing them into a Republican party that greeted them with open arms; nonetheless, the majority followed Quincy as they had done the year before. Due to his past battles with the Central Committee, Quincy's recent affiliation with the Federalist party in 1823 could hardly be taken too seriously by knowledgeable Bostonians.

Stressing this point, the Middling Interest's most prominent leaders continued to work vigorously for him. Although Buckingham, Wayland, and Lincoln could no longer deliver Quincy a unified insurgent bloc as they had in 1822, they did hold the majority. Their candidate's unrestrained and independent positions on various municipal policies provided them with weighty material to work with. Quincy had forged his own sovereign course that withstood the electorate's cynicism and disorientation toward Boston's chaotic political environment. He wisely had not precisely categorized himself as a "Federalist" or a "Republican" or even as a "Middling Interest man." Instead, he ran as an incorruptible outsider—an individual who had taken the nonpartisan ideology first expressed by the Middling Interest and lived up to it. When certain cells within the insurgency allowed themselves to be coopted by the Republican party, they betrayed the Middling Interest's founding principle of antipartyism—to be beyond the pettiness of party interests. Quincy's actions, it seemed to many Bostonians, were unsullied by the local partisan warfare that had destroyed or seriously damaged all three parties in Boston.

Indeed, after the election, Francis Wayland came to Quincy to congratulate him on his victory and offer some advice to the mayor-elect. According to Eliza Quincy, Wayland advised Quincy "not to lose his popularity, which gave him such . . . power to be useful.—But Mr. Quincy only laughed," Eliza recalled, "and told him popularity was the last thing he should think of, he should do whatever he considered his duty, & the people might turn him out as soon as they pleased."[39] After the baffling and often vengeful provincial politics that had dominated Boston for the past five years, these sentiments were exactly what many jaded Bostonians longed for in a leader.

IX • BOSTON'S CAESAR AND THE FORMATION OF THE MODERN MUNICIPAL STATE

Reform, Renewal, and Order.

[T]he Mayor . . . swept the rioters from the street by mere force of muscle.
—Edmund Quincy, 1869

On May 1, 1823, citizens of Boston gathered in Faneuil Hall to observe their city's second mayoral inaugural ceremony. After John Phillips administered the oath of office to Josiah Quincy, Boston's second mayor rose to address the crowd. Although this speech would be the shortest and most guarded of all his inaugural addresses, it would prove to be his most important. The new mayor's oration foretold the ambitious and autocratic approach that would soon become his signature. Quincy's speech also reflected the gratitude he felt toward those Middling Interest men who had supported him as well as the antiparty principles that the insurgency had fostered in him. On this, the city's new mayor was determined. "Of local, sectional, party, or personal divisions," Quincy exclaimed, I will "know nothing, except for . . . healing the wounds they inflict." He promised to run the city with a self-confident and independent "zeal"—a zeal predicated upon his own conception of what was good for the city and its people. Because Boston's insurgents had forged a new, more advanced democracy—one devoid of past deferential patterns—Quincy believed he had been given a free hand to run the city; if Bostonians ever disapproved of his activism, they could always vote him out of office. This guaranteed, Quincy asserted, that final authority and responsibility in Boston ultimately rested with its people. They alone would judge his actions and not an exclusive caucus controlled by the old Federalist political establishment.[1] Placing full responsibility for his election on the now free and independent electorate, the new mayor then revealed his future plans. For even his supporters in the crowd, the degree of activism promised must have been a shock.

Quincy explained that because the city charter had passed with "considerable opposition," causing "many jealousies, hard to overcome," the Phillips administration had been "wise to shape the course of the first administration . . . by the spirit of the long-experienced constitution of the town, [rather] than by that of the . . . charter of the city." But now, with the city system firmly in place and he in office, all would change. In a veiled threat to the same independent municipal boards that successfully undermined the Phillips administration, Quincy announced: "In every exigency it will be my endeavor to imbibe . . . , in purpose and in act, the spirit of the city charter." The "spirit of the charter," as Quincy saw it, gave the mayor exclusive power to execute city law, "improve the city finances, police, health, security, cleanliness, comfort and ornament," control all municipal subordinate officers, and ensure that "all negligence, carelessness, and positive violations of duty [be] prosecuted and punished." As Quincy envisioned it, the "spirit of the charter" endowed the mayor with a staggering degree of executive power, not the least of which could be used to wrest authority from Boston's five independent municipal boards.[2]

If there was any doubt about the future of the municipal board system, Quincy quickly extinguished it when he vowed to consolidate all municipal powers within his office. "One great defect," he argued, that prevailed in Boston's municipal government "was the division of the executive power among many." He accused all five boards (the Board of Health, the Board of Firewards, the Overseers of the Poor, the Surveyors of the Highways, and the School Committee) of self-indulgence and incompetence. The weblike structure of the independent municipal board system allowed them to shield one another from any accountability. The specific responsibilities of each, according to Quincy, were so vague that, when a municipal problem arose and nothing was done, each would blame another board or the mayor for neglect, avoiding any individual responsibility while acquitting the whole system. The result, Quincy argued, was that the people were "at a loss whom to blame for the deficiency in the nature or execution of the provisions for their safety." Thus, "public service, was either . . . neglected, or, if performed at all, could only be executed occasionally, and in a very general manner."[3]

The system was intolerable because it had proven so inadequate to the public service needs of the growing metropolis. In addition, since no one person or board was held accountable for the system's consistent failures, it was contrary to the hard-won democratic principles of Boston's new political culture. With no accountability for the rampant delinquency in basic public services, how could the electorate correct a dangerously flawed municipal services system? How could the people control the most basic public necessities in their city? These were not peripheral questions, Quincy explained, for they amounted to a serious public concern to the vast majority. In an ever-expanding city—one geographically limited by the claustrophobic configuration of the Shawmut peninsula—which, by 1823, held upward of 50,000 people, municipal public services were vital to future health and prosperity.

Quincy believed that Boston would be better served if the boards were done away with and their responsibilities shifted to the mayor's office. With the summer just a month away, the mayor offered a particularly timely example that was symptomatic of the endemic problems he saw. Directly attacking the Board of Health and relying on the class-based rhetoric of the Middling Interest, Quincy squarely linked his ambition to consolidate municipal power with the most basic needs of the city's poor-to-middling population. "To those whose fortunes are restricted, these powers [which are to be taken by me], . . . ought to be peculiarly precious. The rich can fly from the generated pestilence [allowed to accumulate and ripen in the hot summer months due to the inept Board of Health]. In the season of danger, the sons of fortune can seek refuge in purer atmospheres. But necessity," Quincy concluded, "condemns the poor to remain and inhale the noxious effluvia." Without immediate change in municipal authority, the mayor predicted that Boston's less fortunate would grow ill or die from substandard municipal public services. Although Boston had been spared a major epidemic since 1792 and maintained a remarkably low death rate relative to other urban centers of its size, by the early nineteenth century the city began to swell with people. According to historian Oscar Handlin, the average number of Bostonians living under one roof by 1820 had crested to nine. With the city's bulging population and its horribly inadequate municipal services, Quincy's solution for Boston's public health problems was logical. With "noxious affluvia" hovering over the city, the spread of disease and eventual epidemic among the city's poor did not seem to be an unreasonable forecast.[4]

Quincy also understood the dubious legacy left by the Phillips administration. Phillips had been hobbled by Boston's semiautonomous municipal boards, shamed by his aldermen's and councilmen's complicity in the ward-voting affair, and spurned by the people for his failure to act. The city's first mayoral administration had been an utter failure. Quincy was not going to allow this to happen to his. Unlike Phillips, he refused to operate by the "letter" of the charter but instead would perform according to its "spirit." With his detailed denunciation of the Board of Health and his broader condemnation of the board system in general, the new mayor brashly declared open warfare on one of Boston's most powerful bureaucracies. He also had guaranteed Bostonians an activist administration that would make dramatic changes. Finally, Quincy instilled in the electorate a deep sense of political responsibility. From his perspective, the electorate wanted him to be an independent and highly aggressive leader. They had handed him the reins to guide the transformation of Boston into a safe, efficient, productive, and ordered community. As the mayor's son explained, by making Quincy mayor they had provided him with the authority to "claim the privilege of doing the . . . work [of the city] himself." If Bostonians eventually decided to revoke such "privilege," then it was their responsibility and theirs alone.[5] For those who studied the mayor's 1823 speech, two dominant themes stood out: first, there could be no doubt in anyone's mind who intended to be in control of Boston; and second, the new mayor did not plan to leave office any time soon.

Despite Quincy's spin on his slim majority of 325 in the election, it was no mandate. Yet, after he was seated in the mayor's office, he would run five more consecutive times, and as his first four elections show, his appeal among the electorate expanded into the unequivocal mandate he so wanted. For four years he dominated Boston politics. In 1824 and 1825 (a year in which two mayoral elections were held due to a charter change), Quincy's popularity proved so overwhelming that he ran uncontested three times. In 1826 and 1827, the Republicans mounted two separate candidates, but the mayor handily routed both. He consistently and successfully presented himself as a thoroughly independent municipal leader whose main objective was neither personal nor political ambition but the material progress and safety of Boston and its citizens. Indeed, it was the public service institutions established by Mayor Quincy that had persuaded Alexis de Tocqueville's traveling companion, Gustave de Beaumont, in 1831 to give Quincy's city a glowing review, claiming it to be "the head" of all the eastern cities.[6]

Quincy's political success can also be attributed to his highly effective and systematic skirmishes with Boston's independent municipal boards. Carrying out the promises made in his 1823 inaugural address, Quincy seized their municipal functions and eventually placed their authority and responsibilities within the mayor's office. Thus, while Quincy incrementally consolidated power, he also incrementally accepted virtually all municipal responsibilities. Contesting such power was a bold move, yet the mayor's various coups d'etat should not have surprised anyone. In large measure, insurgents who supported Quincy's election in 1823 had voiced their disillusionment with the Phillips administration's timid acquiescence to the boards by voting for the outspoken judge. When Quincy first declared war on them in 1823, he set into motion a plan that would establish him as Boston's most powerful mayor of the nineteenth century; he also had made himself its most accountable.

The first of the municipal boards to be purged was the relatively powerless Surveyors of the Highways. One of Quincy's initial actions as mayor was to appoint a Superintendent of the Streets whose authority superseded that of the Surveyors. The superintendent marshaled gangs of laborers who set to work nightly to clean and repair the streets. Though this directly infringed on the Surveyors' jurisdiction (and to a lesser extent, the Board of Health's), the superintendent and his crews did the job much more effectively than the Surveyors. Having proven the efficiency and superiority of this new system, just two weeks after his 1823 inaugural address Quincy called a general meeting of the people to vote on a referendum to abolish the board and place responsibility for the maintenance of the streets under the authority of the mayor and city aldermen. As Quincy later explained, "[i]t was thought important that the city should undertake the operation necessary to cleaning the streets itself, not because this mode was certainly the most economical, but because it would be certainly the most effectual." Quincy's referendum passed, and on June 11, 1823, the legislature approved the measure. On May 1, 1824, the mayor could report that by selling the "seven thousand tons . . . of filth" collected from Boston's streets as fertilizer, "[t]here can be no question, that . . . the city will receive the full value of the whole expense." Although Quincy said that this was a happy coincidence, he firmly reiterated that making the city money was not "the chief object of the system." The most essential goal was to keep Boston in "a general state of cleanliness satisfactory to the inhabitants." By cleaning the streets, the mayor had effectively gained control of them. Next, he moved on to the much more powerful Board of Health.[7]

As Quincy revealed in his inaugural address, with the growth and urbanization of Boston the Board of Health no longer adequately prevented disease or its spread. He thus declared it obsolete and expendable. Also, like all the municipal boards, its members were elected amateurs whom Quincy accused of using their positions to dole out patronage rather than protect public health. In Quincy's Boston such a situation was totally unacceptable. The health of the city should be managed by a trained professional, answerable to the mayor. Much as he had done to garner public support for abolishing the Surveyors of the Highways, Quincy unilaterally assumed all responsibilities for the health of the city. Under the mayor's direction, the city bought a fleet of carts and horses and hired a squad of laborers to remove any potential health hazards within the city. Justifying his actions, Quincy fell back on the "spirit of the charter" argument: "If the powers vested [in me] seem too great, let it be remembered that they are necessary to attain the great objects of the city,—health, comfort, and safety." Having successfully justified to Bostonians his cooptation of the board's responsibilities by proving the efficiency of his own system, in 1824 Quincy unceremoniously abolished the Board of Health and officially placed all its responsibilities on the shoulders of the city marshal, a mayoral appointee. Remarkably, the board went down without putting up a fight.[8]

Ever since Quincy had proposed the House of Industry to better house imprisoned debtors in South Boston, the Overseers of the Poor had challenged the idea, yet the House of Industry was not completed until 1823, so conflict was avoided during the Phillips administration. By the time of Quincy's ascension to the mayoralty, construction of the House of Industry was completed, and the new mayor demanded that the Overseers empty the Leverett Street Jail and prepare its debtor inmates for transfer to South Boston. The Overseers refused to follow Quincy's executive order on the grounds that they were popularly elected by the people and, therefore, did not have to follow the mayor's directive. This was the first serious challenge to Quincy's executive authority.[9]

When Quincy's landslide election of 1824 gave him a ringing popular mandate, he laid the groundwork for an ambitious plan to break the stalemate between the

Overseers and the mayor's office. In his second inaugural address, Quincy declared that the authority of the mayor "should enable him to apply a remedy upon the instant . . . and to effect this, . . . not by writing supplicatory letters to independent boards, but personally, by application of means in his own hands." For, "[i]f there be any advantage in the form of a city over that of a town government, it lies in one single word,—*efficiency*. . . . Now," Quincy continued, "efficiency means nothing more than *capacity to carry into effect*. Whatever . . . tends to deprive the executive of the city of the power to carry into effect the laws . . . has a direct tendency to encourage the executive in ignorance, inactivity, or imbecility." The mayor assured his audience that this would not happen to him. Suspecting the Overseers of corruption, Quincy immediately ordered an audit of the board's finances. When the Overseers refused to allow the mayor's municipal officers to examine their books, Quincy publicly cried corruption and called for a citywide referendum that proposed altering the city charter to grant the mayor unequivocal supremacy over the Overseers. When the referendum failed, Quincy took matters into his own hands, defying the Overseers by selling the Leverett Street Jail. With that, the Overseers found themselves in the awkward position of having no choice but to move inmates to South Boston's House of Industry. Although the Overseers of the Poor remained a state-sanctioned municipal board, Mayor Quincy had undercut all its authority while significantly increasing his own.[10]

By the end of 1824, Mayor Quincy had successfully abolished or dismantled three of the five municipal boards that had ensnared the Phillips administration. Next to face the onslaught was the powerful municipal board responsible for fire prevention: the Board of Firewards. Although Quincy had had misgivings about the Middling Interest's successful struggle to repeal Boston's old ten-foot fire law, he understood that any attempt to meddle with that particular hard-fought issue would alienate much of his insurgent support. Indeed, it was the reform of the ten-foot fire law that had proven one of the Middling Interest's most effective rallying points. Also, Quincy saw wooden buildings higher than ten feet as largely inconsequential to the genuine problem. This was confirmed when he, as Speaker of the House, had signed the reformers' repeal of the "ten foot" fire law back in 1821. When it came to devastating urban fires, the most significant stumbling block to a safer Boston rested with the city's antiquated fire-fighting system.

Traditionally, sixteen squadrons of highly competitive volunteer fire-fighter companies, supervised by the Firewards, contended with each other to gain the honor and "booty" of putting fires out around the city. Competition between these companies was fierce and extremely inefficient. All too often, competing companies would meet each other while rushing to a fire, only to engage in street fights over which of them was to put out the fire. Furthermore, customary etiquette dictated that the use of water hoses to fight fires was dishonorable and unmanly. Instead, bucket brigades were used because the volunteer firemen believed that the "nearer the fire the higher the honor." Naturally, under such a system, fires often spread out of control as contending firemen's fraternities waged war blocks away or when "honor" and small pails of water were no help.[11]

Quincy believed that for the safety of Boston this out-dated system required significant reform. Yet the volunteer fire companies were a popular cultural custom in Boston that had a legacy predating the Revolution. Generations upon generations of Bostonians maintained deep loyalties to these firemen's fraternities. Fraternal membership was passed down from father to son to grandson. Thus Quincy faced overwhelming opposition when he first went after the Board of Firewards by suggesting the professionalization of fire fighting. It would take a devastating urban disaster to wrest control from this powerful and popular municipal board.[12]

In 1825 an enormous fire burned out of control, spreading down State and Broad streets. The volunteers proved totally ineffective in fighting a blaze of such magnitude. When the fire finally burned itself out, fifty stores were lost and, when the smoke cleared, the city had incurred $1,000,000 in damage. Although Quincy's earlier efforts at reform had failed, after the inferno of 1825, in a hotly debated citywide referendum, his proposal for the abolishment of the Board of Firewards and the creation of a new, modernized fire department finally passed.[13]

During his third administration Quincy placed the volunteers under his authority. He appointed a chief engineer to replace the city's Firewards. Coordination of Boston's volunteer fire fighters would no longer be haphazard. Instead, the chief engineer would have direct control over both the professional and volunteer fire fighters. At first, the mayor continued to face stiff criticism for abolishing the fraternal orders of volunteer firemen, yet after the city hired some 1,200 firemen on either a part-time or full-time basis, censure of Quincy's action quieted to impotent mutterings. Also, the modernization of Boston's system of fighting fires significantly reduced the ravages of fire. With twenty engines, a professional "hook and ladder company, eight hundred buckets, seven thousand feet of hose, and twenty-five hose carriages," Boston's semiprofessional fire fighters proved much more effective in stopping outbreaks and protecting lives and property.[14]

Quincy's reform in fire prevention illustrates the fierce activism of his administrations. Not only had he frankly addressed the problem of fires within the city without imposing "oppressive" municipal building codes that threatened middling entrepreneurial interests, as had the city fathers of the past, but he had confronted the city's high unemployment rate by establishing a municipal department that offered Boston's lower sort wage-earning municipal jobs. Needless to say, dispensing municipal patronage on such a wide scale did not hurt Quincy's annual reelection bids.

With the adoption of a professionalized fire department that held both volunteers and fire-fighting specialists, Quincy further consolidated his political power through his use of municipal patronage. Unimpeded by any structured party organizations, Quincy single-handedly dictated an active urban policy between 1823 and 1828—one totally devoid of partisan concerns yet loyal, all the same, to the insurgent movement that had helped catapult him back into the public spotlight in 1822–23. Quincy's activist stand on the redevelopment of Faneuil Hall Market confirmed his fidelity to an extremely important sector of the Middling Interest and its antiaristocratic principles.

By significantly expanding Boston's central marketplace, and under heated and powerful opposition, Quincy planned to carve out a place to accommodate the city's struggling truckmen. His proposal for enlarging Faneuil Hall Market would serve their interests and also, as Quincy later explained, help "reduce the prices of provisions, for the poorer classes." This, coupled with his judicial ruling in the *Levengston* case, further indicated that Quincy understood the profound impact the city ordinance restricting truckmen had had not only on the truckmen but also on Boston's extralegal urban economy—an economy many depended on. When the truckmen ordinance was first proposed, the Middling Interest demanded that the city at least "provide [the truckmen] a suitable place . . . to stand." In 1822 the truckmen's demands were ignored; under the Quincy regime their voices would be heard.[15]

During Quincy's first months as mayor, the city quietly began acquiring private properties on the market's periphery while the mayor's office consulted with various architects. In January 1824, Quincy was ready to announce his plans. At a projected cost of over $1,000,000, the city would buy approximately 142,000 square feet of "flats, docks, and wharf-rights" between Long Wharf and the Town Dock; fill in a substantial amount of that area and cover it with one huge, three-square-acre wharf; build six new streets and expand a seventh; and finally, erect a "granite market-house, two stories high, five hundred and thirty-five feet long, fifty feet wide, covering twenty-seven thousand feet of land." Without doubt, this was the largest public works program ever imagined in Boston's history, and as such it faced ardent opposition. The Federalist-leaning *New England Palladium* immediately denounced Quincy's proposal as fiscally irresponsible, while the Republican *Boston Patriot* declared that Quincy's urban renewal plan would so inflate Boston's property values that the poor would be squeezed for low-income housing. Thus, according to the critics, the city would be thrown into massive debt from which it would take years to recover while the wealthy would prosper at the expense of the poor.[16]

Although the attacks on the city's enormous public works project came from both Republican and Federalist quarters, as early as April 1824—some three months after the mayor had publicly announced his plans—Josiah Quincy was reelected mayor in a resounding mandate. Bostonians clearly knew of the mayor's massive project months before the election; equally telling, considering Quincy's overwhelming mayoral victory, they heartily approved of it. Thus, with Quincy's reelection, his most ambitious and dynamic plan for urban progress was affirmed by the people. His unchallenged election further testifies to the vast political vacuum that remained in Boston after five years of partisan warfare. Although these years of upheaval were significant in destroying traditional partisan politics, little effectual policy had been achieved in a city reeling from the ruinous effects of economic depression. Neither former Federalists nor Republican partisans could mount even the semblance of a viable campaign against the independent and popular mayoral regime of Josiah Quincy. Although the mayor's style could be accurately categorized as boldly autocratic and paternalistic, Boston seemed on the move again with Quincy.

If the project succeeded, not only would a single politician bring hundreds of new public-sector jobs to the city, but the truckmen would be satisfied as well. These small-time peddlers and their shady economy would be given a new legitimacy and respectability—not to mention the opportunity for upward mobility. The very proposition that this much could be accomplished by a duly elected municipal government without the influence or permission of Boston's traditional Federalist elite establishment was a unique and fresh concept. If Quincy succeeded, it seemed, a nonpartisan government bureaucracy sanctioned by ordinary voters would surpass in power those who had dictated public policy for years. Because of the sheer size and scope of Quincy's public works project, its fruition would signify the ascendancy of public municipal government over private interests. Although the private sector would surely benefit from the project, the profits reaped from the new market would go not to the rich but to petty merchants, truckmen, and the municipal government itself. In other words, unlike the past, the lower-to-middling classes would receive aid not from the benevolence of a paternalistic economic elite but from a new democratically determined city government that ordinary Bostonians themselves had created. In the city's proposed new Faneuil Hall public marketplace, private development would give way to public, municipal investment on a scale that had never before been imagined, let alone achieved. Boston would experience the benefits of the modern municipal state.[17]

After his landslide in 1824, Quincy responded to his critics with predictable arrogance and flair. Answering the most substantive attacks on the question of debt, Quincy rejoined that an effective mayor must pursue "the spirit of the charter" and not its "letter." Although the charter said nothing on the subject of debt, the mayor claimed that "[t]he right to create a debt, is a power vested by our charter." Municipal debt, in and of itself, Quincy argued, was not inherently evil or irresponsible but should be judged "according to the objects to which it is applied." Shrugging off his critics as unenlightened and antiprogressive, he lectured that "a debt is no more an object of terror than a sword. Both are very dangerous in the hands of fools or madmen. [But] both are very safe, innocent, and useful in the hands of the wise and prudent. . . . So in the case of Faneuil Hall Market; what possible object of rational apprehension can there be in a debt created for the purpose of purchasing a tract of territory" that, once developed, would generate rental "incomes . . . wholly within the control of the city authorities?" According to Quincy, only a fool would try to stop his project. The issue was moot anyway, the mayor informed his audience. The city's building committee, which he chaired, had already approved the project and secured the needed loans to begin work. Again lecturing his critics, Quincy defined his role as chief executive of all the city's public works projects: "Once decided, in execution he [the mayor] should be as firm and rapid as in council he has been slow and deliberate."[18] True to his word, Mayor Quincy doggedly supervised every aspect of the project until Boston finally had a well-designed and structurally sound new public market. As we shall see, without Quincy's leadership the project would never have gotten farther than the planning stages.

Problems immediately arose after the blueprint for the new market was made public in the winter of 1823. The most significant impediment came from the twenty-four owners of the land and water rights slated to be bought by the city. Some refused to sell their land to the city at any cost. Quincy wanted to employ the power of eminent domain to force the issue, yet the city charter did not expressly confer this power to the municipal government. Although Quincy had effectively employed his view of "the spirit of the charter" in his various battles with the city's municipal boards, he recoiled from using this line of attack specifically against these private property holders. To take over the authority of an incompetent municipal board with this defense was one thing; to use it to force landowners off their property was quite another. The mayor needed more ammunition.[19]

In mid-January 1824, Quincy successfully appealed to the state legislature to grant the city the power of eminent domain. Using his skills as a lawyer, Quincy made a highly convincing argument. If "property is the creature of the social state," the mayor argued, then "[w]here there is no society, there is no property. . . . It follows [then] that property is in relation to society, a dependent interest. It follows also, that the exigencies or necessities of society are paramount to the rights of property." In an ironic twist that did not go unnoticed by those in the legislature, the mayor cited earlier requests for eminent domain made by some of his project's most vocal opponents. Assisting the legislature's memory, Quincy recounted that some of the market's critics had petitioned the General Court for eminent domain leverage over property owners in an attempt to develop water power sites. The mayor reminded the legislature that the memorial had been granted, resulting in the venture's eventual success. Why should the private sector, Quincy asked, be granted eminent domain powers by the legislature and not the democratically elected municipal government of Boston? Such logic proved hard to counter in the highly politically sensitive General Court. It should also be noted that by 1824 the Republicans had made significant headway in the General Court, and Quincy's past nonpartisan approach as Speaker of the House certainly must have helped predispose some legislators to his position. Both these factors contributed to the city easily winning the right to force the sale of the needed property.[20]

Yet the mayor's victory in the General Court did not end the controversy. The city had gained the authority to apply the power of eminent domain, but it still had to haggle with the owners over a "fair price" for their property. The "demagogues," as Edmund Quincy characterized the owners, took advantage of the public works project by dramatically inflating the prices of their properties. Property owners believed that the mayor would pay whatever they asked, rather than have his pet project stalled due to potential legal battles between the city and the owners over the definition of "fair price." As one of the stubborn property owners, John Codman, wrote to Daniel Webster in an appeal to retain Webster's legal services, "[i]t is the object of the Mayor &c to obtain these Estates by an appraisement, predicated on their present income—. . . in my opinion, nothing can be more unjust. My estate, in particular, has great *capability* of improvement, & is rising & must rise every day in value. I am unwilling to sell it unless I can obtain a price, predicated on its *capability* of improvement rather than its present income." Codman's estimation to Webster that his estate, "in particular," would substantially increase in value was not without foundation. He understood that the success or failure of Quincy's market hinged on the city wresting his property from him. He owned the largest parcel on the city's proposed market site. Indeed, the 535-foot-long, granite-built market edifice—the jewel of Quincy's project—was to rest on "Codman's Wharf." As the spokesman for the "demagogues," Codman believed the property owners (and especially he) had the city between a rock and a hard place. He counseled his group to hold out to the highest bidder.[21]

Unfortunately for the Codman group, it seriously underestimated the tenacity of the mayor. Quincy flatly refused to negotiate. Instead, he returned to the legislature for help. Having to pay the owners an estimated postdevelopment price for their property, the mayor argued, would totally undermine the purpose and intent of the power of eminent domain. If postdevelopment price determined "fair value," eminent domain would be rendered virtually useless. According to Quincy, every time the right of eminent domain was employed, property owners would threaten court action to ratchet up prices. In the end, Quincy reasoned, the courts and not professional real estate appraisers would become the arbitrators of property values. This, the ex-judge and mayor argued, was not the desired role of the courts. Once again, Quincy's logic convinced the General Court, and it passed a statute in February 1824 decreeing that a fair price for property in eminent domain cases would be determined by existing estimated valuation. Quincy had not only saved his project but established the legislative view of eminent domain throughout the Commonwealth.[22] Most importantly for the future of Boston, Quincy had significantly strengthened the institutional and jurisdictional powers of municipal government. Under the Quincy regime, Boston's organizations and institutions of city management were modernized at the same frenetic pace as the city's physical transformation.

With the legislature's latest decree on eminent domain, the city began negotiations with the Codman group over fair price as defined by the statute. In June, Codman and one other proprietor agreed to sell their combined properties to the city for $286,000, though three others in the group held out for more. After two years of unproductive dickering with the city, all three were thrown off their land by a thoroughly fed-up Quincy administration and compensated for their property at a price determined by the city. Later that year, in 1826, the new Faneuil Hall Market opened to the public. Finally, the truckmen were given a central location in which to sell their wares. What came to be appropriately known as Quincy Market proved such a success that by 1829 Quincy reported that it generated an annual income of $26,000 for the city. Also, with the new market's erection, the mayor sold the properties the city had acquired back in 1823 on the periphery of the old market at staggering profits. The city, Quincy announced, had applied these profits to help pay the debt incurred in building the project. Thus, in 1828, the mayor could report that Boston not only had successfully completed its largest public works project to date but had also paid for it.[23]

Considering Boston's fractured and ineffectual governance of the past, Mayor Quincy's achievements in defining the new role of urban municipal government were quite remarkable. During his regime, he did more than usher in an expanded standard of responsibility and activism for city government; he had pushed and shoved it to the fore with an arrogant, almost obsessive aggressiveness. This could be no better seen than in the mayor's belligerent approach to vice and crime. Bostonians became used to seeing their mayor charging around on his horse in the wee hours of the morning in his daily inspection of the city. It became commonplace to observe the mayor apprehending, arresting, and delivering criminals to the city jail. He would personally issue summonses to merchants who violated city ordinances. And, in his boldest move, Quincy formed an ad hoc security force made up of Boston's truckmen to police neighborhoods too dangerous even for Boston's official constabulary. Although the new Faneuil Hall Market—the municipal project that promised to advance the truckmen more than any other occupational group—had not yet opened when Quincy first organized his force, these "very substantial and respectable, as well as burly and resolute set of men," as Edmund Quincy described them, sincerely appreciated and respected his activism. When the mayor went "casting about for a proper [security] force," the truckmen enthusiastically volunteered by the dozens.[24]

In the summer of 1825, a series of riots broke out in the notorious West End. The city's marginal official police force proved totally ineffective in quelling the mob. According to one observer, 200 "comical-looking fellows . . . dressed in all kinds of costume, their faces [painted] blacker than the bottom of a tar kettle" and armed with pitchforks, poles, and axes rushed down Hanover Street to besiege Boston's most infamous whorehouse, the "Beehive." The whorehouse was ransacked by the mob. According to the *Commercial Gazette,* "What became of the wretched females who inhabited the [Beehive], we have not heard, nor do we wish to hear." What provoked the riot and what actually occurred within the pillaged Beehive were not reported by Boston's press. Yet, recalling the event, one participant reportedly claimed that "in less than ten minutes there was not a piece of door or window or furniture left of the beehive. I tell you . . . it was a scene for a life time." The next night, the rioting picked up where it had left off. Having been given fair warning that the rioting would continue, Quincy rallied the truckmen. As Boston's *Masonic Mirror* reported, "the Mayor having been timely advised to suppress [the riot,] with his usual alacrity . . . was on the spot at an early hour . . . and with the assistance of the *truck men,* whom he had, we understand previously requested to attend him, succeeded in dispersing the rioters." As Edmund Quincy recalled, "[a] word to one or two of the leaders among [the truckmen] brought the brotherhood to the aid of the Mayor, who, placing himself at their head, . . . swept the rioters out of the street by mere force of muscle." Quincy would call on the security force of truckmen he marshaled to suppress rioting in the city on at least two more occasions during his mayoralty.[25] The spectacle of the mayor policing the city both individually and with his personal security force backing him up symbolized, perhaps more than any other actions taken by the mayor, the extent of his municipal activism. Although the city would not have a professional police force until 1837, the mayor and his truckmen successfully imposed order on Boston's streets.

As mayor, Quincy established himself as a leader who transcended trivial partyism and partisanship and led his constituents on an independent course of his own design. If his annual reelections—elections Quincy consistently won with remarkably high margins—are any indication, the vast majority in Boston endorsed the new direction. Also, the mayor carefully avoided contradicting any of the founding principles of the old Middling Interest insurgency that propelled him to such heights. During his five-year reign as chief executive of the city, he refused to touch the ward-voting provision that the Middling Interest had fought so hard for. Nor did he try to revoke the repeal of the ten-foot fire law, and he remained an outspoken critic of section 30.

Clearly, the "Great Mayor," as Quincy would later be called, dictated municipal policy based upon his own assumptions and prejudices. At least one student of the Quincy mayoralty has described it as a "dictatorship," and in many ways it was.[26] Yet Bostonians armed with ward voting and an empowered political consciousness, one forged from the arduous insurgent struggle of the not-too-distant past, could always overthrow their despot in annual elections. Quincy may have run the city like a dictator, but the democratization of Boston, a process that he had helped instigate, guaranteed that Boston would never become a dictatorship. By 1823 and partially due to his past political activism in the Middling Interest,

Boston's voters had matured into an independent and self-confident electorate that shed its past deferential behavior. Because Boston's traditional party organizations lay in chaos, each year Bostonians evaluated their mayor from an independent viewpoint, judging his worthiness by his actions—not his class, pedigree, or party. For year after year, Quincy successfully withstood the test. Despite his aristocratic roots, in the eyes of Bostonians Quincy had become a populist.

Reflecting back on Boston's complex political culture when the Federalist elite's hegemony in the state was firmly in control, Josiah Quincy Jr., the mayor's second son, wrote in 1888 that "men of the stamp of Sullivan and his friend Otis were more conspicuous for what they *were* than for what they *did.* They were predominant men, and gave the community its quality, shaping, as if by divine right, its social and political issues. . . . [W]e have lost that lay priesthood who were once the accepted models of high living, and whose qualifications to direct the State were eminent and undisputed."[27] Although the younger Quincy does not offer an opinion as to when such "divine" authority came under dispute, by 1823 Boston's "lay priesthood" found its authority politically vanquished and culturally overwhelmed by the political will of an unruly congregation which liked neither its imposing political style nor its elitist culture. To sustain itself, the Federalist elite establishment would have to do something that it could not—change with the democratic current and engage the dominant populist forces which proved the harbingers of Jacksonian political culture. No longer would authority simply be bestowed on leaders because of who "they *were.*" Indeed, it was who Harrison Gray Otis *was* that had largely destroyed both his 1822 mayoral run and his gubernatorial campaign of 1823, taking with him the Federalist party of Massachusetts. Tipping Boston's past political culture on its head, the electorate mandated that leadership and authority be granted to individuals based upon "what they *did*" as opposed to who "they *were.*"

Josiah Quincy believed that he was born to lead, and, in this sense, he should not be seen as exempt from elitist pretensions. But, as Bostonians of the early nineteenth century understood, Quincy's political pretension was different from most other local elites. Unlike the Federalist elites who had spawned him, Quincy did not fear the people. Indeed, his very self-confidence as a leader was predicated on the people's approval of him. He not only was unafraid of democratization but embraced it because it was this unencumbered democracy and not party loyalty and partisanship that reinforced and justified his right to lead.

During the course of his career as a Federalist operative, the party leadership came to be disappointed with Quincy's service and then wholly dismissive of it. Eventually, the party of Otis, Perkins, and Sullivan barred him altogether, purging Quincy even from their lesser ranks. Or, as Quincy himself described his banishment: "He was snug in his birth when these gentlemen . . . tumbled him overboard . . . making shark's meat of [him]."[28] Deeply resentful, yet thoroughly convinced of his righteousness, Quincy turned to ordinary Bostonians to reaffirm what his own party and class would not. These peculiar events paved an equally peculiar path for the middle-aged patrician politician to follow. Quincy was an unlikely candidate to provoke a political insurgency, yet this is exactly what he had done.

What would soon be identified by contemporaries as Jacksonian values of ascendancy, hard work, independence, productivity, and accomplishment displaced inherited wealth, leisure, and pedigree in setting the criteria for community authority and leadership. This is not to say that many future elites would not be elected to high positions of authority in Boston and the state. Indeed, the patrician Quincy himself is proof enough of this. But in the future, these leaders would earn power because they were viewed as proficient—they understood that their authority depended on a discriminating electorate more than willing to snatch that authority away if policy did not match popular needs. After the upheavals of 1819–23, these emergent Jacksonian values would give the community its "quality," not the "divine right" of a self-ordained "lay priesthood." In this sense, the political rebellion ignited by the Middling Interest and led by Josiah Quincy was a token of the politics to come. The popular democratic political culture inspired by the populist insurgency in Boston proved a forerunner of Jacksonian political principles that soon dominated the country.

Harrison Gray Otis and other aristocratic Federalists remained blind to Boston's early displays of the tenor democracy would take throughout the country. Their ignorance and tenacious dependency on the cultural politics of the past, more than any other factor, marked not only the death of Boston Federalism but the end of an era. At the very least, during the Jacksonian period, politicians emerging from the economic elite would be forced to apply Jacksonian rhetoric of equality to appeal to Boston's voters. At their best, such men would have to pay attention to the collective voice of a new generation of voters that held values very different from its fathers.

According to Buckingham, the principal responsibility for Federalism's demise in the Bay State rested in the hands of the "great body of intelligent young men in Massachusetts . . . who are now coming forward in life, [and] do not feel all the excitements, that govern the conduct of their fathers." Because "the course of the federal[ist leadership] . . . [was] not calculated to perpetuate its existence, by extending the hand of patronage and friendship [to this powerful new electorate] without distinction of *person* and *family* . . . ; and so long as [Federalism is] reserved only for the rich, or the sons of the rich, as a sort of [archaic] hereditary possession," Buckingham explained, "it is not very strange that the power of a party, guilty of such impolitic conduct should be on the *wane.*"[29] As the market-driven economy of the Jacksonian period emerged, spawning innovative popular principles of individualism and material ascendancy, old Federalist assumptions about an America that no longer existed, faded into obscurity.

Ever since Josiah Quincy had become involved in local politics, he had proved sensitive to these sprouting middling-class sensibilities. As an ambitious local politician rising to a position of great power within the chaotic and highly cynical urban political culture of Boston in the 1820s, Quincy realized his past loyalty to the old Federalist party had to be abandoned. For many years before 1823, he had set an independent course for himself, offering the Federalist party a new direction. His independence and his advice were disparaged and rejected. With nowhere to go, Quincy, perhaps inadvertently, had helped inspire a democratic force among a growing urban population that felt neglected and ostracized from the corridors of power. In his restless pursuit of position, Quincy had embraced these concerns, exploited them to his advantage, and effectively answered them. His appeals to Boston's lower-to-middling electorate were driven by a combination of his unremitting self-confidence in his ability to lead, his ambition, and his pragmatism. Also, Quincy identified personally with an electorate thoroughly fed up with the pretensions of Federalist leaders. His anger toward such leaders was matched only by the people's. The personal vendetta between the Massachusetts Federalist Central Committee and Quincy that began over Maine statehood and escalated during the populist political warfare of the late 1810s and early 1820s excited the political sensibilities of many ordinary Bostonians. Quincy embodied their resentment toward the "cabal" that had ruled them. And, much like Quincy, they rejected the psychology of political deference that the cabal championed.

The story of the unlikely alliance between the Middling Interest insurgency and Josiah Quincy is significant because together they transformed the political culture of Boston. If viewed in contrast with other dramatic outbreaks of Jacksonian Democracy, on face value this political alteration may seem trivial by comparison, but Boston maintained a uniquely conservative political tradition. Indeed, Andrew Jackson would never carry the state, let alone Boston.[30] But this does not mean that Jacksonian democracy did not influence the city of Boston; it did, but in much less overt and obvious ways than in other American regions. The city went from being ruled by a self-ordained oligarchy of elites who fiercely engaged in partisanship to sustain power to being led by a democratically appointed autocrat—a populist Caesarist. Following a pattern soon to be set on the national level by Andrew Jackson, Quincy achieved power by successfully embracing populism and then exploiting his popularity to unilaterally dictate policy. Armed with an overwhelming popular mandate, he ruled over Boston with unprecedented executive authority. His political authoritarianism brought staggering municipal reforms, renewal, and order to Boston. Despite sporadic charges against the mayor's authoritarian activism, for the most part Boston approved of its Caesar.

Although city politics for years to come would remain dominated by Brahmin elites, these leaders could no longer assume or expect the blanket political authority once bestowed upon their Federalist forebears. Stewardship was no longer automatically conferred on an economic and cultural elite. In Boston, this dramatically altered party structures and strategy. Indeed, for a time in the 1820s it destroyed them.

As Joseph T. Buckingham illustrates, "Our commonwealth and city politics are in a state of . . . confusion. Every tenth man are the leaders of a party;—the blind leading the blind. Republicans and Federalists, Jacksonmen, Adamsmen, Lincolnmen, adminstrationmen, . . . are all are thrown together into the political pot. The fire burns and the caldron bubbles; and many are the weird sisters that are practicing their incantations over the ingredients. Whether any thing will rise from this solemn sorcery, except *scum,* we profess not to foresee." If Buckingham's opinion is in any way reflective of the electorate, Josiah Quincy's authoritarianism was viewed as necessary because it transcended the political "state of . . . confusion" while moving the city forward. Tempering his authoritarianism with a hearty dose of populism, the Quincy regime struck upon a popular political approach to forge a remarkably powerful municipal state—one sanctioned by the people. His activist public policy inspired ordinary Bostonians to re-anoint Quincy annually as their populist leader. He had crushed the aristocratic "cabal" and, as the architect of the modern municipal state, remained the people's protector. He had wrested power from the establishment and placed it in the hands of the electorate. The electorate reciprocated by rewarding him with unprecedented power in its name.[31]

Quincy's unique blend of authoritarianism, populism, and state activism was overwhelmingly reaffirmed between 1823 and 1827. Yet by 1828, when the ingredients of the mix became skewed, even one of his most loyal followers, Joseph Buckingham, lost confidence and ultimately betrayed Boston's Caesar.

X • CONCLUSION

He thinks himself supreme!
—Anti-Quincy Broadside, 1828

Inevitably, the mayor's dictatorial style and autocratic use of executive power would get him into trouble. Utilizing a loose interpretation of the city charter, Mayor Quincy had overwhelmed the municipal boards and seized their powers; he persuaded the state legislature to grant him the power of eminent domain, thus bestowing on his office license to force citizens from their property; and with his own security force he policed the streets, maintaining strict order in Boston. As a result, while the city was pushed into a period of dynamic change, the Quincy administration incrementally acquired new enemies with every mayoral action.

The mayor mandated his own municipal policies, totally unencumbered by any organized partisan opposition. For most of his duration as the city's chief executive, this provided him with significant latitude to operate independently, unentangled by partisan interests, so that he could concentrate exclusively on the interests of the city as he saw them. With the established parties either destroyed or in utter chaos, the mayor simply stepped into the political vacuum.

Such political circumstances were not particularly unique. With only one national party in existence, communities as diverse as Cumberland County, North Carolina, Rochester, New York, and backwaters in Alabama struggled for a political voice that would articulate both traditional and new, unfamiliar community conflicts that had recently arisen due to the effects of an evolving market revolution. During this transitional period, these conflicts were difficult to express without clear party structures. On face value, the country seemed finally to have fulfilled Jefferson's famous 1801 decree that "[w]e are all Republicans, we are all Federalists," but on the state and local level conflicting interests remained a vivid reality. Yet there was no coordinating force. Although, in Massachusetts by 1827, former Federalist and moderate Republican leaders were calling for the political "amalgamation" of past partisan enemies, the newly empowered voters of Boston resisted the charge. Presumably, all might be "Republican" on national issues, but contestation on local and state affairs found the electorate fractured into myriad single-issue factions, causing much political confusion. It was one thing to "amalgamate" during the twilight of the Era of Good Feelings in presidential elections, as had happened in the 1824 campaign between the state's own John Quincy Adams and the western upstart, Andrew Jackson, but quite another when it came to local decisions.[1]

The antipartyism of the insurgency remained influential in many Boston voters' minds, widening the political void when local elections occurred and shrinking during national races. As mayor, Josiah Quincy remained loyal to insurgent nonpartisanship, practicing his fierce municipal activism. The result was that municipal governance did not get bogged down in what Buckingham described as the "solemn sorcery" of single-issue partisan politics. In the activist and focused Josiah Quincy, the electorate discovered a single man who unified the people, not a single issue that forced their division. In his role as an irreverent municipal operative who achieved tangible success, Mayor Quincy transcended the "solemn sorcery" as municipal visionary. Bostonians found this clarifying. This is not to say that the confusion of single-issue politics no longer existed. It did. But when Bostonians annually chose a mayor, they buried their single-issue causes and placed their collective trust in Quincy. This would not last forever. After the 1827 election, new forces threatened to dismantle the Quincy administration. At the close of the decade, the sorcery's venom began to weaken even the mayor.

In 1827, when Quincy successfully coopted Boston's last remaining independent municipal board, the Boston School Committee, hostile forces saw a chance to destroy "the Great Mayor." Ever since Quincy first centralized power in his office, certain sectors in Boston had grown increasingly suspicious of the new and greatly expanded role of city government. Disgruntled property owners angered by the city's use of eminent domain, vengeful ex-Firewards, fiscal conservatives worried about the city's increasing debt and high taxes, antigovernment zealots who feared the modern new face Boston was taking, those who still associated him with the abhorred Federalist Central Committee, and those who refused to forget Quincy's betrayal of that party stewed in their indignation toward the mayor. Yet, with neither a viable party system in place to mount an oppositional campaign nor a charismatic leader to rally the people against the mayor, Quincy's critics remained scattered and thus totally ineffective.[2]

All this changed when the mayor took on the public schools. The city's discontents effectively charged that the mayor's role in the controversy symbolized his wanton abuse of power. Quincy's conduct in public education, claimed his opponents, finally exposed, for all of Boston to see, what his opponents had known all along—that he was a tyrant. After six landslide elections that seemed to indicate the people's unanimous and unconditional acceptance, Quincy was totally taken by surprise when, in 1828, his administration faced a blistering attack that it could not weather. Shocked and utterly despondent, Josiah Quincy, in January 1829, found himself out of a job. Having lost enough of the people's trust, he was summarily dismissed by the electorate.

The Boston Public School Committee had a long legacy of success. Established in 1789, the committee could rightfully boast of having America's first and best public school system, one that catered to all children.[3] For the mayor unilaterally to dismantle this particular independent municipal board would be tantamount to political suicide. Yet Quincy believed that school reform was badly needed. By the 1820s, Boston's growing population had produced scores of children who were described by one Bostonian as "idlers, truants, and, such as have no viable or known employment, and who do not habitually attend any school." In Quincy's Boston this was not acceptable. As he stated in his first inaugural address, the health of Boston's public schools was essential to an ordered and free society. "Be it," Quincy declared, "the endeavor of this metropolis to educate better men, happier citizens, more enlightened statesmen; to elevate a people, thoroughly instructed in their social rights, deeply imbued with a sense of their moral duties, . . . unyielding as fate to unconstitutional impositions." Since this was not being achieved, the mayor concluded that, "[a]bove all" his other priorities, Boston's "schools . . . should engage his utmost solicitude and unremitting superintendence."[4] Taking control of Boston's public schools would be a high priority for Mayor Quincy, but he also knew it would have to be done cautiously.

To harness the municipal power of the School Committee and engage his ideas of educational reform, Quincy appointed himself committee chairman and successfully campaigned for his political allies to win seats on the committee. Slowly, the committee came to be filled with Quincy collaborators. The mayor had been impressed with the progress of an experimental public school organized and run by William B. Fowle in the city's Fort Hill neighborhood, one of Boston's poorest. Worried about the number of uneducated children who ran wild in Boston's streets, Fowle had established a school for these children by employing a new and inexpensive, yet controversial, teaching method called the monitorial system. The system had already been introduced to New York's public schools where it was hailed as a great success. For Quincy, the great advantage of the monitorial system was that it promised to educate the city's growing population of poor youth economically. A master teacher would instruct a school's upperclassmen, who would then teach (or "monitor") fellow students in the lower grades. Under such a system there would be less need for expensive teachers. Thus, with more disposable city funds, municipal resources could be allocated for building more badly needed schools. Not only would more of Boston's children be educated, but juniors and seniors would be tutored in teaching. As one master teacher and proponent of the monitorial system put it, "[g]ive me twenty-four pupils to-day, and I will give you back twenty-four teachers to-morrow."[5]

In 1828, as chairman of the School Committee, Quincy proposed gradually initiating the system in all of Boston's public schools. Politically, the mayor was under pressure to cut costs; after all, his public works programs were weighing heavily on Boston's taxpayers. In mid-December 1828, the city auditor estimated that the municipal debt rested at $1,076,100, a remarkable sum for the time. As the *Patriot* announced, Bostonians "were promised in public town meetings by his Honor the Mayor not only a reduction of taxes, but almost their entire extinction. . . . [Yet, the people] see great public works completed long since; the Streets paved, School-houses built, a new Jail and Court-house, Engine-houses without number; . . . and on the other hand, a great increase of taxable property all over the city; yet there appears no reduction in our taxes."[6] Shifting to the monitorial system would allow Quincy to slash the public school system's annual budget significantly in the name of educational reform.

In another cost-cutting measure, the mayor proposed elimination of Boston's only high school for girls. Quincy ordered a thorough evaluation of the girls' school, which had been established as an experimental program only a few years earlier. The mayor reckoned that if it could be shown to be a failure he could easily justify abolition. Every year, between 1826 through 1828, the school's headmaster, Ebenezer Bailey, had demanded from the School Committee a raise in salary and more city funds to expand the school. On each occasion, the committee rejected Bailey's requests. Bad blood developed between Bailey and the School Committee's chairman, Mayor Quincy, and on November 13, 1828, Bailey resigned his headmastership in protest. With the girls' school operating without a headmaster, the School Committee's subcommittee charged with the responsibility of evaluating the school's performance (a subcommittee also chaired by the mayor) predictably returned with a recommendation to discontinue the "experiment."[7]

Upon reading a published copy of what would become known as "the Mayor's Report" and its conclusions to abolish the girls' school and establish the monitorial system, an embittered Ebenezer Bailey published his "Review of the Mayor's Report on the Subject of Schools"—a 54-page invective that attacked the mayor, his administration, the School Committee, and Quincy's support of the monitorial system. Despite "the testimony of a majority of the teachers [who were] in favor of the High School for Girls," Bailey accused the mayor of single-handedly plotting to destroy the school. The attacks on the girls' school "have been effected by his [Quincy's] influence and authority and management,—yes," Bailey reiterated, "*management;* for he has, in *every instance* . . . either assumed the office of chairman himself, or appointed as chairman a person supposed to be hostile to the institution."[8] For those waiting for a public issue to hang Quincy on, Bailey's "Review of the Mayor's Report" was exemplary. It charged the mayor with abusing his executive power and falsifying the subcommittee's report to conclude that the "whole system of public education is radically wrong," out of date, and wasteful. The mayor, Bailey contested, conspired to fire the majority of public school teachers and, finally, exposed his vicious sexism and venomous elitism.[9]

Although Quincy did display overt sexism in his report and had manipulated it to provide justification for dismantling Boston's High School for Girls, the mayor was sincerely concerned with answering the charges that his administration borrowed and spent too freely. The real reason for the abolition of the girls' school, as Quincy later admitted, was that it had proven to be such a resounding success. "It may be truly said," Quincy revealed in 1829, "that its [the school's] impracticability was proven before it went into operation. The pressure for admission [was so overwhelming that it] satisfied every reflecting mind that, however desirable, the scheme of giving a high classical education equal . . . to a college education to all the girls of a city whose parents would wish them to be thus educated at the expense of the city was just impracticable. . . . No funds of any city could endure the expense."[10] The assault on the mayor's educational policies may provide some insight into the forces bent on ending his mayoral regime, but, considering the patriarchal world of the early nineteenth century, Quincy's abandonment of the High School for Girls does not adequately explain his critics' true motivations.

Underlying the public school dispute lurked powerful reactionary resentment toward the mayor's progressive municipal agenda and his autocratic approach to leadership. Indeed, the Republican *Patriot* proclaimed, Quincy "is the master spirit in City concerns, and according as his feeling, his propensities, his *impulses* are good or bad, so will the administration of the City concerns. . . . Upon a careful and impartial examination of Mr. Quincy's official career as Mayor, its two prominent features appear to us to be: aggression and expense. . . . By taking advantage of the public necessity for change, the Mayor was here enabled to obtain full, and, . . . permanent gratification to his appetite for a concentration of power in himself, as the mainspring of the city government machinery." The mayor's aggressive cooptation of both the Overseers of the Poor and the School Committee were just two of a great number of clear indications of how, according to the *Patriot,* "the patronage and power of the Mayor, [have] under Mr. Quincy's administration alarmingly increased. . . . TAXES TOO HIGH—Why?" The editorial answered: "The cause is our increased and increasing debt,—the city owes money, and pays more interest, than its income. . . . Every foot of real estate in Boston is mortgaged to pay these taxes." The mayor, concluded the *Patriot,* "rashly embark[ed] in projects that he has not coolly examined [with] all the rashness of children chasing after a butterfly." In another anti-Quincy editorial, "Franklin" accused the mayor of "lowering" the "standard" of city government. "[T]he best and most independent men," Franklin claimed, "have retired one after another, unable to resist and unwilling to follow the mad career of their . . . leader." Although the formerly Federalist *Columbian Centinel* supported Quincy's 1828 mayoralty over hard-line Republican hopefuls, even it could not excuse the mayor's dictatorial behavior. "[H]e is too domineering, and . . . will have things done in his own way" or no way, it concluded.[11]

Hostility toward the mayor reached an apex between mid-November and the December 8 mayoral election. Quincy supporters scrambled to confront the opposition. Led by an old Middling Interest supporter, William Sturgis, Quincy operatives had one distinct advantage over the opposition. The anti-Quincy insurgency was hopelessly disorganized and fractured. Its supporters came from all over the political spectrum, victims of Buckingham's "solemn sorcery." Even the anti-Quincy *Patriot* admitted that, although Boston was supposedly united against the mayor, "too great a diversity of views in relation to the most suitable successor" existed to form a united front. "The elements of former parties are now in a very unsettled state," the *Patriot* confessed, "yet it may be hoped some reasonable compromise will be the means of bringing forward a man who may unite some of the essential qualities for the office." Trying to take advantage of chaos, Sturgis and other Quincy operatives presented the mayor as an "amalgamation" candidate. By affiliating him with John Quincy Adams, Quincy partisans hoped to unite the wide range of single-issue groups around their candidate. This had worked in Boston just a month earlier during the presidential campaign, when former Federalists and all but a small faction of disorganized Jacksonian Republicans had united around John Quincy Adams. Indeed, though Adams had lost to Andrew Jackson nationally, the Massachusetts native son had overwhelmingly won Boston, garnering votes from every segment of the electorate.[12]

The anti-Quincy insurgents counterattacked with article after article refuting Quincy's claim to be a true "amagamationist" and announcing that the mayor's strategy was an election ploy. Boston's *Jackson Republican* flatly stated: "One of the most unfortunate mistakes which has been made in our domestic politics is the habit of connecting all our political interests with the presidential question. This connection is unnatural and absurd." Sticking to its objections of high taxes and the city debt, the *Patriot,* in an equally blunt statement, argued: "The weak attempt, that some of the partisans of Mr. Quincy are making, to identify adhesion to Mr. Quincy with adhesion to Mr. Adams, is undeserving of even the mention we have now made of it." "The question . . . presented to the voters we do not regard as a party question,—a question between Adams or Jackson,—republican or federal[ist]; but rather as a question of dollars and cents."[13] Although Quincy may have been thrown off guard by the level of hostility expressed by the insurgents, the enemy was scattered and directionless. Indeed, it could not even decide on a candidate. Also, Joseph Buckingham could be relied upon to support his reelection, or so the mayor must have thought.

Even as he had ascended in both the publishing world and in politics, Buckingham had remained supportive of Quincy. In 1824 Buckingham established the daily *Courier,* which ran in tandem with the *Galaxy* for four years. The *Courier* almost immediately became as successful as the *Galaxy,* reaching a circulation of close to a thousand by 1826. Burdened by the demands of editing and publishing two newspapers, and thinking of running for political office, in 1827 Buckingham offered coeditorship of the *Courier* to his eldest son and sold the *Galaxy;* then he decided to run for a seat on the General Court in 1828. In May 1828 he was elected to the state House of Representatives as an Adams Republican. During the Quincy years, the struggling master printer and editor had risen to middle-class respectability.[14]

Perhaps reflective of Boston's political fragmentation or a result of the schizophrenic nature of coediting the newspaper, Buckingham's *Courier* first gave a taciturn endorsement for Quincy's reelection, then seemed to revoke it, before running a celebratory posthumous review of the mayor's long reign after the mayoralty had been stripped from him. On the eve of the election, the *Courier* advised its readers how to vote. Despite its halfhearted endorsement of Quincy just a week earlier, on December 5, three days before the election, the *Courier* turned on the mayor. According to Buckingham, three major issues were at stake: debt, taxes, and the public schools. The "city is saddled with an enormous debt, and taxes are enormously high," Buckingham asserted, while "[t]he only object of this [school] committee . . . was to help their [the Quincy administration's] friends." By choosing these three particular subjects to criticize the Quincy administration, Buckingham affirmed earlier anti-Quincy insurgent rhetoric and legitimized the mayor's opposition. Indeed, on the morning of the election, insurgents flooded Boston with a broadside called "LOOK TO YOUR INTERESTS!!" that attacked the mayor on these very same issues.[15]

Thus, within a month, anti-Quincy insurgents pulled support from all sectors of Boston's fragmented political spectrum. Although Eliza Quincy intimated that "a combination of private interests & political managements" had coalesced to destroy her father's mayoralty, it was much less organized and conspiratorial than she believed. As the *Patriot* attests, the opposition before the balloting had failed to agree on a compromise candidate and remained in chaos. Yet, because of elections rules this would not matter. "If the first vote should fail to elect a Mayor," the *Patriot* advised, "the second would be likely to bring about that compromise; it is desirable then that the first vote may be very independent."[16]

On December 8, 1828, when the polls opened, there were six mayoral candidates to choose from: Quincy, who ran as the official "amalgamation"–John Quincy Adams administration man; J. C. Amory, nominated by the ex-Firewards and their allies; Andrew Dunlap, the Jacksonian (who had defended Solomon M. Levengston before Quincy's court in 1823); and three other marginal candidates, one of whom garnered only 289 votes. Ironically, this candidate was Harrison Gray Otis. Quincy captured 1,958 votes, beating his closest competitor, J. C. Amory, by 674 solid votes, yet the mayor, as in his race in 1822, did not have a majority. The splintered opposition combined received 2,028 votes to Quincy's 1,958. By a mere 70 votes, the opposition denied the incumbent the mayoralty and forced a runoff.[17]

Although old Middling Interest spokesman William Sturgis tried to rally the mayor's traditional partisan base, Francis Wayland had left the city to take over the presidency of Brown University, and Sturgis's efforts were in vain. With the loss of Buckingham's unqualified support and Wayland's departure from Boston, Quincy had lost two vital spokesmen who linked him with the old insurgency—a crucial popular base. As George Shattuck, a Quincy supporter, recognized, the people of Boston "have made the astonishing discovery that [Quincy] is not perfect [and] are determined to change, . . . as [they] never know when they are well off."[18] Yet Quincy refused to give up. With a week until the December 15 runoff election, he frantically tried to regroup his partisans, but the opposition heightened its attacks on the incumbent and his administration.

In an attempt to dampen his critics, Quincy ordered a prompt audit of the municipal books to counter charges that he had plunged the city into massive debt. Unfortunately for the mayor, the city auditor delivered his findings four days before the runoff election, and the news was damning. The city was over a million dollars in debt, which exceeded the estimations of even Quincy's most excessive critics. On December 12, three days before the second balloting, a broadside exposing the audit's findings circulated around Boston. After a thorough analysis of the audit that exposed that the city debt was accruing thirty-two cents every minute, the broadside concluded: "Mr. Quincy has excersized [*sic*] a tyranny . . . unparralled [*sic*] in the history of our country . . . Look at Mr. Quincy's *overbearing* and even *imperious* manner of doing business with every department of the City Government. He thinks himself supreme! Look at his haughty and anti-republican manners to the citizens generally. . . . HE *lacks* JUDGEMENT. . . . But he is determined to hold his office during [the tenure of his] life!"[19] On the night of December 12, Sturgis tried to organize a pro-Quincy mass rally to defend the mayor's municipal spending. By all accounts it was a lackluster event. As Charles Francis Adams reported it, the gathering was "a tame affair."[20]

The field had narrowed substantially in the December 15 runoff. Andrew Dunlap, the Jacksonian, dropped out, as had one other marginal candidate, the gubernatorial-appointed sheriff of Boston, Charles Pinckney Sumner. Amory, Charles Wells (one of the earlier marginal candidates), and Otis all remained in the race to keep Quincy from the mayor's office. In the second balloting, the anti-Quincy forces prevailed, much as they had in the first election. The mayor got 2,561 votes to Amory's 1,400, Wells's 970, and Otis's 236. Although Quincy amassed 603 more votes, it proved to be too-little-too-late. By a handful of 45 votes, the obstructionist candidates together had forced yet another runoff. The *Columbian Centinel* blamed the obstructionists' second victory on a passive electorate that expected the mayor to win and thus did not vote.[21]

Humbled by his second defeat, Quincy announced to Boston that he would not run in the third election. Claiming that "no consideration would induce me again to accept that office," he announced he would step down from his five-and-a-half-year reign as Boston's mayor. After his announcement, both Wells and Amory followed suit, indicating that both their campaigns had been launched not to gain the mayoralty but to stop the "tyrant" Quincy. As Buckingham's *Courier* concluded with great clarity, "The object of Mr. Quincy's opponents has been attained—which has been avowed by many of them to be *his defeat* rather than the success of any one of the competitors which has been brought into the field. Under these circumstances, it is hoped that the triumphant party—or, rather, parties—will set themselves soberly to work to find some candidate who is likely to be generally acceptable to the public without the imputation of being the candidate of a particular *interest,* or a particular *class.*"[22] As we shall see, Buckingham's words were not heeded. Indeed, with Quincy, Wells, and Amory out of the race, only one candidate remained, Harrison Gray Otis.

In the first two mayoral ballots, Otis had thrown in with unlikely allies to defeat Quincy but was considered by all of Boston's press a marginal candidate. He placed in the bottom tier in both elections, averaging a mere 263 votes. But now, with an open field, Otis jumped at the chance for a political rebirth. In fact, the same day the results of the second balloting were announced and Quincy abdicated, the *Columbian Centinel* ran an editorial calling for Otis's election, claiming Otis was "the only man in the city of Boston, who will at the present time, unite the suffrages of the people." The *Courier* had warned of this as far back as November. Buckingham alerted Bostonians of the danger presented by opposition candidates. Although the *Courier,* in the end, betrayed Quincy, on November 27 it had counseled caution. There were, according to Buckingham, dark figures "looking with an envious squint at the office of Mayor—from all which added to certain whisperings about the streets, is presumed that an effort is to be made to displace that active magistrate [Mayor Quincy], and give his office with all its power and prerogative, to someone who is *pining for want of place,* or to another who is good-naturedly pliant enough to be the tool of the discontented, the ambitious, and the disorganized." By 1828 Harrison Gray Otis fit both descriptions. Ever since the old Federalist Central Committee had betrayed him by supporting Quincy's mayoralty in 1823, political power had been stripped from Otis. If anyone in Boston "pin[ed] for want of place," it was Otis. He remained politically driven by old bitterness and certainly would be "good-naturedly pliant" if his political honor was restored to him.[23]

Under the direction of his son Harry and nephew William Foster Jr., the Otis mayoral campaign began in earnest. The first essential step taken by his handlers was to solicit the support of the "amalgamationists," many of whom had backed Quincy a week earlier. In a brilliant speech before the "amalgamation" caucus on December 19, William Foster acknowledged his complicity in destroying Mayor

Quincy but now called for peace and unity behind his candidate. "It is well known," Foster proclaimed, "that I have taken an active part in the opposition to Mr. Quincy's re-election; [but in] the best interests of the city, . . . I would . . . hope that all minor considerations may yield for one short year to the ardent wishes, and imperious wants of the City; and that the man pronounced most capable by all parties, of healing our wounds, and laying a solid foundation for our future prosperity, may be elected. Need I say, that man is HARRISON GRAY OTIS? My family connection with that Gentleman, I assure you," Foster pledged, "does not weigh a scruple in my decision."[24] Foster and Harry Otis also held an ace that would virtually ensure their candidate the mayoralty if they got amalgamationists support.

In 1825 the city charter went through what at the time seemed a harmless and practical revision. Mayoral elections would no longer be held in the spring but in December. It was thought that voter participation would increase because work generally slowed in the winter, and the spring and summer exodus of Bostonians to the country would no longer affect the elections. Also, it seemed practical that a mayor's term should coincide with the calendar year. Although this had meant that Mayor Quincy had had to run in two elections in 1825, he did not object to the charter change because his popularity in 1825 was at an all-time high. In 1828, after two inconclusive elections that had taken up two thirds of December, Bostonians began to fear the consequences if they could not decide on a mayor by the end of the calendar year. Buckingham as well as the editor of the *Columbian Centinel* had looked into this and discovered that if Boston did not choose a mayor by the end of the month—the time allowed by the charter—the city charter was automatically abrogated and the city would be thrown into a sort of receivership controlled by the General Court. Thus, if the city could not decide on a mayor by the last day in December, it would no longer legally exist and would be controlled by the state legislature. Certainly, this was in nobody's interest.[25] Because the two previous indecisive elections had carried Boston into the latter third of the month, speed on every level of the decision-making process was of the essence.

Fearful that the municipality would lose its autonomy and partly due to Foster's and Harry Otis's determination, the amalgamations nominated Harrison Gray Otis as their candidate. The opposition cried foul, as they had when Quincy ran on the John Quincy Adams administration–amalgamationist ticket, stating that most of Otis's "supporters are not Adams men and we know, that many of Mr. Adams' best and most sincere friends are decidedly opposed to the election of Mr. Otis." Although much of Otis's support must have come from Adams men, the opposition's charge that Otis could hardly be considered an administration man held much truth. Otis and Adams historically loathed each other. When Otis defended Federalist actions at the Hartford Convention in 1818, John Quincy Adams responded with his own interpretation of the convention, totally debunking Otis's more pacific claims. Adams attacked Otis's defense as totally disingenuous and self-serving while arguing that the events in Hartford were clearly motivated by secessionist, anti-American, regional impulses. By 1828 neither Otis nor Adams had forgotten their rhetorical warfare, and certainly neither had worked toward any sort of reconciliation. They remained personal, if not political, enemies up until Otis's death. Thus, for most Bostonians, Otis's attempt to jump on the Adams bandwagon should have seemed spurious.[26]

Although the obstructionists had been perfectly happy to have Otis running with them to crush the "Great Mayor," the thought of him actually achieving the mayoralty horrified them. When it became clear that Otis was engaged in a serious bid for the post and seemed to have wooed significant numbers of supporters from the amalgamationists, the Republican opposition scrambled to catch up. On December 22 it published a broadside that expressed its horror and utter astonishment that Boston would even consider such a candidate after the bloody partisan warfare of the recent past in which Otis represented the worst of Federalist extremism. "Arise, the Philistines be upon ye!" the opposition desperately proclaimed. It had been "[y]ears since you doomed . . . HARRISON GRAY OTIS, to the shades of retirement, for political offenses of a grander cast than even those of Josiah Quincy. . . . Will you now call him from his banishment?" the broadside asked in desperation. "Will you bend your backs for a stepping stone by which he mounts above you to command you? . . . Will you now be insulted and duped by such artifice?" And finally it pleaded: "Will you suffer the Aristocracy thus to outwit you?"[27] Frantically searching among its ranks to find a last-minute candidate, the Republicans came up with Caleb Eddy.

In the mayoral elections of 1828, the *Patriot* had stood against the amalgationists' nomination of Josiah Quincy, yet this moderate Republican organ had strongly supported the amalgamation candidate for president, John Quincy Adams, in both 1824 and 1828. It had also campaigned for the amalgamation candidate in the governor's race, moderate Republican Levi Lincoln Jr. The *Patriot,* unlike its more radical Republican competitor, the *Jackson Republican,* saw value in combining with moderate former Federalists to forge a new "union" party predicated on an economic agenda that called for both government support and control of the region's economic growth and development—growth that, unlike free-trade advocates, would be both harnessed and promoted by government regulation.[28] When the amalgamationists endorsed Harrison Gray Otis for mayor, the *Patriot* groaned in dismay. "We had hoped, after the events of last week [when the opposition had forced Quincy to submit], that such a course would have been taken as would have secured . . . the election of some unobjectionable individual. . . . We are very disappointed. Our objections to Mr. Otis are wholly political, but they are plenary and conclusive. . . . [Otis] cannot be supported for the Mayoralty by those, who a few years back decidedly resisted his election to higher office."[29]

When, the next day, Otis was elected mayor under the amalgamationist banner, culling 2,978 votes to Eddy's 1,283, the *Patriot* abandoned the amalgamation cause altogether. "[W]hen the determination is announced," the *Patriot* explained, "to select a federalist candidate, and no other federalist can be thought of but the one who has been, on every occasion, the favorite and leader of the junto . . . the candidate of the 'exclusives,' and who has never testified his readiness to be in fellowship with [his] former political opponents," then, the *Patriot* declared, "the project of 'amalgamation' . . . has been abandoned by those who concurred in the nomination and election of Mr. Otis." In a bid for the support of furious ex-amalgamationist Republicans, on the day after Otis's election an announcement ran in the city's newspapers declaring the foundation of Boston's own chapter of the Jackson Republican party.[30]

Although Eddy's operatives charged voter fraud, Harrison Gray Otis's victory can be best explained by his cooptation of the amalgamationists. This had been achieved by the very real threat that Boston's city charter would become invalidated and the General Court would take control of the city if the third ballot could not produce a victor. After discovering the charter's flaw, Buckingham counseled that "it would be well to have the charter revised." But in the meantime, the *Courier* had advised the people of Boston to avoid another election stalemate at all costs.[31] With the backing of the amalgamationists and with the threat of throwing the city into receivership, the vast majority of Bostonians had little choice but to turn to Otis. When they did so, the city system that earlier democratic insurgents had fought so hard for had been saved, but the fragile "union" party, the amalgamationists, splintered apart.

Trying to explain what had just happened, the *Jackson Republican* admitted its own bewilderment. Otis's election "will probably surprise and puzzle our readers . . . We can only say that this city has been in a state of political chaos for the past five years. . . . The confusion of parties, we have had here [has created] no sort of real, legitimate distinction. . . . We cannot trust [party] names to express our ideas, for a confusion of names first led . . . to a confusion of things. . . . [T]he political movements here . . . confound the cooled calculations of the most careful and experienced party men." The editorial concluded by calling on all "good" Republicans to flock to the Jacksonian ranks.[32]

The amalgamationists' nomination of Otis had caused them to break apart and pushed some Republicans into the Jacksonian camp; yet this would not lead to a viable Democratic party in Boston. In future national and state elections, the Boston electorate would reject the party of Jackson and follow Adams Republicans into the National Republican party and then eventually settle on the Whigs. Yet, unlike the past when Federalist hegemony ruled Boston, this path was one determined by a coalition of interests with a deep commitment to independent, anti-deferential values. Indeed, the Middling Interest's third-partyism anticipated an enduring political pattern that advocated a wide variety of reforms by forging cross-class coalitions.[33]

Despite the fear that Otis inspired in those Republicans represented by the *Jackson Republican* and the *Patriot,* Bostonians would not revisit the deferential politics of Federalism's past, as some predicted. Even Harrison Gray Otis recognized this much. As Boston's third mayor acknowledged in his inaugural address, his ascension to office was largely the result of half-hearted support he had garnered from past political enemies who remained highly skeptical of the man they had just voted into office. Realizing his tenuous position, Otis understood that his appointment from the people was highly provisional. He knew that he would be banished if he stepped out of line. As his speech indicates, this once dominant political figure, by 1828, was hobbled. As he explained, "[w]ith the friends of former days, whose constancy can never be forgotten, others have been pleased to unite (and to honour me with their suffrages,) who hold in high disapprobation the part I formerly took in political affairs. Their support of me on this occasion is no symptom of a change of their sentiment in that particular," Otis confessed, and only confirms their frustration with Quincy's dictatorial activism. "I . . . admit," concluded a humbled Otis, "that I am not indifferent to the desire of removing doubts and giving satisfaction to the minds of any who by a magnanimous pledge of kind feelings towards me, have a claim upon me for every candid explanation and assurance in my power to afford." Finally, stating that he hoped "our beloved city prove an exception" to the partisan "antipathies" and the "torch of discord [that] blazes while the fire of patriotism expires" under the suffocating weight of partisan warfare, Otis called for peace in Boston.[34]

Harkening back to the more "judicious" Phillips administration, the new mayor promised the people of Boston that his would be a passive administration, unlike his predecessor's. Otis promised "[t]o reconcile by gentle reform, not to revolt by startling innovation," as Quincy had done. Citing the city's burdensome debt, Otis declared a reversal of the past mayor's "radical reformation" of Boston and promised his overriding policy would be based on "strict economy . . . [f]or the gradual extinguishment of this debt." Reassuring his audience, Otis pledged to balance the budget and follow John Phillips's example by allowing the city to run a natural course without his interference.[35]

Although he aided the obstructionists in toppling Josiah Quincy, Joseph Buckingham was shocked by Boston's choice. In an editorial after the election of 1828, he chastised the selection of Otis as mayor. "The old federal[ist] party is declared to be defunct," Buckingham explained, "and its odor remaineth only as an offence to a few individuals, who have survived its dissolution. If it be indeed so, we derive some consolation from the hope that, phoenix-like, a new party may arise from its ashes, possessing the wisdom, the magnanimity, the prudence, the disinterestedness, the patriotism, which rendered the original an object of admiration and respect while in its vigor of manhood; *but* without any of the weakness, meanness, or infidelity to friends and benefactors, that disgraced its decline." Then, in a thinly veiled attack on Otis's reemergence in politics, Buckingham scolded Boston for resurrecting what he believed to be the worst that Federalism ever had to offer. "The dotage of the Sage and the imbecility of the Giant may excite compassion; the affected humility of an aristocrat in fetters, like the morality of a superannuated libertine, produces only disgust."[36] Certainly, Josiah Quincy would have agreed.

Boston exiled its assertive and imposing "tyrant" in favor of a passive strawman who rose on the wreckage of what the *Patriot* described as "this poor exhausted body politic."[37] The Otis mayoralty would satisfy Boston's desire for a dull government of inaction. According to Otis family legend, the old "Sage's" one achievement as mayor was to banish grazing cows from Boston Common. Other than this, the municipal bureaucracy established under the leadership of Mayor Quincy continued to sustain the needs of the city. Otis did not strengthen or weaken these city municipal mechanisms that had brought Boston kicking and screaming into the Jacksonian era. This machinery, put into place by Quincy, continued to serve the needs of Bostonians during Otis's tenure as mayor. After years of political chaos and disorientation coupled with the fierce activism of the city's second mayor, Mayor Otis served a valuable function in Boston—like the reassuring voice of a grandfather, he promised Bostonians political and civic tranquility. Exhausted from a decade of political upheaval, Boston had tired of its popular crusading Caesar and given itself to the calm promised by a humbled and submissive leader from the past.

The legacy of Josiah Quincy remains an ambivalent one. On one hand, his rise to power can be viewed as the triumph of popular democracy. Yet, on the other, his political odyssey illustrates an all too familiar irony inherent to populist politics. In the quest for inclusive democracy, Boston surrendered itself to a dominating Caesarist. Quincy not only justified but championed his political authoritarianism as the proper fruition of popular democracy. Defending his actions as the genuine affirmation of Boston's democratic uprising, Quincy unilaterally transformed a city to conform with his own urban vision of the future. Under the guise of democracy and the antiaristocratic principles of the Middling Interest, he captured control of a city and forced his will on its people. The defender of democracy had become a demagogue. In spite of this, the political conflict of the 1820s had brought a more advanced democracy to Boston, and it was this new democratic form that ensured the demagogue's decline. The same populist forces that Quincy had kindled banished him in the end, providing the ultimate testimony of democracy's ascendancy in Boston.

The Middling Interest spokesmen who cut their teeth in the stormy, depression-era politics of Boston between 1818 and 1824 provide insight into the painful political, economic, and social transformation that American society went through during the early Jacksonian period. This period marks a divide between differing conceptions of democracy. By the time Harrison Gray Otis ironically stepped into the mayor's office, Boston had gone from a democracy of the few to a democracy of the many. First, Bostonians successfully toppled an oligarchy that demanded the people's deference. After victory, they placed their trust in a populistic Caesarist who successfully grappled for power in his quest to fulfill his individual vision of a modern metropolis. When Boston's Caesar was perceived as too autocratic, overstepping the people's authority, the city exiled him for a malleable replacement, illustrating an ironic, yet enduring pattern in American populist politics.

The events that Boston experienced between 1814 and 1828 provide a narrative of democracy's development during the early nineteenth century. Almost everything changed in Boston between 1800 and 1828. It had gone from a provincial town predicated on an organic notion of community to a dynamic, burgeoning, democratic metropolis. Manufacturing interests and the emerging market economy took over a past economy based on maritime trade. The urban transformation proved the death knell of a dominant political party and signaled the rise and fall of an incendiary third party. These years marked the decline of an elitist conception of cultural politics and the emerging tide of an inclusive form of democratic politics that would never ebb away. The most important development can be found in the activism of a new generation of voters whose political energy was matched only by the intensity of Boston's urban transformation. During these decades, ordinary Bostonians shook off the established political culture, forced further democratization, weathered a populist Caesarist, and in the end established an advanced and more inclusive democracy. Viewed in this context, Harrison Gray Otis had been right when he described the political upheavals of the 1820s as "revolutionary." For Boston, everything had, in fact, changed.

NOTES

1. THE SETTING FOR INSURGENCY

1. Ronald P. Formisano, "From Deferential-Participant to Party Politics," in Ronald P. Formisano and Constance K. Burns, eds., *Boston, 1700–1980: The Evolution of Urban Politics* (Westport, Conn.: Greenwood Press, 1984), 29–58. Samuel Eliot Morison, *Harrison Gray Otis, 1765–1848: The Urbane Federalist,* (Boston: Houghton Mifflin, 1969), 249–253, 433–437; and Samuel Eliot Morison, *The Life and Letters of Harrison Gray Otis, Federalist, 1765–1848,* 2 vols. (Boston: Houghton Mifflin, 1913), passim. James M. Banner, *To the Hartford Convention: The Federalists and the Origins of Party Politics in Massachusetts, 1789–1815,* (New York: Alfred A. Knopf, 1970), 127–131, 268–269. Linda K. Kerber, *Federalists in Dissent: Imagery and Ideology in Jeffersonian America* (Ithaca: Cornell University Press, 1970), esp. 135–215. Shaw Livermore Jr. *The Twilight of Federalism: The Disintegration of the Federalist Party, 1815–1830* (Princeton: Princeton University Press, 1962), 26. David Hackett Fisher, *The Revolution of American Conservatism: The Federalist Party in the Era of Jeffersonian Democracy* (New York: Harper Torchbooks, 1965), see esp. chap. 6, "Federalists and the 'French System of Fraternity': The Birth of the Washington Benevolent Societies," 110–128. Virginia Cardwell Purdy, *Portrait of a Know-Nothing Legislature: The Massachusetts General Court of 1855* (New York: Garland, 1989), 47–49, for an overview of Massachusetts party politics.

2. Formisano, "Deferential-Participant to Party Politics," in Formisano and Burns, *Boston,* 30. *An Exposition of the Principles and Views of the Middling Interest in the City of Boston* (Boston, May 1822), 1–8, American Antiquarian Society, Worcester, Mass.

3. Most historians of Massachusetts use Federalist Harrison Gray Otis's defeat to Republican William Eustis in the 1823 gubernatorial race as the indicator of Federalism's death in the state, yet I argue the 1822 mayoral race foretold the fate of Federalism before the governor's race.

4. Frederic Cople Jaher, *The Urban Establishment: Upper Strata in Boston, New York, Charleston, Chicago, and Los Angeles* (Urbana: University of Illinois Press, 1982), chap. 2.

Edward Pessen, *Riches, Class, and Power before the Civil War* (Lexington, Mass.: Heath, 1973), passim. Peter Dobkin Hall, *The Organization of American Culture, 1700–1900: Private Institutions, Elites, and the Origins of American Nationality* (New York: University of New York Press, 1984), chaps. 4 and 9. Ronald Formisano, *The Transformation of Political Culture: Massachusetts Parties, 1790s–1840s* (New York: Oxford University Press, 1983), chap. 12. Ronald Story, *Harvard and the Boston Upper Class: The Forging of an Aristocracy* (Middletown, Conn.: Wesleyan University Press, 1980), chaps. 1 and 9. Robert F. Dalzell Jr., *Enterprising Elite: The Boston Associates and the World They Made* (Cambridge: Harvard University Press, 1987), 165–174. Betty G. Farrell, *Elite Families: Class and Power in Nineteenth-Century Boston* (Albany: State University of New York Press, 1993), 3, 13–15, 21–37. Harlow E. Sheidley, "Sectional Nationalism: The Culture and Politics of the Massachusetts Conservative Elite, 1815–1836" (PhD. diss., University of Connecticut, 1990), iv. Oscar and Mary Handlin, *Commonwealth: A Study of the Role of Government in the American Economy: Massachusetts, 1774–1861*, rev. ed. (Cambridge: Harvard University Press, Belknap Press, 1969), 184–191. Kinley J. Brauer, *Cotton versus Conscience: Massachusetts Whig Politics and Southwestern Expansion, 1843–1848* (Lexington: University of Kentucky Press, 1967), chap. 1. Samuel Eliot Morison, *The Maritime History of Massachusetts, 1783–1860* (Boston: Houghton Mifflin, 1921), 129.

5. Robert A. McCaughey, *Josiah Quincy, 1772–1864: The Last Federalist* (Cambridge: Harvard University Press, 1974), 17. McCaughey's is the best and most thorough biography of Josiah Quincy yet written, although he tends to down-play Quincy's significant role in local party politics during the crucial years covered in this book.

6. John Lothrop Motley to Edmund Quincy, Aug. 7, 1864, in Edmund Quincy, *The Life of Josiah Quincy of Massachusetts* (Boston: Fields, Osgood, 1869), 547.

7. Richard G. Hewlett, "Josiah Quincy: Reform Mayor of Boston," *New England Quarterly*, 27 (1951), 179–196, argues: "The basis of Josiah Quincy's career as reform mayor of Boston was to be found in his own social philosophy and the society in which he lived. . . . Josiah Quincy's reform program [as mayor] was but one manifestation of the social ferment of his age" (195–196).

8. George Dangerfield, *The Era of Good Feelings* (New York: Harcourt Brace Jovanovich, 1952), 175–179. George Dangerfield, *The Awakening of American Nationalism, 1815–1828* (New York: Harper Torchbooks, 1965), 72–75.

9. Dangerfield, *Era of Good Feelings*, 178. Douglass C. North, *The Economic Growth of the United States, 1790–1860* (New York: W. W. Norton, 1966), 182–185.

10. Dangerfield, *Era of Good Feelings*, 178–179. North, *Economic Growth*, 186, 185. Carl Seaburg and Stanley Paterson, *Merchant Prince of Boston: Colonel T. H. Perkins, 1764–1854* (Cambridge: Harvard University Press, 1971), 287–289.

11. Dangerfield, *Era of Good Feelings*, 176–177.

12. For the effects of the auction system on Boston, see Andrew R. L. Cayton, "The Fragmentation of 'A Great Family': The Panic of 1819 and the Rise of the Middling Interest in Boston, 1818–1822," *Journal of the Early Republic*, 2 (Summer 1982), 148–150. Dangerfield, *Era of Good Feelings*, 176–178.

13. Samuel Rezneck, "The Depression of 1819–1822: A Social History," *American Historical Review*, 39 (1933), 33. *Evening Gazette*, as reported in the *Portsmouth* (N.H.) *Journal of Literature and Politics*, June 6, 1822, American Antiquarian Society, Worcester, Mass. (all sources from the American Antiquarian Society hereafter cited as AAS). Morison, *Mari-*

time History, 215. Cayton, "Fragmentation of 'A Great Family,'" 145–146. Murray N. Rothbard, *The Panic of 1819: Reaction and Policies* (New York: Columbia University Press, 1962). For an extremely detailed contemporary explanation of the depression and its effects on Boston, see "The Prospect before us, or Facts and Observations illustrative of the past and present situation and future Prospects of the United States, embracing a View of the Causes of the late Bankruptcies in Boston: to which is added a sketch of the restrictive Systems of the principle Nations of Christendom. By a Pennsylvanian," *North American Review,* 8 (July 1823), 186–220, American Periodical Series microfilm (all material from this source hereafter cited as APSmicro). For a general overview, see North, *Economic Growth,* 177–188; Thomas H. O'Connor, *Lords of the Loom: The Cotton Whigs and the Coming of the Civil War* (New York: Charles Scribner's Sons, 1968), 22–24; Handlin and Handlin, *Commonwealth,* 168–166. *Castigator* (Boston), Aug. 7, 1822, AAS. For debt imprisonment and bankruptcy, see Peter J. Coleman, *Debtors and Creditors in America: Insolvency, Imprisonment for Debt, and Bankruptcy, 1607–1900* (Madison: State Historical Society of Wisconsin, 1974), 37–52.

14. Formisano, "Deferential-Participant to Party Politics," in Formisano and Burns, *Boston,* 29–30.

15. Fisher, *Revolution of American Conservatism,* 70–71, 126–128, 61–66, 142–144.

16. Formisano, *Transformation of Political Culture,* 68–72. Fisher, *Revolution of American Conservatism,* 271. Morison, *Otis: Urbane Federalist,* 95–169, 247–248, 257–259, 266.

17. "Aristocracy," *New England Galaxy,* Sept. 22, 1820, AAS. It should be noted that the *Galaxy*'s full title until the end of 1820 was the *New England Galaxy and Masonic Magazine.* By the end of 1820, it dropped "Masonic" from its title. For brevity, I have abbreviated the title even when using it as a source before the newspaper's change.

18. For Harrison Gray Otis's investments between 1818 and 1823, see Matthew Edel, Elliot D. Sclar, and Daniel Luria, *Shaky Palaces: Homeownership and Social Mobility in Boston's Suburbanization* (New York: Columbia University Press, 1984), 202–204, which provides a table showing Otis and partners' purchases and sales from 1783 through 1823. For Thomas H. Perkins's investments in 1819, see Seaburg and Paterson, *Merchant Prince,* 287–288.

19. Lawrence W. Kennedy, *Planning the City upon the Hill: Boston since 1630* (Amherst: University of Massachusetts Press, 1992), 27–41. Morison, *Otis: Urbane Federalist,* 218–232. Formisano, *Transformation of Political Culture,* 68–71. Handlin and Handlin, *Commonwealth,* 108–109, 172–177, 184. Dalzell, *Enterprising Elite,* 62, 85, 58. Seaburg and Paterson, *Merchant Prince,* 263–267. Thomas G. Cary, ed., *Memoir of Thomas Handasyd Perkins, containing Extracts from his Diaries and Letters* (1856; rpt., New York: Burt Franklin, 1971), is an uncritical, contemporary account of Perkins's life.

20. Morison, *Otis: Urbane Federalist,* 205. Hall, *Organization of American Culture,* 108. The grip of these Boston elites extended into national politics as well as operating on the local level; see Alfred S. Konefski and Andrew J. King, eds., *The Papers of Daniel Webster, Legal Papers: The Boston Practice,* 4 vols. (Hanover, N.H.: University Press of New England, 1983), 2:175–275; and Carl E. Prince and Seth Taylor, "Daniel Webster, the Boston Associates, and the U.S. Government's Role in the Industrializing Process, 1815–1830," *Journal of the Early Republic,* 2 (Fall 1982), 283–299.

21. Harrison Gray Otis to William Sullivan, Mar. 21, 1822, Harrison Gray Otis Papers, 1691–1870 New York Public Library, Massachusetts Historical Society, microfilm (all material from this source hereafter cited as Otismicro).

22. Frederic Cople Jaher, "The Politics of the Boston Brahmins, 1800–1860," in Formisano and Burns, *Boston,* 67.

23. Sheidley, "Sectional Nationalism," 34.

24. Handlin and Handlin, *Commonwealth,* esp. 51–86 and 106–133.

25. Fisher, *Revolution of American Conservatism,* 274.

2. NEW ENGLAND FEDERALISM ON THE ATTACK

1. Fisher, *Revolution of American Conservatism,* xvii, xvi.

2. Fisher Ames to Thomas Dwight, Feb. 29, 1804, quoted in Winfred E. A. Bernhard, *Fisher Ames: Federalist and Statesman, 1758–1808* (Chapel Hill: University of North Carolina Press, 1965), 339.

3. Eliza S. (Morton) Quincy to Abigail Adams, Apr. 6, 1806, Quincy Family Papers, Massachusetts Historical Society microfilm, Papers Relating to the Quincy, Wendell, Holmes, and Upham Families at the Massachusetts Historical Society together with the Quincy, Wendell, Holmes, and Upham Family Papers in the Collection of Hugh Upham Clark, of Arlington Virginia, (hereafter cited as Quincymicro).

4. Ibid. Fisher, *Revolution of American Conservatism,* 1–49, argues that this division was generational. Younger Federalists saw the need to expand the social composition of the party at the expense of older Federalists' most basic conceptions of party ideology.

5. Harrison Gray Otis to T. H. Perkins [?], 1818, quoted in Edmund Quincy, *Life of Josiah Quincy,* 376.

6. For Jonathan Mason quotation, see Fisher, *Revolution of American Conservatism,* 252. Harrison Gray Otis to Woodbury Storer, Aug. 29, 1804, quoted in ibid., 59. For distinctions and differences between old guard and nontraditional Federalists, see ibid., 1–72, 245–277.

7. Josiah Quincy to John Quincy Adams, Nov. 23, 1804, quoted in ibid., 273.

8. McCaughey, *Quincy: The Last Federalist,* 54. Fisher, *Revolution of American Conservatism,* 273. For details on the Custom House issue, see James Walker, "Memoir of Josiah Quincy," *Proceedings of the Massachusetts Historical Society,* 9 (Mar. 1866), 97–100. Henry Clay quoted in James Spear Loring, *The Hundred Boston Orators Appointed by the Municipal Authorities and Other Public Bodies, from 1770 to 1852; Comprising Historical Gleanings, Illustrating the Principles and Progress of our Republican Institutions* (Boston: John P. Jewett, 1852), 261.

9. Quincy quoted in "Rebellion Threatened," *Independent Chronicle* (Boston), Jan. 24, 1811, Massachusetts Historical Society microform copy, (hereafter cited as MHSform). Also see Walker, "Memoir of Josiah Quincy," 100–103, for Quincy's explanation for the speech. He claims he was trying to shock the majority party so it would listen to his constitutional arguments against Louisiana statehood. For a constitutional defense of the speech, see Josiah P. Quincy, "The Louisiana Purchase; and the Appeal to Posterity." *Proceedings of the Massachusetts Historical Society,* 38 (Nov. 1903), 48–59.

10. "Rebellion Threatened," *Independent Chronicle,* Jan. 24, 1811, MHSform.

11. Josiah Quincy to Harrison Gray Otis, Nov. 26, 1811, quoted in Morison, *Life and Letters of Otis,* 2:33–36. McCaughey, *Quincy: The Last Federalist,* 58–76. Quincy to Otis, Nov. 8, 1811, Quincymicro.

12. Walker, "Memoir of Josiah Quincy," 104.

13. Josiah Quincy to William Sullivan, Dec. 21, 1810, reel 36, Quincymicro.

14. Josiah Quincy to Eliza (Morton) Quincy, Mar. 22, 1812, quoted in McCaughey, *Quincy: The Last Federalist*, 75.

15. Henry Clay's speech cited in Theodore Clarke Smith, "War Guilt in 1812," *Proceedings of the Massachusetts Historical Society*, 64 (June 1931), 324.

16. Edmund Quincy, *Life of Josiah Quincy*, 306. "Tadmor" is a reference to Christopher Marlowe's 1587 play, *Tamburlaine*, about the Mongol conqueror of Persia, India, and Mesopotamia, Timur Lang, aka Tamburlaine, aka Tadmor (c. 1336–1405).

17. Ibid., 365. See Eliza Susan Quincy, 1820, Commonplace Book, 1818–1825, reel 7, Quincymicro, for more on Josiah Quincy's "obsessive" behavior. Josiah Quincy, *Essay on the Soiling of Cattle* (Boston, 1859). Tamara Plankins Thornton, *Cultivating Gentlemen: The Meaning of Country Life among the Boston Elite, 1785–1860* (New Haven: Yale University Press, 1986), 2–56.

18. Thornton, *Cultivating Gentlemen*, 1, 22, 155, 67–69. Fisher, *Revolution of American Conservatism*, 252.

19. Thornton, *Cultivating Gentlemen*, 2–56.

20. Ibid., 114.

21. Edmund Quincy, *Life of Josiah Quincy*, 369. Eliza Susan Quincy, 1820, Commonplace Book, 1818–1825, reel 7, Quincymicro.

22. Eliza Susan Quincy, 1820, Commonplace Book, 1818–1825, reel 7, Quincymicro. Eliza's reaction is echoed by Henry Adams in *The Education of Henry Adams: An Autobiography* (1918; rprt., Boston: Houghton Mifflin, 1961), 9–10, where Adams explains: "Quincy was in a way inferior to Boston and . . . socially Boston looked down on Quincy. . . . Quincy had no Boston style." Edmund Quincy, *Life of Josiah Quincy*, 390. John Phillips had inherited all of his father's estate, none of which filtered down to Josiah Quincy or his family. As Edmund explained (384), "William Phillips . . . influenced by the desire of keeping together the large fortune he had accumulated, bequeathed it almost entire to his only son, leaving to my father, the only representative of one of his daughters, absolutely nothing."

23. Richard Peters to Josiah Quincy, Jan. 24, 1813, quoted in Edmund Quincy, *Life of Josiah Quincy*, 367.

24. Harrison Gray Otis to John Phillips [?], 1818, quoted in ibid., 376. Although Otis is referring to Quincy's nomination to the senate chairmanship in 1818 and not his 1813 nomination, Quincy's liabilities to the party were the same in 1818 as 1813. He was haunted throughout his life by his call for Jefferson's impeachment and his threat of northern secession on the House floor. In 1814 the Boston press was still debating his secessionist comments of 1811; see "The Integrity of the United States Must Be Preserved, No. I–IX," *Boston Spectator*, Feb. 19, 1814–Apr. 23, 1814, APSmicro, which carried front-paged articles for three months on Quincy and the issues he first raised in 1811. In the midst of the 1814 Hartford Convention, the *Spectator*, as well as many other newspapers, returned to the logic or illogic that Quincy had used to justify secession in 1811. Thus Otis's concerns about Quincy in 1818 were the same as in 1813—Quincy had spoken too rashly and openly while in Congress, and many people, even in 1818, had not forgotten. If his congressional stands remained a liability in 1818, clearly, they would not have been forgotten in 1813.

25. Edmund Quincy, *Life of Josiah Quincy*, 365.

26. "Journal of the Washington Benevolent Society of Massachusetts," Washington Benevolent Society of Massachusetts Records: 1812–1824, Massachusetts Historical Society,

Boston (hereafter cited as WBS Records, MHS). The two best accounts of the Washington Benevolent Society are Fisher, *Revolution of American Conservatism,* chap. 6, and William Alexander Robinson, "The Washington Benevolent Society in New England: A Phase of Politics during the War of 1812," *Proceedings of the Massachusetts Historical Society,* 49 (Mar. 1916), 274–286.

27. Harrison Gray Otis to Woodbury Storer, Aug. 29, 1804, quoted in Fisher, *Revolution of American Conservatism,* 59. "Minutes, of the Washington Benevolent Society: 1812–1824," WBS Records, MHS.

28. Fisher, *Revolution of American Conservatism,* chap. 6. William A. Robinson, *Jeffersonian Democracy in New England* (1916; rpt., New York: Greenwood Press, 1968), 89–91. See George D. Luetscher, *Early Political Machinery in the United States* (1903; rpt., New York: Da Capo Press, 1971), for a description of Republican party organization and the Federalist response. The loss of the governorship and both houses of the General Court in 1811, according to Morison, *Otis: Urbane Federalist,* 315–316, was due to Federalism's extremist position that the Non-Intercourse Act should be nullified by Massachusetts. Republican Elbridge Gerry, on the eve of the War of 1812, lost in the spring of 1812 to Federalist Caleb Strong.

29. Francis X. Blouin, Jr. *The Boston Region, 1810–1850: A Study of Urbanization* (Ann Arbor: UMI Research Press, 1980), 137. Peter R. Knights, *Yankee Destinies: The Lives of Ordinary Nineteenth-Century Bostonians* (Chapel Hill: University of North Carolina Press, 1991). Fisher, *Revolution of American Conservatism,* 120. Article 17, "Constitution of the Washington Benevolent Society," "Journal of the Washington Benevolent Society," WBS Records, MHS. Robinson, "Washington Benevolent Society in New England," 278–282. Fisher, *Revolution of American Conservatism,* 119.

30. "Constitution of the Washington Benevolent Society," 1, in "Journal of the Washington Benevolent Society," WBS Records, MHS.

31. Fisher, *Revolution of American Conservatism,* 121. "Washington Benevolent Society Correspondence, etc., 1812–1818," doc. 15, "Minutes of the Washington Benevolent Society, Nov. 10, 1812, p. 23 MHS; also see "Constitution," Article 16, in "Journal of the Washington Benevolent Society," WBS Records, MHS, which states that all moneys given "shall be exclusively appropriated for the relief of the members & their families."

32. J. Welles to Andrew Ritchie, Mar. 23, 1815, doc. 102, "Washington Benevolent Society Correspondence, etc., 1812–1818," docs. 17, 25, WBS Records, MHS.

33. "Journal of the Washington Benevolent Society," "Minutes of the Washington Benevolent Society," Mar. 28, 1812, p. 7, WBS Records, MHS. Although I have found no direct evidence that the WBS directly communicated with the Central Committee, it seems impossible that it did not, considering that Thomas H. Perkins and William Sullivan were both members of the Central Committee, Perkins was a WBS founder, and Sullivan was its president in 1813 and 1814; also, it should be mentioned that Harrison Gray Otis's son worked his way up in the organization, serving as its secretary in 1819; see "Journal of the Washington Benevolent Society," WBS Records, MHS.

34. Fisher, *Revolution of American Conservatism,* chap. 6. "Minutes of the Washington Benevolent Society," Oct. 12, 1813, p. 37. Khilborn Whitman to William Sullivan, Apr. 20, 1812, doc. 60, "Washington Benevolent Society Correspondence, etc., 1812–1818," WBS Records, MHS.

35. See Fisher, *Revolution of American Conservatism,* 188, which shows voter participation

in 1812 stood at 68 percent; in 1813, 64 percent; in 1814, 64 percent; in 1815, 50 percent. The point is that after the WBS's formation in the state, voting participation rose and Federalists were getting elected (after 1812 Federalism held the governor's seat until 1823). The part played by the WBS in getting out the vote thus seems quite remarkable.

36. Benjamin Merrill [of Salem] to Lemuel Shaw, Mar. 26, 1812, doc. 44; Rufus King Page and Hiram A. Bement [both of Hallowell] to Arnold Welles, Mar. 31, 1813, doc. 50; William Garland [of Portsmouth] to B. T. Tilden, Mar. 28, 1812, doc. 49; and see docs. 59, 63, 66, 69–70, and 75 (all contained in "Washington Benevolent Society Correspondence, etc., 1812–1818," WBS Records, MHS) for Federalists from Plymouth, Gloucester, Marblehead, Easton, and Keene, N.H., asking for advice on how to set up their own societies.

37. "The 'Art' of Faction," *Independent Chronicle,* May 6, 1813, MHSform.

38. There is evidence that the Boston Hussars were formed by the WBS and served as the society's primary protection force. The Hussars were trained by an individual named Roulstone, a stable keeper and riding school instructor who served as the Hussars' cavalry instructor. Roulstone also was one of the original members of the WBS; see John T. Prince, "Boston's Lanes and Alleys," *Bostonian Society Publications,* 7 (1910), 22–24. Also, Josiah Quincy served as the Hussars' first "Captain of the Company" while he was the WBS's vice-president; see Prince, "Boston's Lanes and Alleys," 24. "Washington Benevolent Society Correspondence, etc., 1812–1818," doc.15; "Minutes of the Washington Benevolent Society," Apr. 14, 4, and 30, 1812; G. H. Steuart to Lemuel Shaw, Aug. 18, 1812, doc. 77, "Washington Benevolent Society Correspondence, etc., 1812–1818," WBS Records, MHS. Fisher Ames quoted in Formisano, *Transformation of Political Culture,* 133.

39. *Boston Patriot,* July 15, 1815, quoted in Robinson, "Washington Benevolent Society in New England." 280.

40. Ibid., 282.

41. "Constitution," in "Journal of the Washington Benevolent Society," WBS Records, MHS.

42. Otis Williams to Arnold Welles, June 1, 1812, doc. 70; William Gordon to Lemuel Shaw, June 1, 1812, doc. 75, "Washington Benevolent Society Correspondence, etc., 1812–1818," WBS Records, MHS.

43. Josiah Quincy to Lemuel Shaw, Mar. 20, 1820, doc. 44, ibid.

44. "Washington Benevolent Society," *Columbian Centinel,* May 1, 1813, MHSform, estimated the parade held 2,000 people; the *Independent Chronicle,* May 6, 1813, MHSform, estimated the number to be 1,700. See Morison, *Life and Letters of Otis,* 2:93, for Strong's reelection numbers. For a breakdown of the procession, see "The 'Art' of Faction," *Independent Chronicle,* May 6, 1813, MHSform. See Edmund Quincy, *Life of Josiah Quincy,* 308–309, for another description of the march. Morison, *Otis: Urbane Federalist,* 255–257, describes the Apr. 30, 1814, WBS parade, which proved larger than the 1813 celebration. Eliza Quincy's description is taken from Walter Muir Whitehill, *Boston: A Topographical History* (Cambridge: Harvard University Press, Belknap Press, of Harvard University Press, 1959), 66. It should be noted that Eliza's description is of the WBS's Washington's Birthday parade in 1815, though there is no reason to believe that the social composition of the 1813 parade was any different.

45. "The 'Art' of Faction," *Independent Chronicle,* May 6, 1813, MHSform. *Boston Yankee,* Apr. 30, 1813, quoted in Robinson, "Washington Benevolent Society in New England," 278, n. 1.

46. For Sullivan's comments, see Morison, *Life and Letters of Otis,* 1:300, n. 1. John G. Weld, "Sidelights of the Old Boston Militia Companies," *Proceedings of the Bostonian Society,* 68 (Jan. 1949), 34, which describes the Hussars as "the most extravagant" of all the militia; Weld claims the membership cost was $800, not including the expense of one's horse. Also, Weld identifies Quincy as its first captain. Also see Prince, "Boston's Lanes and Alleys," 24, which inaccurately identifies "John" Roulstone as the trainer of the Hussars instead of "Michael" Roulstone. Prince also provides the name of William Sturgis as a member of the Hussars. Sturgis was also a member of the WBS and became a leader in the Middling Interest party in 1821. McCaughey, *Quincy: The Last Federalist,* 79, suggests that the Hussars might fight against U.S. troops if they came to crush Boston's antiwar sentiments. Edmund Quincy, *Life of Josiah Quincy,* 346–347. For Roulstone's connection to the WBS, see "Journal of the Washington Benevolent Society of Massachusetts," WBS Records, MHS.

47. Josiah Quincy, Apr. 30, 1813, quoted in Edmund Quincy, *Life of Josiah Quincy,* 309–316.

48. Eric Foner, *Free Soil, Free Labor, Free Men: The Ideology of the Republican Party before the Civil War* (New York: Oxford University Press, 1970), chap. 1. McCaughey, *Quincy: The Last Federalist,* 80–82.

49. For favorable reviews, see *Columbian Centinel,* May 1, 1813, MHSform; "The 'Art' of Faction," *Independent Chronicle,* May 6, 1813, MHSform.

50. William J. Cooper Jr., *Liberty and Slavery: Southern Politics to 1860* (New York: Alfred A. Knopf, 1983), 124.

51. For tonnage of shipping owned in custom houses, see Dalzell, *Enterprising Elite,* 62–63; Morison, *Maritime History,* 378; and Handlin and Handlin *Commonwealth,* 58, 126–127. For fishing decline, see Handlin and Handlin, *Commonwealth,* 60.

52. George Ticknor quoted in Morison, *Life and Letters of Otis,* 1:58. Francis Bassett quoted in ibid., 59. Caleb Strong quoted in ibid., 68–69. Joseph Buckingham, *Personal Memoirs and Recollections of an Editorial Life* 2 vols. (Boston: Ticknor, Reed, and Fields, 1852), 1:32–33; for a biographical sketch of Buckingham, see Robert J. Zboray, "Buckingham, Joseph Tinker," thumbnail biography in author's possession; also, Gary J. Kornblith, "Becoming Joseph T. Buckingham: The Struggle for Artisanal Independence in Early Nineteenth-Century Boston," in Paul J. Gilje and Howard Rock, eds., *American Artisans: Explorations in Social Identity* (Baltimore: Johns Hopkins University Press, 1995), 125–126. For Charles Bulfinch's imprisonment for debt, see Kennedy, *Planning the City,* 40. "Politick Measures," *Boston Spectator,* Oct. 15, 1814, APSmicro. For general descriptions of the economic problems the War of 1812 caused in New England, Massachusetts, and Boston, see Oscar Handlin, *Boston's Immigrants, 1790–1880,* rev. ed. (New York: Atheneum, 1975), 3–10. Handlin and Handlin, *Commonwealth,* 58. Morison, *Maritime History,* 191–193. Dalzell, *Enterprising Elite,* 62.

53. Morison, *Life and Letters of Otis,* 2:104, provides a tally of the General Court vote, which breaks down the legislative vote for or against the Hartford Convention by district; see 104, n. 20.

54. Edmund Quincy quoted in Walker, "Memoir of Josiah Quincy," 106. Josiah Quincy as quoted in ibid., 105. Also see James Loring, "Josiah Quincy," *Hundred Boston Orators,* 266–268, for a different description of the same events.

55. For Republican press reaction, see Walker, "Memoir of Josiah Quincy," 105. For Holmes's request that Quincy's remarks be struck, see Loring, "Josiah Quincy," *Hundred*

Boston Orators, 267. For the Federalist leadership's irritation and Edmund Quincy's remarks on his father and the convention, see Walker, "Memoir of Josiah Quincy," 104, 106.

56. Fisher, *Revolution of American Conservatism,* 180, n. 115.

57. Formisano, "Deferential-Participant to Party Politics," in Formisano and Burns, *Boston,* 33. Kennedy, *Planning the City,* 38.

58. "Journal of the Washington Benevolent Society," leadership lists; J. Welles to Andrew Ritchie, Mar. 23, 1815, doc. 102, "Washington Benevolent Society Correspondence, etc., 1812–1818," both in WBS Records, MHS. Fisher, *Revolution of American Conservatism,* 128.

3. MILITIAMEN, DEBTORS, DOWNEASTERNERS, AND "DEMIGODS"

1. Rezneck, "Depression of 1819–1822," 29. Formisano, *Transformation of Political Culture,* 187–190. "The Prospect before us, or facts and observations . . . ," *North American Review,* July 1823, 210, APSmicro. Coleman, *Debtors and Creditors,* 50, n. 17.

2. Coleman, *Debtors and Creditors,* 50, n. 17.

3. Ibid.

4. "The Poor Debtor's Journal," *New England Galaxy,* Sept. 1, 1820, APSmicro, is a public announcement of the forthcoming journal, which states that the paper's purpose is to "open . . . discussions upon the subjects of *Bankruptcy, poor debtors, debtor's laws,* &c." Its publishers were Clark and Brown. *Debtor's Journal,* Sept. 23, 1820, APSmicro. Also see Formisano's discussion of the debtor's movement in *Transformation of Political Culture,* 187–190.

5. *Debtor's Journal,* Sept. 23, 1820, APSmicro. For information on Orne, see Arthur B. Darling, *Political Changes in Massachusetts, 1824–1848: A Study of Liberal Movements in Politics* (1925; rpt., Cos Cob, Conn.: John E. Edwards, 1968), 62–67. Formisano, *Transformation of Political Culture,* 189.

6. *Debtor's Journal,* Sept. 23, 1820, APSmicro.

7. *Columbian Centinel,* Oct. 6 and Sept. 29, 1819, MHSform.

8. Zboray, "Buckingham, Joseph T.," passim. Kornblith, "Becoming Joseph T. Buckingham," 124–26, in Gilje and Rock, *American Artisans. New England Galaxy,* Mar. 9, 1821; for the consistency of the *Galaxy* on this issue, see Mar. 9 and 16, June 22, July 6, 1821, and Mar. 22, 1822, all in APSmicro. For the *Galaxy*'s commitment to the debt issue, also see Buckingham, *Personal Memoirs,* 1:102.

9. Letter to Editor, *New England Galaxy,* Oct. 27, 1820, AAS. Kornblith, "Becoming Joseph T. Buckingham," 126–127.

10. "Imprisonment for Debt," *New England Galaxy,* June 22, 1821, APSmicro.

11. Buckingham, *Personal Memoirs,* 2:36–37.

12. See above, chap. 2, n. 38, for the partisan basis of militias. For the militia reform movement, see "Our Militia," *New England Galaxy,* Mar. 31, 1820, APSmicro. Weld, "Sidelights of Boston Militia Companies," 336, and Fisher, *Revolution of American Conservatism,* 184; both argue that militias were extremely partisan. Ebenezer W. Stone, *Digest of the Militia Laws of Massachusetts, and Extracts Relating to the Militia from the United States and State Constitutions and Laws of the United States* (Boston: Dutton and Wentworth, State Printers, 1851), 5, 12, 15, 24, 25. Prince, "Boston's Lanes and Alleys," 9–32. The militia reform movement spread throughout the state, as indicated by "The Militia," *Hampshire Daily Gazette,* Mar. 27, 1822, microfilm, W.E.B. Du Bois Library, University of Massachusetts, Amherst.

13. "Our Militia," *New England Galaxy,* Mar. 31, 1820, APSmicro. For a listing of exemptions, see Stone, *Digest of the Militia Laws,* 23.

14. "Our Militia," *New England Galaxy,* Mar. 31, 1820, APSmicro.

15. "Militia," *Columbian Centinel,* Jan. 15, 1820, MHSform. Rezneck, "Depression of 1819–1822," 187–190.

16. "Militia Law," *New England Galaxy,* June 23, 1820, APSmicro.

17. For the authoritarian style of the Federalist party leadership, see Fisher, *Revolution of American Conservatism,* 62–65; and Sheidley, "Sectional Nationalism," 8–10.

18. See Formisano, *Transformation of Political Culture,* 152, for the Republican majority in the Maine district. See also Edmund Quincy, *Life of Josiah Quincy,* 373–375. Morison, *Life and Letters of Otis,* 2:234. Alan Taylor, *Liberty Men and Great Proprietors: The Revolutionary Settlement on the Maine Frontier, 1760–1820* (Chapel Hill: University of North Carolina Press, 1990), 241–244.

19. Eliza Susan Quincy to Justin Winsor, July 7, 1880, Winsor Family Papers, reel 63, in Quincymicro. Edmund Quincy, *Life of Josiah Quincy,* 374–375. Walker, "Memoir of Josiah Quincy," 106–107. McCaughey, *Quincy: The Last Federalist,* 84–85. For a detailed analysis of Maine's separation attempts and final success in 1820, see Edward Stanwood, "The Separation of Maine from Massachusetts," *Proceedings of the Massachusetts Historical Society,* 41 (June 1907), 125–164. It should be noted that an earlier attempt in 1816 to separate Maine from Massachusetts proper was spearheaded by Harrison Gray Otis while serving in the state senate. As in 1819, Quincy in 1816 voted against separation.

20. Edmund Quincy, *Life of Josiah Quincy,* 374–375. Stanwood, "Separation of Maine from Massachusetts," 161–162.

21. *Daily Advertiser* quoted in Stanwood, "Separation of Maine from Massachusetts," 161–162, which also provides much information on Quincy's legislative tactics opposing the Maine bill.

22. Stanwood, "Separation of Maine from Massachusetts," 162–163.

23. *Bostonian and Mechanics Journal,* Apr. 26, 1823, AAS.

24. Edmund Quincy, *Life of Josiah Quincy,* 375. For the Federalist Central Committee's justification and the Phillips quotation, see Eliza Susan Quincy, 1820, Commonplace Book, 1818–1825, reel 7, Quincymicro.

25. Eliza Susan Quincy to Robert C. Winthrop, June 30, 1879, Winthrop Family Letters, reel 63, Quincymicro, ibid. Harrison Gray Otis to John Phillips, as quoted in Eliza Susan Quincy to Robert C. Winthrop, ibid. Edmund Quincy, *Life of Josiah Quincy,* 375–76. Eliza Susan Quincy, 1820, Commonplace Book, 1818–1825, reel 7, Quincymicro.

26. For third-party activity see *Columbian Centinel,* Apr. 1 and 8, 1820, MHSform.

27. "Era of Good Feelings," *New England Galaxy,* Mar. 10, 1820, APSmicro.

28. "Communication," *New England Galaxy,* Mar. 17, 1820, APSmicro; also see "Letter to the Editor," *New England Galaxy,* Apr. 20, 1820, APSmicro, which also endorses ward voting as a means of empowering the electorate.

29. "General, alias Central Committee," *New England Galaxy,* Apr. 14, 1820, APSmicro.

30. "Central Committee," *Columbian Centinel,* Mar. 18, 1820, MHSform.

31. For election results, see *Columbian Centinel,* Apr. 8, 1820, MHSform.

32. For Quincy's response to being dumped, see Eliza Susan Quincy, 1820, Commonplace Book, 1818–1825, reel 7, Quincymicro; and Edmund Quincy, *Life of Josiah Quincy,* 375–376.

33. *Daily Advertiser* quoted in Eliza Susan Quincy, 1820, Commonplace Book, 1818–1825, reel 7, Quincymicro. "Mr. Quincy," New England Galaxy, Apr. 6, 1821, APSmicro.

34. Cayton, "Fragmentation of 'A Great Family,'" 149–151. Editorial, *New England Galaxy,* Nov. 3, 1820, AAS.

35. Edmund Quincy, *Life of Josiah Quincy,* 377. Eliza Susan Quincy, 1820, Commonplace Book, 1818–1825, reel 7, Quincymicro.

36. Edmund Quincy, *Life of Josiah Quincy,* 376–377. Unfortunately, Quincy's speech before the Federalist caucus in 1820 has not survived; yet, according to his son in 1869, it was remembered at that late date by those who attended the 1820 caucus. In a story run by the *New England Galaxy* on Apr. 6, 1821, APSmicro, entitled "Mr. Quincy," an account is given of a speech made by Quincy on Apr. 1, 1821, at the Federalist caucus. The similarities between Edmund's and Eliza's account of the 1820 speech and the 1821 speech reported by the *Galaxy* are striking and, perhaps, indicate that Edmund (who based much of his biography of Quincy on the records and diaries of his sister) may have confused 1820 with 1821. McCaughey's *Quincy: The Last Federalist,* 89, concurs with Edmund's 1820 date for the speech, but according to McCaughey's notes, he is also relying on Eliza's diary. In any case, if the *Galaxy*'s date for the speech is accurate, Quincy was still embittered about the Central Committee's treatment of him as late as 1821. For the rise of anti-Maine-separation sentiment in Massachusetts by the spring of 1820, see Stanwood, "Separation of Maine from Massachusetts," 162–63.

37. Eliza Susan Quincy, Diary, 1820, Commonplace Book, 1818–1825, reel 7, Quincymicro. For elite Federalists who supported Quincy, see Edmund Quincy, *Life of Josiah Quincy,* 377–378; and McCaughey, *Quincy: The Last Federalist,* 101–102, 88–89. Federalist extremist John Lowell surprisingly wrote a very positive editorial on Quincy's speech; see *Daily Advertiser* (Boston), Apr. 18, 1820, quoted in Walker, "Memoir of Josiah Quincy," n. 107.

38. Josiah Quincy, Diary, 1818–1828, June 6, 1820, reel 5, Quincymicro; unfortunately, Quincy's diary during this period, unfortunately provides little insight into his own partisan/political actions or the politics of the day; mostly the diary contains material relating to his in depth readings of Cicero, and other classical writers, as well as, material relating to his discussions on the Revolutionary era with John Adams. Merrill D. Peterson, ed., *Democracy, Liberty, and Property: The State Constitutional Conventions of the 1820s* (New York: Bobbs-Merrill Co., 1966), 3, 4–5.

39. Morison, *Life and Letters of Otis,* 2:235. See Peterson, *Democracy, Liberty, and Property,* 6–7, where Peterson concludes that Quincy played a conservative role in the convention, upholding the Federalist cause against liberal reformers. I disagree with Peterson's conclusion. He neglects to mention that Quincy was the first to propose restructuring the constitution, and he does not place into context Quincy's deflated role within the Federalist leadership. As we shall see, Quincy gained such significant Republican support while serving in the convention that at its conclusion he was elected president of the lower house of representatives with the strong backing of the Republican leadership; see Eliza Susan Quincy, Jan. 27, 1821, Commonplace Book, 1818–1825, reel 7, Quincymicro.

40. John Brooks, *Daily Advertiser,* Jan. 14, 1820, quoted in Harlow Walker Sheidley, "Preserving 'The Old Fabrick': The Massachusetts Conservative Elite and the Constitutional Convention of 1820–1821," *Proceedings of the Massachusetts Historical Society,* 103 (1991), 121–122. For the Constitutional Convention, see also Sheidley, "Sectional Nationalism," chap.

2. For Federalist press opposition to a convention, see *Daily Advertiser,* June 12, Jan. 14, 1820; *Columbian Centinel,* Apr. 19, 1820; *Hampshire Daily Gazette* (Northampton), July 18, 1820; *Massachusetts Spy* (Worcester), Aug. 9, 1820; all as cited in Sheidley, "Preserving 'The Old Fabrick,'" 122.

41. Morison, *Life and Letters of Otis,* 234–235. *Independent Chronicle* (Boston), June 7, 1820; also see June 10, 14, and 20, 1820, as quoted in Sheidley, "Preserving 'The Old Fabrick,'" 122. The referendum vote came to 11,756 for and 6,593 against; see Peterson, *Democracy, Liberty, and Property,* 18.

42. Sheidley, "Sectional Nationalism," 72; "The Bill of Rights," *New England Galaxy,* Dec. 29, 1820, APSmicro, which attacks state-sponsored religion; Peterson, *Democracy, Liberty, and Property,* 6–17. See Formisano, *Transformation of Political Culture,* 141, on suffrage rights.

43. Joseph Story to Jeremiah Mason, Jan. 21, 1821, Oliver Family Papers, Massachusetts Historical Society, microfilm, W.E.B. Du Bois Library, University of Massachusetts, Amherst. Morison, *Life and Letters of Otis,* 2:235. Peterson, *Democracy, Liberty, and Property,* 6. Sheidley, "Sectional Nationalism," 78.

44. For Story's difference of opinion with the Republican party, see Joseph Story to Edward Everett, Nov. 1, 1832, cited in William W. Story, *Life and Letters of Joseph Story,* 2 vols. (Boston: Charles C. Little and James Brown, 1851), 1:135. "The Convention," *New England Galaxy,* Jan. 5, 1821, APSmicro. For Josiah Quincy's views of Story, see Josiah Quincy Jr., *Figures of the Past: From the Leaves of Old Journals* (Boston: Roberts Brothers, 1888), 188–189, where Quincy's second son, Josiah, reports his father describing Story as a "country pettifogger."

45. For a full description of Story's antireform position before and during the convention, see William W. Story, *Life and Letters of Joseph Story,* 1:127–130, 386–397, 402.

46. Morison, *Life and Letters of Otis,* 2:235. Sheidley, "Preserving 'The Old Fabrick,'" 126–127.

47. P. F. Degrand to John Quincy Adams, Oct. 4, 1820, quoted in Sheidley, "Sectional Nationalism," 78.

48. Sheidley, "Preserving 'The Old Fabrick,'" 114–137, and "Sectional Nationalism," 77–80. It should be noted that my discussion of the Constitutional Convention in this section relies heavily on the thorough and extensive research and analysis of Harlow Sheidley in both his unpublished dissertation and his article in the *Proceedings of the Massachusetts Historical Society.* I am indebted to his remarkably revealing exposition of the tactics employed by the Federalist conservative elites during the convention. For the structure of the convention, see Peterson, *Democracy, Liberty, and Property,* 3–17 and n. 46.

49. Sheidley, "Sectional Nationalism," 77–80, and "Preserving 'The Old Fabrick,'" passim.

50. *Pittsfield Sun,* Nov. 26, 1820, quoted in Sheidley, "Sectional Nationalism," 80–81.

51. "The Chief Justice's Charge," *New England Galaxy,* Oct. 20, 1820, APSmicro.*Boston Patriot* quoted in the *New England Galaxy,* Oct. 20, 1820, APSmicro.

52. McCaughey, *Quincy: The Last Federalist,* 91–92. *Columbian Centinel,* Dec. 27, 1820, quoted in Sheidley, "Sectional Nationalism," 97–98. The views on Harvard that Quincy adopted at the convention are remarkably similar to those expressed much later by Ralph Waldo Emerson on New England's exceptional role in spreading its culture and "civ-

ilization" throughout the country; see George M. Fredrickson, *The Inner Civil War: Northern Intellectuals and the Crisis of the Union* (New York: Harper Torchbooks, 1965), 176–178.

53. Joseph Richardson, *Journal of Debates,* Nov. 24, 1820, quoted in Sheidley, "Sectional Nationalism," 98.

54. Peterson, *Democracy, Liberty, and Property,* 119. Sheidley, "Sectional Nationalism," 99. Also see Edmund Quincy, *Life of Josiah Quincy,* 379, for Quincy's liberal opinions on freedom of religion. He, like John Adams, had never approved of the Commonwealth's marriage of church and state.

55. Peterson, *Democracy, Liberty, and Property,* 11. Eli A. Glasser, "Government and the Constitution (1820–1917)," in Albert Bushnell Hart, ed., *Commonwealth History of Massachusetts,* 5 vols. (New York: State History Company, 1928–1930), 4:5–6.

56. One delegate at the convention explained how the property qualification for voting rights was often gotten around by those who may not have qualified: the question would be asked, "what property have you? have you the tools of your trade? Yes. What else? A pair of steers my father gave me. And if this was not enough, then he said, a note, which is never intended to be paid, makes up the balance"; quoted in Formisano, *Transformation of Political Culture,* 141. As this quotation clearly indicates, the qualifications for voting easily could be subverted. For Lincoln's position on suffrage during the convention, see Hon. Charles C. Haswell, "Death of Ex-Governor Lincoln," *Boston Journal,* as reprinted in Massachusetts, *A Memorial of Levi Lincoln, the Governor of Massachusetts from 1825 to 1834* (Boston: J. E. Farwell, 1863), 57. Peterson, *Democracy, Liberty, and Property,* 11, 61.

57. Quincy quoted in Peterson, *Democracy, Liberty, and Property,* 65.

58. For an explanation of the origins and perpetuation of this distinction between the "worthy" and "unworthy" poor in Boston, see Eric C. Schneider, *In the Web of Class: Delinquents and Reformers in Boston, 1810s–1930s* (New York: New York University Press, 1992), 4, 23, 25, 30, 45, 106, 190.

59. Peterson, *Democracy, Liberty, and Property,* 66.

60. James T. Austin quoted in ibid., 67.

61. Morison, *Life and Letters of Otis,* 2:235, n. 2, which provides voting statistics for the governor's races between 1815 and 1824. According to Morison's statistics, in 1820, after Maine's separation but before the establishment of the new constitution, the total number who voted was 53,648, compared to 1822, after the new constitution took effect, when the voters numbered 49,664. In the heated gubernatorial race of 1823 that pitted Harrison Gray Otis against William Eustis, the number rose to a total of 64,573, yet Morison's point still stands that the codification of new suffrage laws did not increase the numbers of those who could vote. For historians who reached a similar conclusion, see Formisano, *Transformation of Political Culture,* 141, and Peterson, *Democracy, Liberty, and Property,* 11.

62. For Varnum's role in the convention, see Sheidley, "Sectional Nationalism," 120, n. 44. "Our Militia," *New England Galaxy,* Mar. 31, 1820, APSmicro. For the results of Varnum's committee, see Glasser, "Government and the Constitution," in Hart, *Commonwealth History,* 4:6.

63. Nathan Martin, *Journal of Debates,* Nov. 18, 1820, quoted in Sheidley, "Sectional Nationalism," 86–87.

64. Daniel Webster to Jeremiah Mason, Jan. 12, 1821, in Charles M. Wiltse, ed., *The*

Papers of Daniel Webster: Correspondence, 1798–1824, 15 vols. (Hanover, N.H.: University Press of New England, 1974), 1:280. Joseph Story to Jeremiah Mason, Jan. 21, 1821, Oliver Family Papers, 1419–1946, Massachusetts Historical Society (microfilm ed).

65. See "The Convention," Jan. 5, 1821; Editorials, Jan. 12 and 26, 1821; "For the Consideration of Bostonians," Feb. 2, 1821, all in the *New England Galaxy,* APSmicro.

66. "The Convention," *New England Galaxy,* Jan. 5, 1821, APSmicro.

67. "Massachusetts Peace Society," *New England Galaxy,* Jan. 5, 1821; also see Editorial, *New England Galaxy,* Jan. 12, 1821; both in APSmicro.

68. Levi Lincoln quoted in Eliza Susan Quincy, Jan. 27, Jan. 10, and Jan. 27, 1821, Commonplace Book, 1818–1825, reel 7, Quincymicro.

69. On every partisan issue before the convention of 1820–21, Quincy and Lincoln held diametrically opposite positions. Most representative of their differences are their opposing positions on the War of 1812. Despite many Massachusetts Republicans' hesitation in supporting the war, Lincoln adamantly supported the administration; see Delano A. Goddard, *Daily Advertiser* (Boston), in Massachusetts, *Memorial of Levi Lincoln,* 51.

70. Levi Lincoln to Thomas Jefferson, June 2, 1805, as cited in Robinson, *Jeffersonian Democracy in New England,* 73. Haswell, "Death of Ex-Governor Lincoln," in Massachusetts, *Memorial of Levi Lincoln,* 56–57. It should be noted that Lincoln's opinion on voting qualification (all of-age men who paid taxes should be allowed to vote) was successfully codified in the new constitution; but reform in the basis of representation in the state senate was not achieved. The convention's "Address to the People," on the matter of representation in the senate, states: "We have not thought it expedient . . . to make any fundamental changes in this department." This proved a significant victory for the Central Committee, which would continue to enjoy Federalist domination of the senate due to the overrepresentation of Suffolk and Essex counties; see Peterson, *Democracy, Liberty, and Property,* 114.

71. Quincy and Lincoln both quoted in Eliza Susan Quincy, Jan. 27, 1821, Commonplace Book, 1818–1825, reel 7, Quincymicro.

72. For a full description of the meeting, see ibid.Jan. 27, 1821, Quincymicro.

73. Harrison Gray Otis's opinion of Austin is clearly indicated in Morison, *Life and Letters of Otis,* 2:25. Joseph Story to Jeremiah Mason, July 19, 1821, Oliver Family Papers, 1419–1946, Massachusetts Historical Society (microfilm ed.).

74. *Columbian Centinel,* quoted in *New England Galaxy,* Oct. 20, 1820, APSmicro.

75. Biographical information on Russell and quote from Joseph T. Buckingham, in *Specimens of Newspaper Literature with Personal Memoirs, Anecdotes, and Reminiscences,* 2 vols. (Boston: Charles C. Little and James Brown, 1850), 2:110–115; also see Buckingham, *Personal Memoirs,* 1:121–123.

76. Russell had worked his way up in the WBS organization, serving on the standing committee at the organization's inception in 1812 and becoming its sixth vice-president in 1813; in 1814, he became its fourth-ranked vice-president, and in 1815, he was second vice-president, which proved to be his highest rank; see "Journal of the Washington Benevolent Society of Massachusetts," leadership lists, WBS Records, MHS.

77. Edmund Quincy, *Life of Josiah Quincy,* 389. "Odds between Maine and Massachusetts," *New England Galaxy,* Mar. 23, 1821, APSmicro. "Municipal Election," *New England Galaxy,* Mar. 9, 1821, APSmicro.

4. BOSTON REBELS AGAIN

1. "The Convention," *New England Galaxy,* Jan. 5, 1821, APSmicro.

2. Josiah Quincy speech, Apr. 1, 1821, as quoted in "Mr. Quincy," *New England Galaxy,* Apr. 6, 1821, APSmicro.

3. "Mr. Quincy," *New England Galaxy,* Apr. 6, 1821, APSmicro.

4. Lewis Bunker Rohrbach, comp., Introduction to *Boston Taxpayers in 1821* (1822; rpt., Camden, Me.: Picton Press, 1988), 1–6, in which Rohrbach describes the tax reformist movement as a "revolt."

5. Registry Department (Boston), *A Volume of Records Relating to the Early History of Boston Containing Boston Town Records, 1814 to 1822* (Boston: Municipal Printing Office, 1906), 220–221, (hereafter cited as *Boston Town Records, 1814–1822*).

6. Ibid. For the authority of the Court of Sessions over town affairs, see John Koren, *Boston, 1822–1922: The Story of Its Government and Principal Activities during One Hundred Years* (City of Boston Printing Department, 1923), 7–8. Note that *Boston Town Records, 1814–1822,* 220–221, refers to the "Committee of Finance" and not the Court of Sessions. The Court of Sessions held within it a standing committee (the Committee of Finance) specifically in charge of county tax moneys; see *Boston Town Records, 1814–1822,* Codman Report, 226.

7. *Boston Town Records, 1814–1822,* 221.

8. Ibid., 222.

9. "Town Affairs," *New England Galaxy,* June 22, 1821, APSmicro.

10. *Boston Town Records, 1814–1822,* 222.

11. "Town Affairs," *New England Galaxy,* June 22, 1821, APSmicro.

12. *Boston Town Records, 1814–1822,* 227. For material on Lewis Tappan's Boston years, his best biographer remains Bertram Wyatt-Brown, whose *Lewis Tappan and the Evangelical War against Slavery* (Cleveland: Press of Case Western Reserve University, 1969), 20–21, describes his life as a hardware store owner but does not discuss his actions as a town selectmen.

13. For salaries of justices of the peace, see *Boston Town Records, 1814–1822,* 220.

14. Ibid., 227.

15. Ibid., Tappan Report, 227, which explains clearly the complex nature of taxation in Boston from the 1810s to early 1821. Also see "A Town Meeting," *New England Galaxy,* Sept. 23, 1821, APSmicro.

16. Boston Town Records, 1814–1822, Tappan Report, 227–31. *New England Galaxy,* Oct. 6, 1820, APSmicro.

17. *Boston Town Records, 1814–1822,* Tappan Report, 227–31.

18. Ibid., Tudor Report, 232.

19. Ibid., 231–33.

20. Ibid., 231–34.

21. Letter to the editor, "City Government," *New England Galaxy,* Nov. 23, 1821, APSmicro.

22. *New England Galaxy,* Oct. 6, 1820, APSmicro.

23. Josiah Quincy, *A Municipal History of the Town and City of Boston, during Two Centuries, from September, 17, 1630 to September 17, 1830* (Boston: Charles C. Little and James Brown, 1852), 28. "Town Meeting," *New England Galaxy,* Dec. 7, 1822, APSmicro. "Advantages of City Government," *New England Galaxy,* Dec. 21, 1821, APSmicro.

24. *New England Galaxy,* Oct. 6, 1820, APSmicro.

25. Sullivan's original thirteen-member committee had suggested, at Town Meeting on Dec. 10, 1821, that the Court of Sessions be abolished and an elected-at-large nine-member town council be established to replace the court; see Cayton, "Fragmentation of 'A Great Family,'" 155–156; and *Boston Town Records, 1814–1822,* 254. For an account of the addition of twelve new members to the Sullivan committee, see "The Municipal Affairs of Boston," *New England Galaxy,* Dec. 14, 1821, APSmicro; and *Boston Town Records, 1814–1822,* 254, which lists the additional members: from Ward 1, George Darracott; Ward 2, Redford Webster; Ward 3, Thomas Badger; Ward 4, James Davis; Ward 5, Henry Farnam; Ward 6, Michael Roulstone; Ward 7, John Cotton; Ward 8, Lewis G. Pray; Ward 9, Benjamin Russell; Ward 10, William Sturgis; Ward 11, Daniel Messinger; and Ward 12, Gerry Fairbanks. Also see James Mascarene Hubbard, "Boston's Last Town Meetings and First City Election" *Bostonian Society Publications,* 6 (1910), 93, which states that Town Meeting demanded the drafting of a city charter.

26. "The Municipal Affairs of Boston," *New England Galaxy,* Dec. 14, 1821, APSmicro.

27. Josiah Quincy, *Municipal History of Boston,* iii–iv. Formisano, *Transformation of Political Culture,* 182. Also see Edel et al., *Shaky Palaces,* 198–205, for wealthy Federalists using the municipal government for their own economic interests, especially in real estate.

28. Formisano, *Transformation of Political Culture,* 183.

29. For examples of the *Galaxy*'s editorial position on ward voting, see "General, alias Central Committee," *New England Galaxy,* Apr. 4, 1820; *New England Galaxy,* Apr. 20, 1820; and "Communication," *New England Galaxy,* Mar. 17, 1820; all in APSmicro.

30. For the Central Committee's view of a city system, see Harrison Gray Otis to William Sullivan, Dec. 17, 1821; Gerry Fairbanks to Otis, Dec. 26, 1821; Sullivan to Otis, Jan. 6, 1822; Otis to Sullivan, Jan. 8, 1822; Sullivan to Otis, Jan 13, 1822; Sullivan to Otis, Jan. 18, 1822; Otis to Sullivan, Jan. 19, 1822; all in Otismicro.

31. For Otis's ineffectiveness in the U.S. Senate, see Morison, *Otis: Urbane Federalist,* chap. 19. [Harrison Gray Otis,] "One of the Convention," *Letters Developing the Character and Views of the Hartford Convention* (Washington, 1820); microform, Pamphlets in American History, W. E. B. Du Bois Library, University of Massachusetts, Amherst. Biographical material on Theodore Dwight can be found in Fisher, *Revolution of American Conservatism,* 296–297. Harrison Gray Otis to Theodore Dwight, 1821, quoted in Morison, *Otis: Urbane Federalist,* 412.

32. Morison, *Otis: Urbane Federalist,* 439–441. Robert A. McCaughey, "From Town to City: Boston in the 1820s," *Political Science Quarterly,* 88 (June 1973), 198. Eliza Susan Quincy to Justin Winsor, July 17, 1880, Winsor Family Papers, reel 63, in Quincymicro. William Sullivan to Harrison Gray Otis, Jan. 6, 1822, Otismicro. Also see Edmund Quincy, *Life of Josiah Quincy,* 393, for Otis's strategy to become governor.

33. The "Lancastrian system" was a new method of experimental education developed by English schoolmaster Joseph Lancaster. Lancaster imposed severe discipline on his hundreds of pupils, who were carefully watched and managed by monitors who applied the switch to any unruly students; see Morison, *Otis: Urbane Federalist,* 436. William Sullivan to Harrison Gray Otis, Jan. 6, 1822; Otis to Sullivan, Jan. 19, 1822, Otismicro; Otis to Sullivan, Dec. 12, 1821, as quoted in Morison, *Otis: Urbane Federalist,* 436. Otis to Sullivan, Dec. 17, 1821, Otismicro.

34. Harrison Gray Otis to William Sullivan, Jan. 8, 1822, Otismicro.

35. For limited biographical material on Roulstone, see Prince, "Boston's Lanes and Alleys," 23–26; for Roulstone's position on the committee, see Harrison Gray Otis to William Sullivan, Mar. 21, 1822, Otismicro. See Thomas H. Perkins to Otis, Apr. 5, 1822, Otismicro, for the Central Committee's opposition to Sturgis; also, McCaughey, *Quincy: The Last Federalist,* 102.

36. Gerry Fairbanks to Harrison Gray Otis, Dec. 26, 1821, Otismicro. My analysis of why Fairbanks threw in with his traditional political enemy, Harrison Gray Otis, is conjecture, but one must ask why he would have done such a thing. If the future growth of the Middling Interest is any indication, Fairbanks (as well as all of the Republican leadership in Boston) should have worried about the party's vulnerability to a populistic third party. Once the Middling Interest developed a coherent platform, it filled with traditional Republicans. In the mayoral elections of 1822 and 1823, the Middling Interest candidates garnered significantly more votes than the Republican candidates, making Republicanism a totally insignificant political identity in Boston during those years. Also, the Middling Interest coopted Republicanism's traditional role as critic of Boston's elite and exploited such class-based animosity much more effectively than the Republicans. Also, a coalition party, consisting of ex-Federalists and ex-Republicans, proved that it could win. The Republican party could never muster enough force in Boston to even come close, even before the formation of this third party; thus Republican voters had found a third party where their vote would not just be thrown after a losing cause. With the Middling Interest, not only were their issues addressed (as they had been by the Republicans), but they could actually gain offices within Boston. For most Bostonians who were traditionally Republicans, party realignment made good sense.

37. Gerry Fairbanks to Harrison Gray Otis, Dec. 26, 1821, Otismicro.

38. For accounts of the debates, see Hubbard, "Boston's Last Town Meetings," 94.

39. For Adams's and Clough's involvement in the Town Meetings, see ibid., 95–98.

40. William Sullivan quoted in ibid., 99. William Tudor quoted in Cayton, "Fragmentation of 'A Great Family,'" 157.

41. Harrison Gray Otis to William Sullivan, Jan. 8, 1822, Otismicro.

42. Cayton, "Fragmentation of 'A Great Family,'" 156.

43. Sullivan quoted in Hubbard, "Boston's Last Town Meetings," 99.

44. Adams quoted in ibid., 101; and Cayton, "Fragmentation of 'A Great Family,'" 157, which proved the best analysis of the various forces and interests involved in the debates. For William Emmons's opposition to a charter, see William Emmons, *Mr Emmons' Speech, Delivered at the Grand Caucus, held in Faneuil Hall, on the Evening of the Third of March, 1822, upon the Acceptance or rejection of the City Charter* (Boston: Published by the Author, 1822), AAS.

45. Hubbard, "Boston's Last Town Meetings," 100.

46. Clough quoted in Cayton, "Fragmentation of 'A Great Family,'" 158–159.

47. Hubbard, "Boston's Last Town Meetings," 100.

48. The total vote on the city charter issue: 2,811 (1,805 for the charter, 1,006 against). The total vote on the ward-voting issue: 4,806 (2,611 for ward voting, 2,195 against); see Cayton, "Fragmentation of 'A Great Family,'" 159.

49. Harrison Gary Otis to William Sullivan, Jan. 19, 1822, Otismicro.

50. William Sullivan to Harrison Gray Otis, Jan. 18, 1822, Otismicro.

51. Harrison Gray Otis to William Sullivan, Jan. 8, 1822, Otismicro.

52. Hubbard, "Boston's Last Town Meetings," 104–105. Cayton, "Fragmentation of 'A Great Family,'" 160, which provides a less-detailed account of the chartering debates in the General Court. Section 30 of *The Charter of the City of Boston, and Ordinances Made and Established By the Mayor, Aldermen, and Common Council, with such Acts of the Legislature of Massachusetts, as Relate to the Government of Said City* (Boston: True and Greene, City Printers, 1827), 20, which gives all authority for amendments to the charter to the General Court.

53. Harrison Gray Otis to William Sullivan, Jan. 8, 1822, Otismicro. For William Tudor's role in guiding the charter through the General Court, see Hubbard, "Boston's Last Town Meetings," 104. For Tudor's loyalty to Otis, see Thomas H. Perkins to Otis, Apr. 5, 1822, Otismicro.

54. *Boston Town Records, 1814–1822,* Quincy Report, 242–243.

55. Ibid., 251, 246. Town Meeting, on Oct. 22, 1821, diverted $6,000, previously allocated for the creation of a new vegetable market, to Quincy's House of Industry. Quincy's committee estimated the whole project would cost $20,000. Considering the large amount instantly diverted to the proposed project, it would seem that Quincy had garnered significant support for his plan in Town Meeting—support he certainly did not want to lose once the authority of Town Meeting was invalidated by a new governmental system. Although Quincy never explicitly stated that he feared the formation of a city government would place his project in a tenuous financial position, a city form of government might have challenged his plans by reallocating funds that Town Meeting had already designated for the House of Industry. As we shall see, if Quincy did not worry about this, he should have. During his first and second terms as mayor of Boston, his battles with powerful city officials over funding stalled the project for years.

56. "Who Shall Be Mayor?" *New England Galaxy,* Mar. 29, 1822, APSmicro.

57. Edmund Quincy, *Life of Josiah Quincy,* 393.

58. Hubbard, "Boston's Last Town Meetings," 106. "City of Boston," *New England Galaxy,* Mar. 1, 1822, APSmicro.

59. Emmons, *Speech, Delivered at the Grand Caucus,* 2, 3, AAS.

60. "City of Boston," *New England Galaxy,* Mar. 8, 1822, APSmicro. Cayton, "Fragmentation of 'A Great Family,'" 160. Hubbard, "Boston's Last Town Meetings," 106–107.

61. *Exposition of the Principles of the Middling Interest,* 4, AAS.

62. For the leadership of the Middling Interest, see Cayton, "Fragmentation of 'A Great Family,'" 164. McCaughey, *Quincy: The Last Federalist,* 102. Eliza Susan Quincy to Robert C. Winthrop, July 7, 1879, Winthrop Family Papers, reel 63, in Quincymicro, and to Justin Winsor, July 7, 1880, Winsor Family Papers, in Quincymicro. Harrison Gray Otis to William Sullivan, Mar. 21, 1822, Otismicro. For the Middling Interest strategy in defeating Federalism in Boston and the state, see Francis Wayland to Alonzo Potter, Apr. 8, 1822, Francis Wayland Papers, 1796–1865, John Hay Library, Brown University, Providence. For a statement of the Middling Interest political philosophy, see *Exposition of the Principles of the Middling Interest,* AAS; and *Defence of the Exposition of the Middling Interest on the Right of Constituents to give Instructions to their Representatives, and the obligation of these to obey them* (Boston, ? July 1822), AAS.

5. "POPULAR HALLUCINATIONS," "TEN-FOOTERS," AND "LORDLY NABOBS"

1. Quincy's resignation speech quoted in "Legislature of Massachusetts," *New England Galaxy,* Jan. 18, 1822, APSmicro. Formisano, *Transformation of Political Culture,* 82. Haswell, "Death of Ex-Governor Lincoln," in Massachusetts, *Memorial of Levi Lincoln,* 56.

2. Quincy's resignation speech quoted in "Legislature of Massachusetts," *New England Galaxy,* Jan. 18, 1822, APSmicro.

3. Eliza Susan Quincy to Robert C. Winthrop, June 30, 1879, Winthrop Family Papers, reel 63, in Quincymicro, and to Justin Winsor, July 7, 1880, Winsor Family Papers, reel 63, in Quincymicro.

4. *Exposition of the Principles of the Middling Interest,* 3–4, AAS.

5. Edmund Quincy, *Life of Josiah Quincy,* 289. Walker, "Memoir of Josiah Quincy," 112–113. McCaughey, *Quincy: The Last Federalist,* 94–95. For a public announcement of Quincy's appointment to the Boston municipal court, see "Municipal Court," *New England Galaxy,* Jan. 18, 1822, APSmicro. Appointments to the municipal courts were made by the governor; see *Charter of the City of Boston,* chap. 15, p. 81.

6. Harrison Gray Otis to William Sullivan, Jan. 19, 1822, Otismicro; also see McCaughey, *Quincy: The Last Federalist,* 94.

7. Darling, *Political Changes in Massachusetts,* 34–37. Robinson, *Jeffersonian Democracy in New England,* 160–170. For Worcester County, see John L. Brooke, *The Heart of the Commonwealth: Society and Political Culture in Worcester County, Massachusetts, 1713–1861* (Amherst: University of Massachusetts Press, 1989), 247–268.

8. For gubernatorial election returns, see Morison, *Life and Letters of Otis,* 2:240. In 1816 Brooks won by his smallest margin (51 percent), beating Dearborn by just 2,194 votes out of a total of 96,962; in 1817, Brooks won by 8,031 votes out of 84,289 (55 percent); in 1818, Brooks faced Crowninshield and won by 9,497 out of 69,579 votes (57 percent); in 1819, Brooks won by 7,604 out of 78,146 votes cast (55 percent); in 1820, Brooks faced Eustis and won by 9,144 votes out of a total of 53,000 votes (59 percent); again facing Eustis, Brooks, in 1821, won by 8,340 votes out of a total of 48,876 (59 percent); and in his final election, in 1822, he beat Eustis by 7,310 out of a total of 49,664 votes cast (57 percent).

9. *Boston Palladium,* Feb. 6, 1816, quoted in Livermore, *Twilight of Federalism,* 35; for Brooks's tenuous position in Massachusetts and his pragmatic decision to support the Virginia Dynasty, see ibid., 81, where Livermore explains that Brooks "beat back successive Republican challenges with a policy of moderation, smooth and continuous praise of the national administration, and constant reminders of his fine Revolutionary War record." Also see Formisano, *Transformation of Political Culture,* 63–65, for a thumbnail sketch of Brooks's political life which confirms that for Brooks to win elections in Massachusetts he had to "'disarm party spirit with talismanic power'" (64). Fisher, *Revolution of American Conservatism,* 246, also offers a thumb-nail sketch of Brooks's involvement in the Federalist party.

10. See above, n. 8 for election returns.

11. For the impact on Bostonians of the wooden building restrictions, see Cayton, "Fragmentation of 'A Great Family,'" 161–162; and Formisano, *Transformation of Political Culture,* 183–184. See Whitehill, *Boston: A Topographical History,* 50, for a brief history of Boston fires and the establishment of the 1803 fire law. See "Wooden Buildings," *New England Galaxy,* Mar. 8, 1822, APSmicro, for a description for the living conditions of Boston's poor.

12. *Boston Town Records, 1814–1822,* 182–183.

13. Ibid., Codman Report, 204–205.

14. Ibid.

15. "To the Mechanics of Boston," *New England Galaxy,* June 29, 1821, APSmicro.

16. "By Authority of the Commonwealth," *New England Galaxy,* June 29, 1821, APSmicro.

17. "To the Mechanics of Boston," *New England Galaxy,* June 29, 1821, APSmicro.

18. *Hampshire Daily Gazette,* July 18, 1821, W. E. B. Du Bois Library, University of Massachusetts, Amherst (microfilm).

19. *Boston Town Records, 1814–1822,* 263–264. "Town Meeting," *New England Galaxy,* Jan. 18, 1822, APSmicro.

20. "Wooden Buildings," *New England Galaxy,* Feb. 1, 1822, APSmicro.

21. Harrison Gray Otis to William Sullivan, Jan. 19, 1822, Otismicro.

22. For Otis's holdings in real estate and rental properties, see Edel et. al., *Shaky Palaces,* 198–205; and Rohrbach, *Boston Taxpayers in 1821,* passim, which provides a listing of all rental properties, owners, rental rates, and tenants who paid taxes in 1821. As evidenced by the tax records, Otis collected rent from significant numbers of Boston rental units.

23. "Wooden Buildings," *New England Galaxy,* Mar. 8 and Feb. 1, 1822, APSmicro. "Town Meeting," *New England Galaxy,* Jan. 18, 1821, APSmicro.

24. "Wooden Buildings," *New England Galaxy,* Feb. 1, 1822, APSmicro.

25. Ibid. For the impact high rents were having on middling Bostonians during the depression, see editorial, *New England Galaxy,* Mar. 8, 1822, and "Wooden Buildings," *New England Galaxy,* Feb. 18, 1822, APSmicro.

26. "A Conversion," *New England Galaxy,* Feb. 22, 1822, APSmicro.

27. *Boston Town Records, 1814–1822,* 265–266. Lewis's petition was widely publicized before it arrived at Town Meeting; see "City of Boston," *New England Galaxy,* Mar. 1, 1822, APSmicro, where Buckingham predicts the petition will come to Town Meeting with over 4,000 signatures.

28. "Wooden Buildings," *New England Galaxy,* Mar. 8, 1822, APSmicro.

29. "Wooden Buildings," *Columbian Centinel,* Mar. 16, 1822, AAS.

30. Ibid. *Daily Advertiser* quoted in editorial, *New England Galaxy,* Mar. 8, 1822, APSmicro.

31. Wooden Buildings," *New England Galaxy,* Mar. 8, 1822, APSmicro.

32. "Wooden Buildings," *Columbian Centinel,* Mar. 16, 1822, AAS. Also see "Wooden Buildings," *Columbian Centinel,* Mar. 10, 1822, AAS.

33. "Wooden Buildings," *New England Galaxy,* Mar. 8, 1822, APSmicro.

34. "Wooden Buildings," *New England Galaxy,* Mar. 8 and Feb. 1, 1822, APSmicro.

35. See Edel et. al., *Shaky Palaces,* 204, for a table showing the holdings of Otis and his partners. Rohrbach, *Boston Taxpayers in 1821,* passim. Morison, *Otis: Urbane Federalist,* 218–226. Kennedy, *Planning the City,* 29–41.

36. "Wooden Buildings," *Columbian Centinel,* Mar. 10, 1822, AAS.

37. Harrison Gray Otis to William Sullivan, Mar. 21, 1822, Otismicro. Otis claims in the same letter that he had already written to Thomas H. Perkins to do the same.

38. "Who Shall Be Senators?" *New England Galaxy,* Mar. 15, 1822, APSmicro.

39. "Electioneering," *New England Galaxy,* Mar. 22, 1822, APSmicro. For Roulstone's and Blake's connection with the wooden building reform movement, see *Boston Town Rec-*

ords, 1814–1822, 202–204, which identifies both as serving on Town Meeting committees that approved Josiah Jones's 1821 wooden building reform petition.

40. "Electioneering," *New England Galaxy,* Mar. 22, 1822, APSmicro. Also see Formisano, *Transformation of Political Culture,* 184–185.

41. "Electioneering," *New England Galaxy,* Mar. 22, 1822, APSmicro.

42. Formisano, *Transformation of Political Culture,* 185.

43. Both Roulstone's and Blake's political careers were strictly local. Both had served on various Town Meeting committees since 1821 (see *Boston Town Records, 1814–1822,* 167, 177–178, 203, 254, 202), but neither was involved, as far as I can tell, in state politics.

44. Francis Wayland, *The Duties of an American Citizen, Two Discourses, Delivered in the First Baptist Meeting House in Boston, on Thursday, April 7, 1825, the Day of Public Fast* (Boston: James Loring, 1825), 8, 17, 35–36, AAS.

45. Francis Wayland and H. L. Wayland, *A Memoir of the Life and Labors of Francis Wayland, D. D., LL.D., Late President of Brown University,* 2 vols. (New York: Sheldon, 1867), 1:12–14, 16–17, 21, 31, 37, 57–58, 61, 76–78, 103, 113. For an explanation of Wayland's impact as an activist educator, see Theodore R. Crane, "Francis Wayland: Political Economist as Educator," *Brown University Papers,* 39 (1962), passim. See also, Theodore R. Crane, "Francis Wayland and Brown University, 1796–1841," (Ph.D. diss., Harvard University, 1959).

46. Wayland and Wayland, *Life and Labors of Francis Wayland,* 1:153, 119, 151, 128, 144–145, 131, 135, 132. For material on the North End, see Kennedy, *Planning the City,* 48; and Whitehill, *Boston: A Topographical History,* 112–113. For Boston artisans' rejection of turn-of-the-century evangelicalism, see Ronald Schultz, "Alternative Communities: American Artisans and the Evangelical Appeal, 1780–1830," in Gilje and Rock, *American Artisans,* 69–70, where Schultz argues that Boston's lower-to-middling classes were unique among their counterparts in other cities in not responding in mass numbers to evangelical appeals.

47. Francis Wayland, "The Death of the Ex-Presidents," July 4, 1826, quoted in Crane, "Wayland and Brown University," 171. Crane, "Francis Wayland: Political Economist as Educator," 8–9.

48. Francis Wayland to Mark Tucker, May 3, 1824, Francis Wayland Papers, 1796–1865, John Hay Library, Brown University.

49. Francis Wayland, "The Death of the Ex-Presidents," July 4, 1826, as quoted in Crane, "Wayland and Brown University," 171.

50. For example, see Francis Wayland to Alonzo Potter, Apr. 8, 1822, Francis Wayland Papers, 1796–1865, John Hay Library, Brown University.

51. Ralph Waldo Emerson to John Boynton Hill, Mar. 11, 1822, as quoted in McCaughey, *Quincy: The Last Federalist,* 102.

52. Francis Wayland, "Remarks on the Quarterly Review of Mrs. Judson's Account of the American Baptist Mission to the Burman Empire," May 1826, quoted in Crane, "Wayland and Brown University," 148–153. Wayland, *Duties of an American Citizen* 17, AAS.

53. Wayland, *Duties of an American Citizen,* 30, AAS.

6. THE MAYORAL ELECTION OF 1822

1. "Federal Caucus," *New England Galaxy,* Apr. 12, 1822, APSmicro. Also, see above, chaps. 1–5.

2. Harrison Gray Otis to William Sullivan, Mar. 21, 1822, Otismicro.

3. *Exposition of the Principles of the Middling Interest,* 1–8, AAS; emphasis added. It should be noted that during the 1810s and 1820s both Otis and Perkins were involved in speculations not only in real estate but in "merchandize." For their investments in land development, see Edel et al., *Shaky Palaces,* 198–205, which concludes that Harrison Gray Otis and his partners (one of whom was Perkins) earned an "excess of $311,115 of sales [in real estate and development] over purchases of $543,199, a gain of just under 60 percent." For investments in mercantile speculation, see Seaburg and Paterson, *Merchant Prince of Boston,* esp. 284–289, which cites Perkins stating his philosophy on speculation in the China trade: "The speculator does not wait for the event which would frustrate his views; he anticipates it, and if his anticipations are warranted he makes a profitable speculation." In 1819 Perkins and his partners invested $765,000 in the China trade and expected to double their initial investment. For further evidence of Otis and Perkins business ventures that directly beneftted from their involvement in government, see Prince and Taylor, "Webster, the Boston Associates, and the U.S. Government's Role in the Industrializing Process," 283–299; and Francis W. Gregory, *Nathan Appleton: Merchant and Entrepreneur, 1779–1861* (Charlottesville: University Press of Virginia, 1975), 194–200.

4. *Exposition of the Principles of the Middling Interest,* 1–8, AAS.

5. "Poverty, Vice, and Crime," *New England Galaxy,* Apr. 25, 1822, APSmicro.

6. Joseph Story to Jeremiah Mason, Jan. 10, 1822, as cited in Story, *Life and Letters of Joseph Story,* 1:411.

7. For popular animosity toward judges of all kinds, see chap. 4, herein, which discusses the perceived corruption on the county level, that is, within the justices of the peace and the Court of Sessions; for charges of corruption in the Massachusetts Supreme Court, see "The Chief Justice's Charge," Oct. 20, 1820, and "The Convention," Jan. 5, 1821, both in *New England Galaxy,* APSmicro, where Buckingham first contends that Supreme Court justices have traded justice for political expediency and then argues that circuit court justices are being paid too much. (See chap. 4, herein, for a fuller discussion of these charges and their political ramifications.)

8. Josiah Quincy, *Remarks on Some of the Provisions of the Laws of Massachusetts, Affecting Poverty, Vice, and Crime* (Cambridge, 1822), as quoted in "Crimes and Punishments," *Boston Recorder,* May 25, 1822, APSmicro. Also see Hewlett, "Josiah Quincy," 181–182, 187–191; and "Poverty, Vice, and Crime," *New England Galaxy,* Apr. 25, 1822, APSmicro, which, like the *Recorder,* provides selected portions of Quincy's charge. Some modern historians interested in forms of institutionalized social control will take exception to my favorable characterization of Quincy's reformist stance—in particular, Peter C. Holloran, *Boston's Wayward Children: Social Services for Homeless Children, 1830–1930* (Rutherford, N.J.: Fairleigh Dickinson University Press, 1989), 24–31. And Eric C. Schneider, *Web of Class,* 32–37, describes Quincy's later "reformist" actions as mayor as simply a means by which to clear from Boston's streets roving poor children and the poor homeless, while at the same time "inviting all groups, regardless of class, to join in opposition to pauperism, and to divide the world between the respectable and the vicious." Although this view of Quincy may, in fact, be perfectly valid, for the average jailed pauper, to be segregated from hardened, violent criminals certainly must have been a relief.

9. "Poverty, Vice, and Crime," *New England Galaxy,* Apr. 25, 1822; "Crimes and Punishments," *Boston Recorder,* May 25, 1822; both in APSmicro. Although both of these editorials came out after the 1822 mayoral election with the public printing of Quincy's charge to the

Suffolk County grand jury in March 1822, the fact that his charge to a jury was published at all clearly indicates that Bostonians were aware of his statement on prison reform before the April mayoral election. Unfortunately for Quincy's mayoral ambitions, the tract was not published until after the election, probably due to time constraints. For Buckingham's opinion of debt imprisonment, see chap. 3, herein, and Buckingham, *Personal Memoirs,* 1:102–104.

10. Quincy, *Remarks on . . . the Laws of Massachusetts,* quoted in "Poverty, Vice, and Crime," *New England Galaxy,* Apr. 25, 1822, APSmicro.

11. "Judge Quincy's Charge," *Portsmouth Journal of Literature and Politics,* June 1, 1822, as reported from Boston by "LABEO," AAS. For Codman's criticism of the judiciary, see above, chap. 5.

12. *Boston Town Records, 1814–1822,* Codman Report, 238.

13. Joseph Story to Daniel Webster, Jan. 10, 1824, as cited in Story, *Life and Letters of Joseph Story,* 1:438–439. According to *Boston Town Records, 1814–1822,* 220, the average salary for judges in Massachusetts was higher than Story's estimate, resting at $3,000; see my discussion on this in chap. 4.

14. For wages in Massachusetts during the early nineteenth century, see Carroll D. Wright, *Comparative Wages, Prices, and Cost of Living* (Boston: Wright and Potter, State Printers, 1889), 54, 48, 59, 47.

15. Ibid., 128, 125, 136.

16. For examples of the suffering debtors, see Buckingham, *Personal Memoirs,* 2:102–105.

17. "Bankrupt Law," *New England Galaxy,* Mar. 22, 1822, APSmicro.

18. William Emmons, *The Inaugural Speech of William Emmons, delivered on the Morning of General Election May 31, 1826. By particular Desire of his Fellow Citizens* (Boston: Published by the Author, 1826), 5, AAS. It should be noted that Emmons was recounting the rise of the "middling interest and the poor . . . for the last twenty years" in his 1826 oration. Emmons, like Quincy, had spoken out against the city charter; see Emmons, *Speech, Delivered at the Grand Caucus,* AAS, which says he stands with the "intelligent decisions of a Quincy." Also, the *Portsmouth Journal of Literature and Politics,* Apr. 13, 1822, AAS, and the *National Gazette and Literary Register,* (Philadelphia), May 18, 1822, AAS, connect the debtor's movement to the Middling Interest agenda.

19. "Judge Quincy's Charge," *New England Galaxy,* May 30, 1822, APSmicro. Also see "Original Communications: Judge Quincy's Charge," *New England Galaxy,* May 17, 1822, APSmicro.

20. Hewlett, "Josiah Quincy," 179–196.

21. *Boston Town Records, 1814–1822,* Quincy Report, 243.

22. *Boston Town Records, 1814–1822,* Quincy Report, 249–250.

23. Arthur Gilman, *The Story of Boston: A Study of Independency* (New York: G. P. Putnam's Sons, 1889), 428–429, which portrays Quincy as a reformist judge.

24. For Roulstone's involvement in the WBS, see "Journal of the Washington Benevolent Society of Massachusetts," leadership lists, WBS Records, MHS. For background on Lincoln, see Formisano, *Transformation of Political Culture,* 158. For Heman Lincoln as a member of the General Court in 1821 while Quincy was also there, see *Boston Town Records, 1814–1822,* 199–200, which show Lincoln receiving 484 more votes than Quincy. For Roulstone's involvement in Boston politics, see *Boston Town Records, 1814–1822,* 167, 178, 203, 254, 275, 276. For both Wayland's and Lincoln's support of the Quincy candidacy, see Eliza

Susan Quincy to Robert C. Winthrop, Oct. 29, 1879, Winthrop Family Papers, reel 63, in Quincymicro.

25. For Quincy's antichartering position, see Eliza Susan Quincy to Justin Winsor, July 7, 1880, Winsor Family Papers, reel 63, in Quincymicro. For Joseph T. Buckingham's antichartering stance, see "City of Boston," *New England Galaxy,* Mar. 1, 1822, APSmicro.

26. "Wooden Buildings," *New England Galaxy,* Feb. 1, 1822, APSmicro. For an example of popular criticism of section 30, see "Unalienable Rights," *New England Galaxy,* Apr. 19, 1822, APSmicro. "Who Shall Be Mayor of the New City?" *New England Galaxy,* Mar. 29, 1822, APSmicro. For Quincy's position on the fire law proposal, see above, chap. 5, and "To the Mechanics of Boston," *New England Galaxy,* June 29, 1821, APSmicro, in which editorialist "Mill Creek Wharf" reports that the "bill . . . received the signature of the . . . Speaker of the House," a position which at the time was filled by Josiah Quincy.

27. See "Massachusetts Peace Society," *New England Galaxy,* Jan. 5, 1821, APSmicro, which gives portions of Quincy's speech and favorably reviews it. Also see Hewlett, "Josiah Quincy," 180–181, which interprets Quincy's speech as a reformist statement.

28. For the activities of the militia reform movement, see above, chap. 3.

29. "Mr. Quincy," *New England Galaxy,* Apr. 6, 1821, APSmicro. See above, chaps. 3 and 4, for a full description of Quincy's break with the Central Committee.

30. Eliza Susan Quincy to Justin Winsor, July 7, 1880, Winsor Family Papers, reel 63, in Quincymicro. For more on the Middling Interest delegation that Quincy received at his house, see "Impartiality of Editors," *New England Galaxy,* Apr. 12, 1822, APSmicro.

31. Hubbard, "Boston's Last Town Meetings," 111–112. Formisano, *Transformation of Political Culture,* 185. The final vote came to 175 for Otis and 170 for Quincy.

32. Unidentified editorial in Hubbard, "Boston's Last Town Meetings," 112. William Sullivan to Harrison Gray Otis, Jan. 13 and 19, 1822, Otismicro. "Federal Caucus," *New England Galaxy,* Apr. 12, 1822, APSmicro. Hubbard, "Boston's Last Town Meetings," 109–113; emphasis added.

33. Buckingham, *Specimens of Newspaper Literature,* 261–263. "City Newspapers," *New England Galaxy,* Sept. 30, 1825, APSmicro. Buckingham, *Personal Memoirs,* 1:122. *Gazette,* as quoted in "Impartiality of Editors," *New England Galaxy,* Apr. 12, 1822, APSmicro.

34. "Who Shall Be Mayor of the New City?" *New England Galaxy,* Mar. 29, 1822, APSmicro. Also see Hubbard, "Boston's Last Town Meetings," 110; emphasis added.

35. Hubbard, "Boston's Last Town Meetings," 112–113.

36. Eliza Susan Quincy to Robert C. Winthrop, Oct. 29, 1879, Winthrop Family Papers, reel 63, in Quincymicro.

37. Thomas H. Perkins to Harrison Gray Otis, Apr. 5, 1822, Otismicro. Also see Morison, *Life and Letters of Otis,* 2:251–253.

38. Leverett Saltonstall to William Minot, Apr. 9, 1822, in Robert E. Moody, ed., *The Papers of Leverett Saltonstall, 1816–1845* (Boston: Massachusetts Historical Society, 1978), 97–98.

39. Daniel Webster to Joseph Story, Apr. 6, 1822, in Wiltse, *Papers of Daniel Webster: Correspondence, 1798–1824,* 1:312.

40. Leverett Saltonstall to James C. Merrill, Mar. 30, 1822, in Moody, *Papers of Leverett Saltonstall,* 97.

41. Harrison Gray Otis to William Sullivan, Jan. 19, 1822, Otismicro. Jaher, "Politics

of the Boston Brahmins," in Formisano and Burns, *Boston, 1700–1980,* 66–67. Sheidley, "Sectional Nationalism," 34. *Portsmouth Journal of Literature and Politics,* Apr. 13, 1822, AAS. The *National Gazette and Literary Register,* May 18, 1822, AAS, in an article in response to Quincy's betrayal, also linked the political and the cultural when it described "the political supremacy of the old 'Boston Stamp.'" My conception of the party as a signifying emblem that provided cultural and class solidarity has been largely informed by Jean H. Baker, *Affairs of Party: The Political Culture of Northern Democrats in the Mid-Nineteenth Century* (Ithaca: Cornell University Press, 1983).

42. Ralph Waldo Emerson quoted in McCaughey, *Quincy: The Last Federalist,* 102. Hubbard, "Boston's Last Town Meetings," 114. Thomas H. Perkins to Harrison Gray Otis, Apr. 5, 1822, Otismicro; and Morison, *Life and Letters of Otis,* 1:252. Leverett Saltonstall to William Minot, Apr. 9, 1822, in Moody, *Papers of Leverett Saltonstall,* 97; emphasis added.

43. Leverett Saltonstall to William Minot, April 9, 1822, in Moody, *Papers of Leverett Saltonstall,* 97–98. *National Gazette and Literary Register,* May 18, 1822, AAS. Webster quoted in McCaughey, *Quincy: The Last Federalist,* 104. Harrison Gray Otis, "Speech before the Federal Caucus," Spring 1822, Otismicro.

44. Thomas H. Perkins to Harrison Gray Otis, Apr. 5, 1822, Otismicro; and Morison, *Life and Letters of Otis,* 2:251–253. Eliza Susan Quincy to Robert C. Winthrop, Oct. 29, 1879, Winthrop Family Papers, reel 63, in Quincymicro.

45. Eliza Susan Quincy to Justin Winsor, July 7, 1880, Winsor Family Papers, and to Robert C. Winthrop, Oct. 29, 1879, Winthrop Family Papers, reel 63, both in Quincymicro.

46. Daniel Webster to Joseph Story, Apr. 6, 1822, and May 12, 1823, in Wiltse, *Papers of Daniel Webster: Correspondence, 1798–1824,* 1:312, 325.

47. Francis Wayland to Alonzo Potter, Apr. 8, 1822, Francis Wayland Papers, 1796–1865, John Hay Library, Brown University.

48. Remarkably, this quotation comes from the *Philadelphia Democratic Press,* as cited in Hubbard, "Boston's Last Town Meetings," 114. Although the source is from Philadelphia, there is no reason to believe the Boston Republicans' response was any different.

49. *Portsmouth Journal of Literature and Politics,* Apr. 13, 1822, AAS.

50. Ibid. Daniel Webster to Joseph Story, Apr. 6, 1822, in Wiltse, *Papers of Daniel Webster: Correspondence, 1798–1824,* 1:312.

51. Eliza Susan Quincy to Robert C. Winthrop, Oct. 29, 1879, Winthrop Family Papers, reel 63, in Quincymicro. For Thomas L. Winthrop's affiliation with the Middling Interest, see "Electioneering," *New England Galaxy,* Mar. 22, 1822, APSmicro, which shows Winthrop as the Middling Interest nominee for the state senate. Also see Mary Caroline Crawford, *Romantic Days In Old Boston: The Story of Its People during the Nineteenth Century* (Boston: Little, Brown, 1910), 8, which presents Winthrop as being thrown into the race as a spoiler.

52. *Portsmouth Journal of Literature and Politics,* Apr. 13, 1822, AAS, provides a remarkably detailed breakdown of the voting. It is particularly important to note, considering earlier historical interpretations of the insurgency's social composition, that the Middling Interest gained its largest support from ex-Republicans. Clearly, the party appealed to more than disaffected Federalists as claimed by Morison, *Life and Letters of Otis,* 2:238–239; McCaughey, *Quincy: The Last Federalist,* 100–106; McCaughey, "From Town to City," 203–

204; Formisano, *Transformation of Political Culture,* 186; Cayton, "Fragmentation of 'A Great Family,'" 439–442 (which, to date, is the most perceptive analysis of the Middling Interest).

53. For Quincy's statement, see *New England Galaxy,* Apr. 12, 1822, APSmicro.

54. "Federal Caucus," *New England Galaxy,* Apr. 12, 1822, APSmicro.

55. Ibid.

56. "City Elections," *New England Galaxy,* Apr. 12, 1822, APSmicro, which offers a section of Perkins's speech and then blasts it.

57. "Impartiality of Editors," *New England Galaxy,* Apr. 12, 1822, APSmicro.

58. *Daily Advertiser* quotation taken from the *National Gazette and Literary Register,* Apr. 13, 1822, AAS. *National Gazette and Literary Register,* Apr. 15 and May 18, 1822, AAS. *Portsmouth Journal of Literature and Politics,* Apr. 13, 1822, AAS.

59. *Evening Gazette,* as cited in the *Portsmouth Journal of Literature and Politics,* June 6, 1822, AAS.

60. Hubbard, "Boston's Last Town Meetings," 115. McCaughey, *Quincy: The Last Federalist,* 13, 105–106. "Electioneering," *New England Galaxy,* Mar. 22, 1822, APSmicro. Josiah Quincy, *Municipal History of Boston,* 41.

61. "Mr. Otis & the MIDDLING INTEREST," *New England Galaxy,* May 17, 1822, APSmicro.

62. Morison, *Life and Letters of Otis,* 1:204, 283.

63. Harrison Gray Otis, "Speech before the Federalist Caucus," Spring 1822, Otismicro. "Mr. Otis & the MIDDLING INTEREST," *New England Galaxy,* May 17, 1822, APSmicro.

64. *Niles' Weekly Register,* June 8, 1822, APSmicro. "Mr. Otis & the MIDDLING INTEREST," *New England Galaxy,* May 17, 1822, APSmicro. "Names," *New England Galaxy,* May 24, 1822, APSmicro.

7. "THE *SIEGE OF BOSTON*"

1. Josiah Quincy, *Municipal History of Boston,* 42–43, 373–374.

2. For biographical material on Phillips, see Koren, *Boston, 1822–1922,* 19; and Fisher, *Revolution of American Conservatism,* 271. Quincy, *Municipal History of Boston,* 55.

3. *Independent Bostonian,* July 27, 1822, AAS. *Bostonian and Mechanics Journal,* Apr. 12, 1823, AAS.

4. For Phillips's inaugural, see Josiah Quincy, *Municipal History of Boston,* 374. James M. Bugbee, "Boston under the Mayors, 1822–1880," in Justin Winsor, ed., *The Memorial History of Boston including Suffolk County, Massachusetts, 1630–1880,* 4 vols. (Boston: James R. Osgood, 1881–83), 3:222–226, provides a thumbnail sketch of the Phillips mayoralty.

5. Phillips as quoted in Quincy, "The Mayor's Inaugural Address, May, 1822," *Municipal History of Boston,* 373–374. See also Boston, *The Inaugural Addresses of the Mayors of Boston, 1822–1851.* 2 vols. (Boston: Rockwell and Churchill, City Printers, 1894), 1:3–5.

6. Harrison Gray Otis to William Sullivan, Dec. 17, 1821, and Jan. 19, 1822, Otismicro.

7. Koren, *Boston, 1822–1922,* 9–10, 49–50. Nathan Matthews Jr., *The City Government of Boston* (Boston: Rockwell and Churchill, City Printers, 1895), 164.

8. *Charter of the City of Boston,* 1–21. Koren, *Boston, 1822–1922,* 10–11. Matthews, *City*

Government of Boston, 166–167. William Sullivan to Harrison Gray Otis, Jan. 13, 1822, Otismicro.

9. For population statistics, see Matthews, *City Government of Boston,* app., table 2, 192. For Irish immigration, see Thomas H. O'Connor, *The Boston Irish: A Political History* (Boston: Northeastern University Press, 1995), 34, 36. Knights, *Yankee Destinies,* 94–95, 98–99.

10. Alfred F. Young, "George Robert Twelves Hewes (1742–1840): A Boston Shoemaker and the Memory of the American Revolution," *William and Mary Quarterly,* 38 (Oct. 1981), 616–617. Alan Rogers, "A Sailor 'By Necessity': The Life of Moses Adams, 1803–1837," *Journal of the Early Republic,* 11 (Spring 1991), 19–50. An example of the type of "alternative sub-communities" these men forged can be found in Rogers, "A Sailor 'By Necessity,'" 30–31, which describes Adams and his fellow apprentices forming the Gander Club where members would eat, talk, and drink together. Knights notes that men of this sort, once established in Boston, become members of various mechanics associations whose membership, I contest, comprised the dominant share of the Middling Interest; Knights, *Yankee Destinies,* 98–99.

11. Quincy, *Municipal History of Boston,* 44. "Acts of the Legislature, Section 17," *Charter of the City of Boston,* 150, 14. Quincy, *Municipal History of Boston,* 60, which outlines the charges of corruption the board faced. The chartering debates of the winter of 1821–22 in Town Meeting were highly charged, and any fiddling of the charter by the General Court faced severe criticism. Although some of the amendments made by the legislature did pass the town vote, all except section 17 provoked discussion and commentary in the Boston press. Because of this, I have hypothesized that the measure received the unqualified support of Boston's voters. McCaughey, *Quincy: The Last Federalist,* 107. Quincy, *Municipal History of Boston,* 64–65.

12. Quincy, *Municipal History of Boston,* 64.

13. Ibid., 64–65.

14. Note that the *Independent Bostonian,* on Oct. 12, 1822, changes its name to the *Bostonian and Mechanics Journal*; see *Bostonian and Mechanics Journal,* Oct. 12, 1822, AAS, for the announcement. Although Formisano, *Transformation of Political Culture,* 424, identifies the *Bostonian* as chiefly a Republican organ, clearly the *Bostonian*'s editors viewed their newspaper as solely in the support of the Middling Interest when they decided to change its name once again in June 1823 to the *Mechanics Journal and Middling Interest Advocate,* see *Bostonian and Mechanics Journal,* June 28, 1823, AAS, for the announcement.

15. For early insurgent activism on this issue see chap. 3 herein. *Independent Bostonian,* July 27, 1822, AAS. "Prison Limits (concluded)," *Independent Bostonian,* Sept. 7, 1822, AAS. For a particularly insightful discussion of debt imprisonment, see David Montgomery, *Citizen Worker: The Experience of Workers in the United States with Democracy and the Free Market during the Nineteenth Century* (Cambridge: Cambridge University Press, 1993), 30–31, 38–39. For a more detailed description of the Massachusetts laws on debt imprisonment, see Coleman, *Debtors and Creditors in America,* 39–52.

16. *Independent Bostonian,* July 27, 1822, AAS.

17. Coleman, *Debtors and Creditors in America,* 40–42.

18. *Independent Bostonian,* July 27, 1822, AAS. *Bostonian and Mechanics Journal,* Mar. 1, 1823, AAS.

19. Quincy, *Municipal History of Boston,* 418–419.

20. Montgomery, *Citizen Worker,* 72.

21. "Prison Limits," *Castigator,* Aug. 7, 1822, AAS.

22. "Imprisonment for Debt," *Bostonian and Mechanics Journal,* Mar. 1, 1823, AAS. For further calls for the abolishment of debt imprisonment during this time period, see *Bostonian and Mechanics Journal,* Mar. 15 and 29, 1823, AAS. Also see *New England Galaxy,* Jan. 21, 1823, APSmicro.

23. "Society for the Relief of the Distressed," *Bostonian and Mechanics Journal,* Mar. 29, 1823, AAS.

24. See "Alfred's" editorial in the *Bostonian and Mechanics Journal,* Apr. 12, 1823, AAS, for the city government's attempt to abolish ward voting by having the General Court use the authority given to it by section 30. For Josiah Quincy's opinion of section 30, see "Who Shall be Mayor of the New City?" *New England Galaxy,* Mar. 29, 1822, APSmicro. *Independent Chronicle,* Mar. 22, 1822, as quoted in McCaughey, *Quincy: The Last Federalist,* 102. For the importance of ward voting to the passing of the city charter and the Middling Interest's role in the chartering, see above, chap. 4.

25. "Mechanics!" *Bostonian and Mechanics Journal,* Apr. 12, 1823, AAS.

26. *Bostonian and Mechanics Journal,* Apr. 12, 1823, AAS.

27. Ibid.

28. *Evening Gazette,* Boston, Mar. 22, 1823, AAS, contains an announcement of the new law. "Miseries of Human Life," *Castigator,* Oct. 9, 1822, AAS, describes the truckmen before the ordinance as already in dire financial straits; it also provides a brief description of what the truckmen's job was.

29. "Agricola" editorial, *Independent Bostonian,* July 27, 1822, AAS.

30. "THE TRUCKMEN," *Bostonian and Mechanics Journal,* Nov. 2, 1822, AAS. "Agricola" editorial, *Independent Bostonian,* July 27, 1822, AAS.

31. "THE TRUCKMEN," *Bostonian and Mechanics Journal,* Nov. 2, 1823, AAS. *Castigator,* Oct. 22, Oct. 16, and Aug. 7, 1822, AAS.

32. "Licenses," *Independent Bostonian,* July 27, 1822, AAS.

33. Ibid. *Independent Bostonian,* July 12, 1822, AAS. For other examples of criticism of the licensing restrictions, see *Castigator,* Aug. 7 and 14, 1822, AAS.

34. "Licenses," *Independent Bostonian,* July 27, 1822, AAS.

35. *Castigator,* Aug. 7 and 14, 1822, AAS.

36. "MIDDLING INTEREST POLITICS, *Bostonian and Mechanics Journal,* Apr. 5, 1823, and *Bostonian and Mechanics Journal,* Apr. 12, 1823, AAS.

37. "MIDDLING INTEREST POLITICS," *Bostonian and Mechanics Journal,* Apr. 5, 1823, AAS.

38. Editorial, *Bostonian and Mechanics Journal,* Apr. 12, 1823; "Mechanics!" *Bostonian and Mechanics Journal,* Apr. 12, 1823. "Election of City Officers," *Bostonian and Mechanics Journal,* Apr. 12, 1823, all in AAS.

39. "Prison Limits," *New England Galaxy,* July 26, 1822, APSmicro. Also see a letter carried by Buckingham "To the Mayor and Aldermen of the City of Boston," *New England Galaxy,* Aug. 9, 1822, APSmicro, that criticized the new law.

40. See "Our Militia," *New England Galaxy,* Jan. 31, 1823; *New England Galaxy,* Feb. 28, 1823; "Militia Law," *New England Galaxy,* Mar. 14, 1823; "The Militia," *New England Galaxy,* Mar. 31, 1823, all in APSmicro.

41. As reported in "The Caucuses," *New England Galaxy,* Nov. 8, 1822, APSmicro. Daniel Webster to Justice Joseph Story, May 12, 1823, in Fletcher Webster, ed., *The Writings and Speeches of Daniel Webster: Private Correspondence,* 18 vols., (Boston: Little, Brown, 1903), 17:325. Daniel Webster to Jeremiah Mason, Nov. 30, 1823, as cited in Formisano, *Transformation of Political Culture,* 123.

42. Benjamin Gorham as cited in "The Caucuses," *New England Galaxy,* Nov. 8, 1822, APSmicro.

43. "Mr. Webster," *Bostonian and Mechanics Journal,* Nov. 2, 1822, AAS.

44. There is some evidence that Webster was in fact sincere in his nonpartisan position in 1822. One year later, he wrote to Jeremiah Mason about dropping his affiliation with the Federalist party and promoting the "amalgamation" of parties in Massachusetts. See Formisano, *Transformation of Political Culture,* 123.

45. "The Caucuses," *New England Galaxy,* Nov. 8, 1822, APSmicro.

46. "Congressional Nomination," *Bostonian and Mechanics Journal,* Oct. 26, 1822, AAS. "Caucuses," *New England Galaxy,* Nov. 8, 1822, APSmicro. "On Monday Next," *Bostonian and Mechanics Journal,* Nov. 2, 1822, AAS. Bostonian and Mechanics Journal, Oct. 19, 1822, AAS.

47. "Congressional Nomination," *Bostonian and Mechanics Journal,* Oct. 26, 1822, AAS. "Caucuses," *New England Galaxy,* Nov. 8, 1822, APSmicro. "Members of Congress," *New England Galaxy,* Nov. 8, 1822, APSmicro.

48. "Members of Congress," *New England Galaxy,* Nov. 8, 1822, APSmicro.

49. "City Affairs," *New England Galaxy,* Apr. 4, 1823, APSmicro.

50. "City Affairs, *New England Galaxy,* Apr. 11, 1823, APSmicro. "The Election," *New England Galaxy,* Apr. 11, 1823, APSmicro.

51. Koren, *Boston, 1822–1922,* 19–20.

52. John Lowell to Harrison Gray Otis, Feb. 26, 1823, Otismicro. Also see Morison, *Life and Letters of Otis,* 2:253–254, which carries the whole letter and is a tribute to Morison's ability to decipher Lowell's handwriting.

53. "Federalist Conspiracy: Extracts from a letter found upon a snow drift in the town of Worcester, on Monday last," *Bostonian and Mechanics Journal,* Apr. 5, 1823, AAS.

54. "To Middling Interest Electors," *Bostonian and Mechanics Journal,* Apr. 5, 1823, AAS.

55. Morison, *Otis: The Urbane Federalist,* 439–442. Morison, *Life and Letters of Otis,* 2:242–244. Formisano, *Transformation of Political Culture,* 186. Voting statistics are based on the numbers reported in the press for the mayoral contest of 1822; see *Portsmouth Journal of Literature and Politics,* April 13, 1822, AAS, and the numbers reported in the *Columbian Centinel,* Apr. 9, 1823, AAS. The governor's race of 1823 saw an increase in voter participation in Boston of 2,021 from the mayoral election of 1822.

56. "Middling Interest," *Bostonian and Mechanics Journal,* Apr. 12, 1823, AAS.

57. Editorial, *Bostonian and Mechanics Journal,* Apr. 12, 1823, AAS.

58. For examples of those who have described Quincy as dictatorial, see James Phinney Munroe, "Josiah Quincy, the Great Mayor," *Proceedings of the Bostonian Society,* 4 (Jan. 1906), 33–54. Mellen Chamberlin, "Josiah Quincy, The Great Mayor," *An Address Delivered before the Massachusetts Society For Promoting Good Citizenship, at Old South Meeting-House, Boston Feb. 25, 1889* (Boston: Published by the Society, 1889), 3–24.

59. "Agricola" editorial, *Independent Bostonian,* July 27, 1822, AAS.

8. PERSONAL PARTISANSHIP

1. "The Election," *New England Galaxy,* Apr. 11, 1823, APSmicro.

2. Daniel Webster to Justice Joseph Story, May 12, 1823, in F. Webster, *Writings of Daniel Webster: Private Correspondence,* 17:325.

3. "Federal Declension," *New England Galaxy,* May 9, 1823. "The Election," *New England Galaxy,* Apr. 11, 1823, both in APSmicro. For Webster, see Daniel Webster to Justice Joseph Story, May 12, 1823, in F. Webster, *Writings of Daniel Webster: Private Correspondence,* 17:325.

4. *Boston Patriot,* Mar. 25, 1823, and *Statesman* quoted in Morison, *Otis: The Urbane Federalist,* 439–440.

5. Morison, *Life and Letters of Otis,* 2:241–243. For the schism between the orthodox Congregationalists and the Unitarians, its effect on Harvard College, and its political implications, see Morison, *Otis: The Urban Federalist,* 440–442; Formisano, *Transformation of Political Culture,* 120–123; Jaher, "Politics of the Boston Brahmins," in Formisano and Burns, *Boston,* 62–64; McCaughey, *Quincy: The Last Federalist,* 163–166; Story, *Harvard and the Upper Class,* 137–140. It should be noted that Joseph Buckingham's *New England Galaxy* remained essentially mute on the religious fissure; yet when, in the rare moment he does discuss religion, he sides with the Unitarians; see *New England Galaxy,* Oct. 6 and 13, Aug. 4, 1820, APSmicro. As a deist and not particularly interested in religion, Buckingham avoided writing or publishing editorials of a religious nature unless he could connect them to a political concern. An example of Federalist Unitarians and Trinitarians consistently uniting under the Federalist banner can be seen in Hampshire and Suffolk counties. Hampshire was squarely orthodox Congregationalist, and Suffolk was equally dominated by Unitarians. As has been stated above, both counties proved, until 1823, to be Federalism's most loyal strongholds. Before 1823, this religion schism did not seem to affect partisanship. The most comprehensive study of such religious division in Massachusetts can be found in Peter S. Field, *The Crisis of the Standing Order: Clerical Intellectuals and Cultural Authority in Massachusetts, 1780–1835* (Amherst: University Press, 1998).

6. Formisano, *Transformation of Political Culture,* 120–123. Morison, *Otis: Urbane Federalist,* 439–442. Story, *Harvard and the Upper Class,* 139.

7. Serious Federalist in the Country, "FEDERAL REMONSTRANCE," 1823, Broadside Collection, Rare Book and Manuscript Room, Boston Public Library; hereafter cited as BPLrbm. *Statesman,* as cited in Morison, *Otis: The Urbane Federalist,* 441; also see Morison, *Life and Letters of Otis,* 2:241–243.

8. I have found no evidence that Otis or the Central Committee influenced in any meaningful way the General Court's denial of Amherst College's charter.

9. For the massive increase in Massachusetts voter turnout in the 1823 gubernatorial race, as compared with the 1822 race, see Morison, *Life and Letters of Otis,* 2:240. "For the Bostonians," *Bostonian and Mechanics Journal,* Apr. 5, 1823; "Middling Interest Politics," *Bostonian and Mechanics Journal,* Apr. 5, 1823, both in AAS. For immense increase in Boston voter participation, I have compared the numbers of the hard-fought 1822 mayoral race with those of the 1823 gubernatorial race; see *Portsmouth Journal of Literature and Politics,* Apr. 13, 1822, and *Columbian Centinel,* Apr. 9, 1823, both in AAS. "Astonishing Conversion," *Bostonian and Mechanics Journal,* Apr. 12, 1823, AAS, which claims 1,000 Boston votes went with the Middling Interest–endorsed candidate, Republican William Eustis.

10. "The Election," *New England Galaxy,* Apr. 11, 1823, APSmicro.

11. "Federal Declension," *New England Galaxy,* May 3, 1823, APSmicro.

12. It should be noted that this perspective differs from other historians' views on the Trinitarian/Unitarian break. Morison, in particular, argues that the Trinitarian abandonment of the Federalist party seriously damaged the Federalists throughout the state. He infers that this denominational split proved to be the straw that broke the party's back; see Morison, *Otis: Urbane Federalist,* 440–442. Although I do not wholly disagree with Morison's analysis, I do contend that deep-seated class issues lay at the heart of the matter, not competing theological doctrines. Also see Field, *Crisis of the Standing Order,* passim, for another interpretation.

13. *Boston Patriot,* as quoted in "Federal Declension," *New England Galaxy,* May 3, 1823, APSmicro. *Young Galaxy,* (Boston), Jan. 10, 1824, AAS. See Morison, *Life and Letters of Otis,* 1:216–218, 242–245, for the Federalist press's partisan coverage of Otis. It should be noted that once the Republicans gained the governorship, ironically, the U.S. Treasury Department, led by Monroe's appointee, William Crawford, finally coughed up half of Massachusetts' war claims.

14. "Astonishing Conversion," *Bostonian and Mechanics Journal,* Apr. 12, 1823, AAS. There is some dispute among the *Bostonian,* the *Columbian Centinel,* and the *Galaxy* and the margin of Otis's victory in Boston. I have used the number that was most often cited in the press—108. For further explanation, see the table at n.35, below.

15. "Federal Declensions," *New England Galaxy,* May 9, 1823, APSmicro.

16. MIDDLING INTEREST POLITICS," *Bostonian and Mechanics Journal,* Apr. 5, 1823, AAS.

17. "Federal Caucus," *Bostonian and Mechanics Journal,* Apr. 5, 1823, AAS. It should be noted that Quincy's speech at the caucus was not reported or even mentioned in the Federalist press.

18. For one example of Quincy stretching the limits of his authority as a municipal judge, see "Judge Quincy's Charge," *New England Galaxy,* May 17, 1822, APSmicro.

19. For material on Maffitt and the *Maffitt* case, see Edmund Quincy, *Life of Josiah Quincy,* 389–290; Buckingham, *Personal Memoirs,* 1:105–110; Walker, "Memoir of Josiah Quincy," 112–114; Daniel Dorchester, "The Methodist Episcopal Church: Its Origin, Growth, and Offshoots in Suffolk County," in Winsor, *Memorial History of Boston,* 3:428. For the *Galaxy*'s criticisms of Maffitt, see "The Rev. Mr. Maffitt," *New England Galaxy,* May 24, 1822, APSmicro; and "Mr. Maffitt," *New England Galaxy,* May 17, 1822, APSmicro. For Maffitt's indiscretions, see "Justice Vindicated," *New England Galaxy,* Mar. 7, 1823, APSmicro.

20. See n. 19, above.

21. Edmund Quincy, *Life of Josiah Quincy,* 390.

22. *Bostonian and Mechanics Journal,* Apr. 12, 1823, AAS.

23. "Legislative Liberality," *New England Galaxy,* May 30, 1823, APSmicro. Eliza Susan Quincy to Robert C. Winthrop, Oct. 29, 1879, Winthrop Family Papers, and to Justin Winsor, July 7, 1880, Winsor Family Papers, reel 63, Quincymicro. For the Federalist caucus that nominated Quincy, see "Report," *Bostonian and Mechanics Journal,* Apr. 26, 1823, AAS.

24. "The Election," *New England Galaxy,* Apr. 11, 1823, APSmicro. "Esprit de Parti," *New England Galaxy,* Apr. 15, 1823, APSmicro. Also see Walker, "Memoir of Josiah Quincy," 112–114, which offers a brief description of Otis partisans discrediting Quincy be-

fore the mayoral election. Eliza Susan Quincy to Justin Winsor, July 7, 1880, Winsor Family Papers, reel 63, in Quincymicro, for Otis partisans' outrage at Quincy's bid for the mayoralty under the Federalist party banner.

25. Walker, "Memoir of Josiah Quincy," 113, posits that the author of "A Letter to . . . Quincy," was not Harrison Gray Otis but his son, Harrison Gray Otis Jr. "Law of Libel," *New England Galaxy,* Apr. 25, 1823, APSmicro, suggests the author very well might have been the senior Otis. "Remarks upon 'A Letter to Judge Quincy, on the Law of Libel, By a Member of the Suffolk Bar,'" *New England Galaxy,* May 9, 1823, APSmicro, contains sections of "A Letter to . . . Quincy" and also indicates that Harrison Gray Otis Sr. authored the pamphlet.

26. Walker, "Memoir of Josiah Quincy," 113–114, claims the Boston press did not cover the pamphlet issue, yet Walker did not review the *Galaxy.* "Law of Libel," *New England Galaxy,* Apr. 25, 1823, which reprinted selections of"Reflections on the Law of Libel, addressed to a member of the Suffolk Bar, by a Citizen," APSmicro.

27. "Original Review: Remarks upon 'A Letter to Judge Quincy, on the Laws of Libel by a Member of the Suffolk Bar,'" *New England Galaxy,* May 9, 1823, APSmicro; "The Law of Libel," *New England Galaxy,* May 2, 1823, APSmicro; "To the Editor of the Galaxy," *New England Galaxy,* May 9, 1823, APSmicro, all provide evidence that *Galaxy* readers were aware of the controversy and that it had become a campaign issue. "Esprit de Parti," *New England Galaxy,* Apr. 15, 1823, APSmicro.

28. For Boston being offended, see "To the Editor of the *Galaxy,*" *New England Galaxy,* May 9, 1823, APSmicro.

29. Emmons, *Speech Delivered at the Grand Caucus,* AAS. "Who Shall Be Mayor of the City?" *New England Galaxy,* Mar. 29, 1822, APSmicro. For insurgent opposition to section 30 in 1823, see *Bostonian and Mechanics Journal,* Apr. 12 and 26, 1823, AAS; "The Election," *New England Galaxy,* Apr. 11, 1823, and "City Affairs," *New England Galaxy,* Apr. 11, 1823, APSmicro.

30. "Law of Peddling," *New England Galaxy,* Apr. 25, 1823, APSmicro.

31. For Dunlap's political affiliation, see Darling, *Political Changes in Massachusetts,* 42–43; Dunlap had arrived in Boston in 1820 from Salem and would become a Republican leader in the city as founder and an editorial contributor to the Jacksonian Republican *Statesman.* "Law of Peddling," *New England Galaxy,* Apr. 25, 1823, APSmicro.

32. "Law of Peddling," *New England Galaxy,* Apr. 25, 1823, APSmicro.

33. "The Election," *New England Galaxy,* Apr. 11, 1823, APSmicro. Josiah Quincy Jr., *Figures of the Past,* 323.

34. "City Election," *New England Galaxy,* Apr. 18, 1823, APSmicro. Boston, *A Catalogue of the City Councisl of Boston, 1822–1908, Roxbury, 1846–1867, Charlestown, 1847–1873 and of the Selectmen of Boston, 1634–1822 also of Various other Town and Municipal Officers* (City of Boston Printing Department, 1909), 212–213.

35. For the 1823 mayoral election returns broken down by wards, see *Columbian Centinel,* Apr. 16, 1823, AAS. For the 1822 mayoral election returns broken down by party affiliation, see *Portsmouth Journal of Literature and Politics,* Apr. 13, 1822, AAS. For the 1823 gubernatorial election returns for Boston and broken down by ward, see *Columbian Centinel,* Apr. 9, 1823, AAS, and "Esprit de Parti," *New England Galaxy,* Apr. 15, 1823, APSmicro. To identify Boston's poorest wards, see Edward Pessen, "Did Labor Support Jackson? The Boston Story," *Political Science Quarterly,* 64 (1949), 264.

Election Returns by Ward:
Comparison of the 1823 Gubernatorial and Mayoral Races in Boston

	Governor's Race		Mayor's Race	
Ward	Otis (Fed)	Eustis (Rep)	Quincy (Fed/MI)	Blake (Rep/MI)
1	124	260	101	207
2	109	236	98	205
3	159	299	139	249
4	313	298	275	230
5	256	268	231	233
6	146	213	138	182
7	395	193	338	161
8	384	204	291	168
9	264	104	201	106
10	270	222	250	166
11	225	187	238	140
12	194	208	204	132
Total	2,839	2,692	2,504	2,179

Source: Columbian Centinal, Apr. 9 and 16, 1823, AAS. *New England Galaxy,* Apr. 11 and 18, 1823, APSmicro. Although the *Galaxy* and the *Centinel* report the results of the governor's race as 2,836 (Otis) and 2,728 (Eustis), my own calculations of the *Centinel*'s detailed returns (as cited above) show the actual vote in Boston as 2,839 (Otis) and 2,692 (Eustis). The *Centinel* seems to have lost 33 votes in its calculations. In looking at the Boston *Palladium,* Apr. 8 and 15, 1823, Formisano finds the vote stood at 2,835 (Otis) to 2,727 (Eustis) (*Transformation of Political Culture* 424 n. 44, and 186). I have followed the totals given in the *Galaxy* and the *Centinel* while employing the *Centinel*'s breakdown of votes by ward, despite the discrepancy between the given total and the total if added up by ward. Also, the *Galaxy* and the *Centinel* disagree over the final 1823 mayoral vote. The *Galaxy* reports the results as 2,505 for Quincy, and 2,180 for Blake, whereas the *Centinel* reports the results as 2,504 for Quincy, and 2,179 for Blake. I have followed the *Centinel*'s numbers.

36. I have identified middling-class wards by looking at tax assessment data from 1830. For voting statistics, see *Columbian Centinel,* Apr. 16, 1823, AAS.

Ward	Average value per person
1	$155.99 (poor)
2	154.49 (poor)
3	209.72 (poor)
4	724.24 (wealthy)
5	237.37 (poor)
6	599.73 (middling)
7	1,074.88 (wealthy)
8	842.37 (wealthy)
9	851.40 (wealthy)
10	404.92 (middling)
11	384.69 (middling)
12	210.37 (poor)

Source: Pessen, "Did Labor Support Jackson?" 264. Although Pessen does not identify middling wards in his article, I have attempted to define "middling" by distinguishing marked disparities of wealth between wards. This was achieved by comparing the average value per person in each ward. Middling wards were thus defined as wards where the average value per person living in them was between $599.73 and $384.69.

37. *Bostonian and Mechanics Journal,* Apr. 26, 1823, AAS. Otis's margin of victory is disputed. The actual numbers and the reported totals do not conform with each other. I have used the reported totals to arrive at 108, despite the discrepancy. See n. 35 for further explanation.

38. "Esprit de Parti," *New England Galaxy,* Apr. 15, 1823, APSmicro.

39. Eliza Susan Quincy to Robert C. Winthrop, Oct. 29, 1879, Winthrop Family Papers, reel 63, in Quincymicro.

9. BOSTON'S CAESAR

1. For brief descriptions of the ceremony, see *Boston Gazette,* May 2, 1823, Boston Public Library, Newspaper Microfilms Collection (hereafter cited as BPLmicro); "City of Boston," *New England Galaxy,* May 2, 1823, APSmicro. Josiah Quincy, "The Mayor's Inaugural Address, May, 1823", as quoted in Josiah Quincy, *Municipal History of Boston,* 377, 376.

2. Josiah Quincy, "Mayor's Inaugural Address, 1823," *Municipal History of Boston,* 375–376.

3. Ibid., 376–377. For a sympathetic account of Quincy's attack on the boards, see Edmund Quincy, *Life of Josiah Quincy,* 394–395.

4. Josiah Quincy, "Mayor's Inaugural Address, 1823," *Municipal History of Boston,* 378. Handlin, *Boston's Immigrants,* 114, and 328–329, n. 45, for chart of "Persons per House in Boston, 1790–1870."

5. Edmund Quincy, *Life of Josiah Quincy,* 394. For Quincy's attitude toward his role as mayor, see Josiah Quincy, "Mayor's Inaugural Address, 1823," *Municipal History of Boston,* 376, where he claims unprecedented power, justifying it by stating, "by his [the mayor's] annual election, security is attained against insufficiency or abuse, in the exercise of his authority"; also see "The Mayor's Inaugural Address, May, 1824," *Municipal History of Boston,* 379–388, in which Quincy reiterates that the only limit to his authority can come from the people though the ballot box.

6. McCaughey, *Quincy: The Last Federalist,* 127–128. In should be noted that due to a change in the charter in 1825 the polling days were switched from the end of April to the end of December. Thus, two elections were held in 1825. Quincy won both, uncontested. Beaumont quoted in J. P. Mayer, Introduction to Alexis de Tocqueville, *Journey To America,* trans. George Lawrence, ed. J. P. Mayer (Garden City, N.Y.: Doubleday, Anchor Books, 1971), x. See Edmund Quincy, *Life of Josiah Quincy,* 395, in which Edmund credits his father's administration as having built the institutions that had impressed both Tocqueville and Beaumont.

7. Josiah Quincy, *Municipal History of Boston,* 65–66, and Josiah Quincy, "Mayor's Inaugural Address, 1824," ibid., 381. McCaughey, *Quincy: The Last Federalist,* 107–108.

8. McCaughey, *Quincy: The Last Federalist,* 108. For Quincy's quotation on the responsibilities of the mayor in maintaining a healthy city, see Josiah Quincy, *Municipal History of Boston,* 64–66.

9. McCaughey, *Quincy: The Last Federalist,* 116–117. Josiah Quincy, *Municipal History of Boston,* 138–140.

10. McCaughey, *Quincy: The Last Federalist,* 116–117. Josiah Quincy, *Municipal History of Boston,* 138–140, and "Mayor's Inaugural Address, 1824," ibid., 385.

11. The credo of the volunteer firemen quoted in McCaughey, *Quincy: The Last Federalist,* 109. Josiah Quincy, *Municipal History of Boston,* 263–265. Edmund Quincy, *Life of Josiah Quincy,* 397–399.

12. McCaughey, *Quincy: The Last Federalist,* 109–111. Josiah Quincy, *Municipal History of Boston,* 186–191. Loring, "Josiah Quincy," *Hundred Boston Orators,* 269–271.

13. McCaughey, *Quincy: The Last Federalist,* 109–111. Josiah Quincy, *Municipal History of Boston,* 186–191. Loring, "Josiah Quincy," *Hundred Boston Orators,* 269–271.

14. McCaughey, *Quincy: The Last Federalist,* 109. Josiah Quincy, *Municipal History of Boston,* 263–265. Edmund Quincy, *Life of Josiah Quincy,* 397–399.

15. Josiah Quincy, *Municipal History of Boston,* 74–77. Editorial, *Independent Bostonian,* July 22, 1822, AAS.

16. For descriptions of the new marketplace that would come to be know as Quincy Market, see Whitehill, *Boston: A Topographical History,* 96–98; Edmund Quincy, *Josiah Quincy,* 398–399, from which Josiah Quincy quotations are taken; Gilman, *Story of Boston,* 433–435. For criticism of Quincy's proposal, see *New England Palladium & Commercial Advertiser,* Aug. 13, 1824, quoted in Hewlett, "Josiah Quincy," 186; and *Boston Patriot,* Jan. 13 and 16, 1824, as provided in McCaughey, *Quincy: The Last Federalist,* 111–113.

17. McCaughey, *Quincy: The Last Federalist,* 114–116, makes a similar point but contends that Mayor Quincy was motivated by his "determination to restore to Bostonians a collective identity." Thus, McCaughey views Quincy's actions as essentially antiprogressive and antimodern, whereas I interpret his actions as the harbingers of the modern, centralized municipal state.

18. Josiah Quincy, "Mayor's Inaugural Address, 1824," *Municipal History of Boston,* 383.

19. Konefski and King, *Papers of Daniel Webster: Legal Papers,* 2:566–568, where the editors provide the only recent analysis of Quincy's appeal for eminent domain. Josiah Quincy, *Remarks on the Constitutionality for the extension of Faneuil Hall Market* (Boston, 1824), passim BPLrbm.

20. Quincy quoted in Konefski and King, *Papers of Daniel Webster: Legal Papers,* 2:566. For Republican gains in the legislature, see Ronald Formisano, *Transformation of Political Culture,* 359.

21. John Codman to Daniel Webster, Jan. 22, 1824, in Konefski and King, *Papers of Daniel Webster: Legal Papers,* 2:567–568. For the plan of Quincy's market and Codman's property, see Whitehill, *Boston: A Topographical History,* 97.

22. Konefski and King, *Papers of Daniel Webster: Legal Papers,* 2:566–567.

23. Josiah Quincy, "Farewell Address as Mayor of Boston, 1829," *Old South Leaflets,* 182 (n.d.), 14–15. McCaughey, *Quincy: The Last Federalist,* 113. Edmund Quincy, *Life of Josiah Quincy,* 398–399.

24. For Quincy's early-morning city inspections, see Loring, *Hundred Boston Orators,* 269. For Quincy's use of the truckmen, see Roger Lane, *Policing the City: Boston, 1822–1885* (New York: Atheneum, 1971), 24; Gilman, *Story of Boston,* 430. Edmund Quincy, *Life of Josiah Quincy,* 397.

25. Lane, *Policing the City,* 24. Edward H. Savage, *Police Records and Recollections; or, Boston by Daylight and Gaslight for Two Hundred and Forty Years* (1872; rpt., Montclair, N.J.: Patterson Smith, 1971), 110–111. "Disturbances in Boston," *Commercial Gazette,* (Boston), as reported in the *Hampshire Gazette,* Aug. 3, 1825, W.E.B. Du Bois Library, University of

Massachusetts, Amherst (microfilm); and "Further Disturbances," *Masonic Mirror* (Boston), as reported in ibid. Edmund Quincy, *Life of Josiah Quincy,* 397. Hewlett, "Josiah Quincy," 190, claims that Quincy called on the truckmen twice in 1826 to suppress rioting.

26. Munroe, "Josiah Quincy, the Great Mayor," 46.

27. Josiah Quincy Jr., *Figures of the Past,* 323.

28. Quincy quoted in "Mr. Quincy," *New England Galaxy,* Apr. 6, 1821, APSmicro.

29. For Buckingham's explanations for Federalism's decline, see "Legislative Liberality," *New England Galaxy,* May 30, 1823; "The Legislature of Massachusetts," *New England Galaxy,* May, 23, 1823; "The Election," *New England Galaxy,* Apr. 9, 1824; "Reflections and Prospective," *New England Galaxy,* Apr. 16, 1824; all in APSmicro.

30. For the most important analysis of Jackson's failure in Boston, see Pessen, "Did Labor Support Jackson?" passim.

31. Buckingham, *Personal Memoirs,* 2:13–14.

10. CONCLUSION

1. Three exceptional community studies of this period are Harry L. Watson, *Jacksonian Politics and Community Conflict: The Emergence of the Second American Party System in Cumberland County, North Carolina* (Baton Rouge: Louisiana State University Press, 1981), esp. 1–109; Paul E. Johnson, *A Shopkeeper's Millennium: Society and Revivals in Rochester, New York, 1815–1837* (New York: Hill and Wang, 1978), esp. 15–78; J. Mills Thornton, *Politics and Power in a Slave Society: Alabama, 1800–1860* (Baton Rouge: Louisiana State University Press, 1978), passim. For a fruitful discussion on third partyism and its effects on political culture, see Bruce Laurie, "'Spavined Ministers, Lying Toothpullers, and Buggering Priests': Third-Partyism and the Search for Security in the Antebellum North," in Gilje and Rock, *American Artisans,* 98–119. For various descriptions of the attempts to "amalgamate" and for opponents of that idea, see "Amalgamation," *Boston Patriot & Mercantile Advertiser,* Dec. 27, 1828, BPLmicro; "REPUBLICAN CAUCUS," Nov. 27, 1828, and "REORGANIZATION," Dec. 2, 1828, *Boston Courier,* BPLmicro.

2. For an indication of which sectors composed Boston's anti-Quincy forces, see "LOOK FOR YOUR INTERESTS!!" Dec. 8, 1828; "WORSE AND WORSE!!" Dec. 12, 1828; and "Arise, the Philistines be upon ye!" Dec. 22, 1828, Broadside Collection, BPLrbm.

3. For the most in-depth discussion of the legacy of the Boston schools, see Stanley K. Schultz, *The Culture Factory: Boston Public Schools, 1789–1860* (New York: Oxford University Press, 1973), 20–25.

4. For quotation about street urchins," see ibid., 264. Josiah Quincy, "Mayor's Inaugural Address, 1823,"*Municipal History of Boston,* 377.

5. Schultz, *Culture Factory,* 263–268; quotation, 268.

6. "The City Elections," *Boston Patriot & Mercantile Advertiser,* Nov. 25, 1828, BPLmicro.

7. Records of the School Committee of Boston: Minutes, 1815–1836, Aug. 8, 1826; Nov. 13, 1827; Oct. 3, 1826; Mar. 23, 1828; Jan. 10, 1828. BPLrbm. E[benezer] Bailey, *Review of the Mayor's Report on the Subject of Schools, so far as it relates to the High School for Girls* (Boston: Bowles and Dearborn, 1828), 5–9, BPLrbm.

8. Bailey, *Review of the Mayor's Report on the Subject of Schools so far as it relates to the High School for Girls,* 28, 34, BPLrbm.

9. Ibid., passim, BPLrbm.

10. Josiah Quincy, *Farewell Address, 1829,* 10.

11. "City Administration," *Boston Patriot & Mercantile Advertiser* Dec. 8, 1828; "THE MAYOR," *Boston Patriot & Mercantile Advertiser,* Dec. 8, 1828; "THE MAYORALTY," *Columbian Centinel,* Dec. 10, 1828; all from BPLmicro.

12. For William Sturgis's leadership in Quincy's 1828 campaign, see "MEETING OF THE FRIENDS OF MR. QUINCY," *Columbian Centinel,* Dec. 13, 1828, BPLmicro; and, McCaughey, *Quincy: The Last Federalist,* 130. "THE MAYOR," *Boston Patriot & Mercantile Advertiser,* Dec. 5, 1828, BPLmicro. For "amalgamation" approach of Quincy's campaign, see "City Administration," *Boston Patriot & Mercantile Advertiser,* Dec. 8, 1828, BPLmicro. For Adams's victory in Boston, see Pessen, "Did Labor Support Jackson?" passim.

13. "For the Jackson Republicans," *Jackson Republican* (Boston), Dec. 13, 1828; "City Administration," *Boston Patriot & Mercantile Advertiser,* Dec. 8, 1828; "The Mayoralty," *Boston Patriot & Mercantile Advertiser,* Dec. 12, 1828; all from BPLmicro.

14. Kornblith, "Becoming Joseph T. Buckingham," in Gilje and Rock, *American Artisans,* 126–128.

15. "THE MAYOR," *Boston Courier,* Nov. 27, 1828, BPLmicro, which stated that although "Mr. Quincy is not a perfect man" his opposition had not found a suitable candidate and, thus, it would support the mayor. "City Elections," *Boston Courier,* Dec. 5, 1828, BPLmicro. "The Mayoralty of Boston," *Boston Courier,* Dec. 23, 1828, BPLmicro. "LOOK TO YOUR INTERESTS!!" Broadside Collection, BPLrbm.

16. Eliza Susan Quincy to Justin Winsor, July 7, 1880, Winsor Family Papers, reel 63, in Quincymicro. "THE MAYOR," *Boston Patriot & Mercantile Advertiser,* Dec. 5, 1828, BPLmicro.

17. For the Dec. 8 election returns, see "City Elections," *Columbian Centinel,* Dec. 10, 1828, which identifies six candidates; and "Municipal Elections," *Jackson Republican,* Dec. 10, 1828, which identifies the partisan affiliation of three candidates; both in BPLmicro.

18. George Shattuck quoted in McCaughey, *Quincy: The Last Federalist,* 130.

19. "WORSE AND WORSE!!" Dec. 12, 1828, Broadside Collection, BPLrbm.

20. For Sturgis rally, see "MEETING OF THE FRIENDS OF MR.QUINCY," *Columbian Centinel,* Dec. 13, 1823, BPLmicro. Charles Francis Adams quoted in McCaughey, *Quincy: The Last Federalist,* 130.

21. Electoral data from "City Elections," *Jackson Republican,* Dec. 17, 1828, BPLmicro; and "City Elections," *Columbian Centinel,* Dec. 10 and 17, 1828, BPLmicro. For reasons for Quincy's defeat, see "The Mayoralty," *Columbian Centinel,* Dec. 17, 1828, BPLmicro.

22. "The Mayoralty," *Boston Courier,* Dec. 18, 1828, BPLmicro.

23. "The Mayor," *Columbian Centinel,* Dec. 17, 1828, BPLmicro. "THE MAYOR," *Boston Courier,* Nov. 27, 1828, BPLmicro.

24. William Foster Jr., "To the Gentlemen composing the late Caucus at the Old Court House," *Columbian Centinel,* Dec. 20, 1828, BPLmicro.

25. For the city charter issue, see "The City Charter," *Boston Courier,* Dec. 22, 1828, BPLmicro.

26. "The Mayoralty," *Boston Patriot & Mercantile Advertiser,* Dec. 22, 1828, BPLmicro. For the personal feud between Otis and J. Q. Adams, see Morison, *Otis: Urbane Federalist,* 422–423.

27. "Arise, the Philistines be upon ye!" Dec. 22, 1828, Broadside Collection, BPLrbm.

28. For the amalgamationists economic platform, see Formisano, *Transformation of Political Culture,* 190–196; and Kornblith, "Becoming Joseph T. Buckingham," in Gilje and Rock, *American Artisans,* 128–132, which does not identify Buckingham as an amalgamationist yet presents his conceptions of economic independence, which mesh with the amalgamationist approach to economic growth.

29. "The Mayoralty," *Boston Patriot & Mercantile Advertiser,* Dec. 22, 1828, BPLmicro.

30. For voting statistics, see "City Elections," *Jackson Republican,* Dec. 24, 1828, BPLmicro. "Amalgamation," *Boston Patriot & Mercantile Advertiser,* Dec. 27, 1828, BPLmicro. "JACKSON REPUBLICAN PARTY, *Jackson Republican,* Dec. 24, 1828, BPLmicro; and *Boston Patriot,* Dec. 29, 1828, BPLmicro, which states that William Ingalls was the founding chair of the Boston Jacksonian Republican party.

31. For Republican charges of voter fraud, see "The Mayoralty," *Columbian Centinel,* Dec. 24, 1828, BPLmicro. "The City Charter," *Boston Courier,* Dec. 22, 1828, BPLmicro.

32. "City Election," *Jackson Republican,* Dec. 24, 1828, BPLmicro.

33. Lee Benson, *The Concept of Jacksonian Democracy: New York as a Test Case* (New York: Atheneum Press, 1964), passim. Laurie, "Spavined Ministers, Lying Toothpullers, and Buggering Priests," in Gilje and Rock, *American Artisans,* passim.

34. Harrison Gray Otis, "An Address to the Board of Aldermen, and the Members of the Common Council of Boston," in Boston, *Inaugural Addresses of the Mayors of Boston,* 1:126–128.

35. Ibid., 1:120–121.

36. Buckingham, *Personal Memoirs,* 2:14.

37. *Boston Patriot & Mercantile Advertiser,* as quoted in McCaughey, *Quincy: The Last Federalist,* 129.

BIBLIOGRAPHY

PRIMARY SOURCES

Archives

American Antiquarian Society, Worcester, Mass.
- Broadside Collection
- Newspaper Collection
- Pamphlet Collection

Boston Public Library, Rare Book and Manuscript Room
- Broadside Collection
- Pamphlet Collection
- Records of the School Committee of Boston: Minutes, 1815–1836

John Hay Library Archives, Brown University, Providence
- Francis Wayland Papers, (1796–1865)

Massachusetts Historical Society, Boston
- Miscellaneous Bound Papers
- Harrison Gray Otis Papers
- Pamphlet Collection
- Thomas Handasyd Perkins Papers, 1789–1824
- Quincy Family Papers
- Leverett Saltonstall Papers
- Washington Benevolent Society Records, 1812–1824
- Moses Williams Papers, 1790–1882
- Winsor Family Papers
- Winthrop Family Papers

New York Public Library, New York
- Otis Family Papers, 1691–1870

Microfilm, Microfiche, and Microform Collections

Adams Family Papers, Massachusetts Historical Society Microfilm, W.E.B. Du Bois Library, Microfilm Room, University of Massachusetts, Amherst.

American Periodical Series, Microfilm, W.E.B. Du Bois Library, Microfilm Room, University of Massachusetts, Amherst.

Boston Public Library Newspaper Microfilm Collection, Boston Public Library, Microfilm Room, Boston.

W.E.B. Du Bois Library Newspaper Collection, Microfilm, W.E.B. Du Bois Library, Microfilm Room, University of Massachusetts, Amherst.

Edward Everett Papers, 1819–1826, Massachusetts Historical Society Microfilm, W.E.B. Du Bois Library, Microfilm Room, University of Massachusetts, Amherst.

Forbes Family Papers, Massachusetts Historical Society Microfilm, W.E.B. Du Bois Library, Microfilm Room, University of Massachusetts, Amherst.

Harrison Gray Otis Papers, Massachusetts Historical Society Microfilm (with materials from the New York Public Library's Otis Family Papers, 1691–1870), W.E.B. Du Bois Library, Microfilm Room, University of Massachusetts, Amherst.

Horace Mann Papers, 1669–1926, Massachusetts Historical Society Microfilm, W.E.B. Du Bois Library, Microfilm Room, University of Massachusetts, Amherst.

Massachusetts Historical Society Newspaper Collection, Massachusetts Historical Society Microform, W.E.B. Du Bois Library, Microfilm Room, University of Massachusetts, Amherst.

Oliver Family Papers, 1419–1870, Massachusetts Historical Society Microfilm, W.E.B. Du Bois Library, Microfilm Room, University of Massachusetts, Amherst.

Pamphlets in American History, Microfiche Collection, W.E.B. Du Bois Library, Microfilm Room, University of Massachusetts, Amherst.

Papers Relating to the Quincy, Wendell, Holmes, and Upham Families at the Massachusetts Historical Society together with the Quincy, Wendell, Holmes, and Upham Family Papers in the Collection of Hugh Upham Clark, of Arlington, Virginia, Massachusetts Historical Society Microfilm, W.E.B. Du Bois Library, Microfilm Room, University of Massachusetts, Amherst.

Thomas Handasyd Perkins Papers, 1789–1892, Massachusetts Historical Society Microfilm, W.E.B. Du Bois Library, Microfilm Room, University of Massachusetts, Amherst.

Newspapers and Periodicals

Boston Courier

Bostonian and Mechanics Journal

Boston Patriot

Boston Patriot & Mercantile Advertiser

Boston Recorder

Boston Spectator

Castigator (Boston)

Columbian Centinel (Boston)

Daily Advertiser (Boston)
Debtor's Journal (Boston)
Evening Gazette (Boston)
Hampshire Daily Gazette (Northampton, Mass.)
Independent Bostonian
Independent Chronicle (Boston)
Jackson Republican (Boston)
Massachusetts Spy (Worcester)
National Gazette and Literary Register (Philadelphia)
New England Galaxy (Boston)
New England Galaxy and Masonic Magazine (Boston)
New England Palladium and Commercial Advertiser (Boston)
Niles' Weekly Register (Washington, D.C.)
North American Review
Philadelphia Democratic Press
Pittsfield (Mass.) *Sun*
Portsmouth (N.H.) *Journal of Literature and Politics.*
Young Galaxy (Boston)

Pamphlets and Addresses

Bailey, E[benezer]. *Review of the Mayor's Report on the Subject of Schools, so far as it relates to the High School for Girls.* Boston: Bowles and Dearborn, 1828.

Chamberlin. Mellen. "Josiah Quincy, The Great Mayor." *An Address Delivered before the Massachusetts Society for Promoting Good Citizenship, at Old South Meeting-House, Boston Feb.25, 1889.* Boston: Published by the Society, 1889.

Defence of the Exposition of the Principles and Views of the Middling Interest on the Right of Constituents to give Instructions to their Representatives, and the obligation of these to obey them. Boston, July 1822.

Emmons, William. *Mr. Emmons' Speech, Delivered at the Grand Caucus, held in Faneuil Hall, on the Evening of the Third of March, 1822, upon the Acceptance or rejection of the City Charter.* Boston: Published by the Author, 1822.

———. *The Inaugural Speech of William Emmons, delivered on the Morning of General Election May 31, 1826. By particular Desire of his Fellow Citizens.* Boston: Published by the Author, 1826.

An Exposition of the Principles and Views of the Middling Interest in the City of Boston. Boston, May 1822.

[Otis, Harrison Gray.] *Letters Developing the Character and Views of the Hartford Convention.* Washington, 1820.

Quincy, Josiah. "An Address Delivered before the Massachusetts Agricultural Society, Oct. 12, 1819." 1819.

———. "Gorget of Washington Address." *Proceedings of the Massachusetts Historical Society,* 4 (Apr. 1853), 43–50.

———. "Farewell Address as Mayor of Boston, 1829." *Old South Leaflets.* Vol. 182. Boston: Published by the Directors of the Old South Church, n.d.

———. *Remarks on the Constitutionality for the extension of Faneuil Hall Market.* Boston, 1824.

———. *Remarks on Some of the Provisions of the Laws of Massachusetts, Affecting Poverty, Vice, and Crime.* Cambridge, 1822.

Wayland, Francis. *The Duties of an American Citizen, Two Discourses, Delivered in the First Baptist Meeting House in Boston, on Thursday, April 7, 1825 the Day of Public Fast.* Boston: James Loring, 1825.

Public Documents and Publications

Boston. *A Catalogue of the City Councils of Boston, 1822–1908, Roxbury, 1846–1867, Charlestown, 1847–1873 and of the Selectmen of Boston, 1634–1822 also of Various other Town and Municipal Officers.* City of Boston Printing Department, 1909.

———. *The Charter of the City of Boston, and Ordinances Made and Established by the Mayor, Aldermen, and Common Council, with such Acts of the Legislature of Massachusetts, as Relate to the Government of Said City.* Boston: True and Greene, City Printers, 1827.

———. *The Inaugural Addresses of the Mayors of Boston, 1822–1851.* Boston: Rockwell and Churchill, City Printers, 1894.

Koren, John. *Boston, 1822–1922: The Story of Its Government and Prinicipal Activities during One Hundred Years.* City of Boston Printing Department, 1923.

Massachusetts. *Constitutional Convention, 1820–1821: Journal of Debates and Proceedings in the Convention of Delegates.* Boston: Daily Advertiser 1853.

———. *A Memorial of Levi Lincoln, the Governor of Massachusetts from 1825 to 1843.* Boston: J. E. Farwell, 1868.

Matthews, Nathan, Jr. *The City Government of Boston.* Boston: Rockwell and Churchill, City Printers, 1895.

Registry Department of the City of Boston. *A Volume of Records Relating to the Early History of Boston Containing Boston Town Records, 1814–1822.* Boston: Municipal Printing Office, 1906.

Rohrbach, Lewis Bunker, comp. *Boston Taxpayers in 1821.* Camden, Me.: Picton Press, 1988. Reprinted from original documents printed by the City of Boston in 1822.

Stone, Ebenezer W. *Digest of the Militia Laws of Massachusetts, and Extracts Relating to the Militia from the United States and State Constitutions and Laws of the United States.* Boston: Dutton and Wentworth, State Printers, 1851.

Wright, Carroll D. *Comparative Wages, Prices, and Cost of Living: From the Sixteenth Annual Report of the Massachusetts Bureau of Statistics of Labor, for 1885.* Boston: Wright and Potter, State Printers, 1889.

Books, Memoirs, and Published Collections

Adams, Charles Francis. *Memoirs of John Quincy Adams Comprising Portions of His Diary from 1795 to 1848.* Philadelphia: J. B. Lippincott, 1875.

Adams, Henry. *The Education of Henry Adams: An Autobiography.* 1918. Rpt., Boston: Houghton Mifflin, 1961.

Buckingham, Joseph T., comp. *Annals of the Massachusetts Charitable Mechanics Association.* Boston: Crocker and Brewster, 1853.

———. *Personal Memoirs and Recollections of an Editorial Life.* 2 vols. Boston: Ticknor, Reed, and Fields, 1852.

———. *Specimens of Newspaper Literature with Personal Memoirs, Anecdotes, and Reminiscences.* 2 vols. Boston: Charles C. Little and James Brown, 1850.

Cary, Thomas G., ed. *Memoir of Thomas Handasyd Perkins, containing Extracts from his Diaries and Letters.* 1856. Rpt., New York: Burt Franklin, 1971.

Channing, Kathrine Minot, comp. *Minot Family Letters.* Sherborn, Mass.: Privately printed by Meridian Gravure, 1957.

Davis, Isaac. *Reminiscences of Past Members of the Worcester Fire Society in an Address by Hon. Benjamin Franklin Thomas at the Annual Meeting in Jan. 1872.* Worcester: Edward R. Fiske, printed for the Society, 1862.

Dearborn, Nathaniel. *Boston Notions, being an authentic and concise account of "that village," from 1630 to 1847.* Boston: Privately printed, 1848.

Emerson, Ralph Waldo. *Selected Writings of Ralph Waldo Emerson.* New York: New American Library, Signet Classics, 1965.

Grund, Francis J. *Aristocracy in America: From the Sketch-Book of a German Nobleman.* Rpt., New York: Harper and Brothers, 1959.

Holmes, Oliver Wendell. *The Autocrat of the Breakfast-Table: Every Man His own Boswell.* 1858. Rpt., N.p.: West Virginia Pulp and Paper, 1965.

Jefferson, Thomas. "The Jefferson Papers." *Proceedings of the Massachusetts Historical Society,* 12 (June 1898), 267–274.

Konefski, Alfred S., and Andrew J. King, eds. *The Papers of Daniel Webster, Legal Papers: The Boston Practice.* 4 vols. Hanover, N.H.: University Press of New England, 1983.

Lawrence, William R. *Extracts from the Late Amos Lawrence with a Brief Account of Some Incidents in His Life.* Boston: Gould and Lincoln, 1855.

Loring, James Spear. *The Hundred Boston Orators Appointed by the Municipal Authorities and Other Public Bodies, from 1770 to 1852; Comprising Historical Gleanings, Illustrating the Principles and Progress of our Republican Institutions.* Boston: John P. Jewett, 1852.

Lowell, Anna Cabot. "Letters of Miss Anna Cabot Lowell." *Proceedings of the Massachusetts Historical Society,* 38 (May 1904), 310–313.

Moody, Robert E., comp., ed. *The Papers of Leverett Saltonstall, 1816–1845.* 5 vols. Boston: Massachusetts Historical Society, 1978.

Quincy, Edmund. *The Life of Josiah Quincy of Massachusetts.* Boston: Fields, Osgood, 1869.

Quincy, Josiah. *Essay on the Soiling of Cattle.* Boston, 1859.

———. *A Municipal History of the Town and City of Boston, during Two Centuries, from September 17, 1630 to September 17, 1830.* Boston: Charles C. Little and James Brown, 1852.

Quincy, Josiah, Jr. *Figures of the Past: From the Leaves of Old Journals.* Boston: Roberts Brothers, 1888.

Quincy, Josiah P. "The Louisiana Purchase; and the Appeal to Posterity," in *Proceedings of the Massachusetts Historical Society,* 38 (Nov. 1903), 48–59.

Quincy, Margaret Morton. *The Articulate Sisters: Passages from Journal and Letters of the Daughters of President Josiah Quincy of Harvard University.* Rpt., Cambridge: Harvard University Press, 1946.

Savage, Edward H. *Police Records and Recollections; or, Boston by Daylight and Gaslight for*
Savage, Edward H. Police Records and Recollections; or, Boston by Daylight and Gaslight for Two Hundred and Forty Years. 1872. Rpt., Montclair, N.J.: Patterson Smith, 1971.

Smith, Charles C., comp. "Letters of Mr. Webster, 1816–1845." *Proceedings of the Massachusetts Historical Society,* 34 (Jan. 1901), 398–413.

Snow, Caleb Hopkins. *A History of Boston, the Metropolis of Massachusetts, from its Origins to the Present Period with some Account of the Environs.* Boston: A. Bowen, 1825.

Story, William W. *Life and Letters of Joseph Story, Associate Justice of the Supreme Court of the United States, and Dane Professor of Law at Harvard University.* 2 vols. Boston: Charles C. Little and James Brown, 1851.

Tocqueville, Alexis de. *Journey to America.* Trans. George Lawrence; ed. J. P. Mayer. Garden City, N.Y.: Doubleday, Anchor Books, 1971.

Walker, James. "Memoir of Josiah Quincy." *Proceedings of the Massachusetts Historical Society,* 9 (Mar. 1866), 83–156.

Washington Benevolent Society. "Washington Benevolent Society of Massachusetts," "Letter from the Committee of the Washington Benevolent Society of Massachusetts to Mrs. Martha Peter," and various other Washington Benevolent Society records. *Proceedings of the Massachusetts Historical Society,* 15 (Dec. 1877), 401–404.

Wayland, Francis, and H. L. Wayland. *A Memoir of the Life and Labors of Francis Wayland, D. D., LL.D., Late President of Brown University.* 2 vols. New York: Sheldon, 1867.

Webster, Fletcher, ed. *The Writings and Speeches of Daniel Webster.* 18 vols. Boston: Little, Brown, 1903.

Wiltse, Charles M., ed. *The Papers of Daniel Webster: Correspondence, 1798–1824.* 15 vols. Hanover, N.H.: University Press of New England, 1974.

Winsor, Justin, ed. *The Memorial History of Boston including Suffolk County, Massachusetts, 1630–1880.* 4 vols. Boston: James R. Osgood, 1881–83.

Winthrop, Robert C. "The Death of Josiah Quincy." *Proceedings of the Massachusetts Historical Society,* 7 (July 1864), 376–405.

Winthrop, Robert T. *Addresses and Speeches on Various Occasions.* Boston: Little, Brown, 1852.

SECONDARY SOURCES

Articles

Cary, Nathaniel H. "Boston Mechanics of 1814." *Proceedings of the Massachusetts Historical Society,* 34 (Apr. 1900), 150–153

Cayton, Andrew R. L. "The Fragmentation of 'A Great Family': The Panic of 1819 and the Rise of the Middling Interest in Boston, 1818–1822." *Journal of the Early Republic,* 2 (Summer 1982), 143–167.

Crane, Theodore R. "Francis Wayland: Political Economist as Educator." *Brown University Papers,* 39 (1962). Pamphlet series distributed by Brown University.

Davis, Andrew McFarland. "Jackson's LL.D.—A Tempest in a Teapot." *Proceedings of the Massachusetts Historical Society,* 40 (Dec. 1906), 490–512.

Eliot, Samuel A. "Being Mayor of Boston a Hundred Years Ago." *Proceedings of the Massachusetts Historical Society,* 66 (1942), 154–173.

Goodman, Paul. "Ethics and Enterprise: The Values of the Boston Elite, 1800–1860." *American Quarterly,* 18 (Fall 1966), 437–452.

Hewlett, Richard G. "Josiah Quincy: Reform Mayor of Boston." *New England Quarterly,* 24 (June 1951), 179–196.

Hubbard, James Mascarene. "Boston's Last Town Meetings and First City Election." *Bostonian Society Publications,* 6 (1910), 91–117.

Jaher, Frederic Cople. "Nineteenth Century Elites in Boston and New York." *Journal of Social History,* 6 (Fall 1972), 32–77.

King, Patricia M. "The Campaign for Higher Education for Women in 19th-Century Boston." *Proceedings of the Massachusetts Historical Society,* 93 (1981), 59–75.

Kruman, Marc W. "The Second American Party System and the Transformation of Revolutionary Republicanism." *Journal of the Early Republic,* 12 (Winter 1992), 509–537.

Lears, T. J. Jackson. "The Concept of Cultural Hegemony: Problems and Possibilities." *American Historical Review,* 90 (June 1985), 567–593.

McCaughey, Robert A. "From Town to City: Boston in the 1820s." *Political Science Quarterly,* 88 (June 1973), 191–213.

McKay, George E. "Faneuil Hall Market." *Proceedings of the Bostonian Society,* 29 (Jan. 1910), 34–47.

Monkhouse, Christopher P. "Faneuil Hall Market: An Account of its Many Likenesses." *Proceedings of the Bostonian Society,* 87 (Jan. 1968).

Moore, Maureen T. "Andrew Jackson: 'Pretty Near a *Treason* to Call *Him* Doctor!'" *New England Quarterly,* 62 (Sept. 1989), 424–435.

Morison, Samuel Eliot. "Our Most Unpopular War." *Proceedings of the Massachusetts Historical Society,* 80 (1968), 38–54.

Munroe, James Phinney. "Josiah Quincy, the Great Mayor." *Proceedings of the Bostonian Society,* 4 (Jan. 1906), 33–54.

Pessen, Edward. "Did Labor Support Jackson? The Boston Story." *Political Science Quarterly,* 64 (Summer 1949), 262–274.

Prince, Carl E., and Seth Taylor. "Daniel Webster, the Boston Associates, and the U.S. Government's Role in the Industrializing Process, 1815–1830." *Journal of the Early Republic,* 2 (Fall 1982), 283–299.

Prince, John T. "Boston's Lanes and Alleys." *Bostonian Society Publications,* 7 (1910), 9–32.

Rezneck, Samuel. "The Depression of 1819–1822: A Social History." *American Historical Review,* 39 (Oct. 1933), 28–47.

Rich, Robert. "'A Wilderness of Whigs': The Wealthy Men of Boston." *Journal of Social History,* 4 (Spring 1971), 263–276.

Robinson, William Alexander. "The Washington Benevolent Society in New England: A Phase of Politics during the War of 1812." *Proceedings of the Massachusetts Historical Society,* 49 (March 1916), 274–286.

Rogers, Alan. "A Sailor 'By Necessity': The Life of Moses Adams, 1803–1837." *Journal of the Early Republic,* 11 (Spring 1991), 19–50.

Sheidley, Harlow Walker. "Preserving 'The Old Fabrick': The Massachusetts Conservative Elite and the Constitutional Convention of 1820–1821." *Proceedings of the Massachusetts Historical Society,* 103 (1991), 114–137.

Smith, Theodore Clarke. "War Guilt in 1812." *Proceedings of the Massachusetts Historical Society,* 64 (June 1931), 320–331.

Stanwood, Edward. "The Separation of Maine from Massachusetts." *Proceedings of the Massachusetts Historical Society,* 41 (June 1907), 124–165.

Weld, John G. "Sidelights of the Old Boston Militia Companies." *Proceedings of the Bostonian Society,* 68 (Jan. 1949), 25–43.

Young, Alfred F. "George Robert Twelves Hewes (1742–1840): A Boston Shoemaker and the Memory of the American Revolution." *William and Mary Quarterly,* 38 (Oct. 1981), 561–627.

Zemsky, Robert M. "Power, Influence, and Status: Leadership Patterns in the Massachusetts Assembly, 1740–1755." *William and Mary Quarterly,* 26 (Oct. 1969), 501–520.

Books

Abbott, Richard A. *Cotton and Capital: Boston Businessmen and Antislavery Reform, 1854–1868.* Amherst: University of Massachusetts Press, 1991.

Aldrich, Nelson W. *Old Money: The Mythology of America's Upper Class.* New York: Alfred A. Knopf, 1988.

Baker, Jean. *Affairs of Party: The Political Culture of Northern Democrats in the Mid-Nineteenth Century.* Ithaca: Cornell University Press, 1983.

Baltzell, Edward Digby. *Philadelphia Gentlemen: The Making of a National Upper Class.* Glencoe, Ill.: Free Press, 1958.

———. *The Protestant Establishment: Aristocracy and Caste in America.* New York: Random House, Vintage Books, 1984.

———. *Puritan Boston and Quaker Philadelphia: Two Protestant Ethics and the Spirit of Class Authority and Leadership.* New York: Free Press, 1989.

Banner, James M. *To the Hartford Convention: The Federalists and the Origins of Party Politics in Massachusetts, 1789–1815.* New York: Alfred A. Knopf, 1970.

Barney, William L. *The Road to Secession: A New Perspective on the Old South.* New York: Praeger, 1972.

Benson, Lee. *The Concept of Jacksonian Democracy: New York as a Test Case.* New York: Atheneum Press, 1964.

Bernhard, Winfred E. A. *Fisher Ames: Federalist and Statesman, 1758–1808.* Chapel Hill: University of North Carolina Press, 1965.

Bernstein, Iver. *The New York Draft Riots: Their Significance for American Society and Politics in the Age of the Civil War.* New York: Oxford University Press, 1990.

Billington, Ray Allen. *The Protestant Crusade, 1800–1860: A Study of the Origins of American Nativism.* New York: Rinehart, 1952.

Blouin, Francis X., Jr. *The Boston Region, 1810–1850: A Study of Urbanization.* Ann Arbor: UMI Research Press, 1980.

Blumin, Stuart M. *The Emergence of the Middle Class: Social Experience in the American City, 1760–1900.* Cambridge: Cambridge University Press, 1989.

Boyer, Paul. *Urban Masses and Moral Order in America, 1820–1920.* Cambridge: Harvard University Press, 1978.

Bowen, Cathrine Drinker. *Yankee from Olympus: Justice Holmes and His Family.* Boston: Houghton Mifflin, 1962.

Brauer, Kinley J. *Cotton versus Conscience: Massachusetts Whig Politics and Southwest Expansion, 1843–1848.* Lexington: University of Kentucky Press, 1967.

Brooke, John L. *The Heart of the Commonwealth: Society and Political Culture in Worcester County, Massachusetts, 1713–1861.* Amherst: University of Massachusetts Press, 1989.

Bushman, Richard., et al., eds. *Uprooted Americans: Essays in Honor of Oscar Handlin.* Cambridge: Harvard University Press, 1973.

Cameron, James R. *The Public Service of Josiah Quincy, Jr., 1802–1882.* Quincy, Mass.: Printed for the Quincy Co-operative Bank, 1964.

Cole, Donald B. *Jacksonian Democracy in New Hampshire, 1800–1851.* Cambridge: Harvard University Press, 1970.

Coleman, Peter J. *Debtors and Creditors in America: Insolvency, Imprisonment for Debt, and Bankruptcy, 1607–1900.* Madison: State Historical Society of Wisconsin, 1974.

Cooper, William J., Jr. *Liberty and Slavery: Southern Politics to 1860.* New York: Alfred A. Knopf, 1983.

Crawford, Mary Caroline. *Romantic Days in Old Boston: The Story of Its People during the Nineteenth Century.* Boston: Little, Brown, 1910.

Cromwell, Adelaide M. *The Other Brahmins: Boston's Black Upper Class, 1750–1950.* Fayetteville: University of Arkansas Press, 1994.

Dalzell, Robert F., Jr. *Enterprising Elite: The Boston Associates and the World They Made.* Cambridge: Harvard University Press, 1987.

Dangerfield, George. *The Awakening of American Nationalism, 1815–1828.* New York: Harper Torchbooks, 1965.

———. *The Era of Good Feelings.* New York: Harcourt Brace Jovanovich, 1952.

Darling, Arthur B. *Political Changes in Massachusetts, 1824–1848: A Study of Liberal Movements in Politics.* 1925. Rpt., Cos Cob, Conn.: John E. Edwards, 1968.

Edel, Matthew; Sclar, Elliot D.; and Luria, Daniel. *Shaky Palaces: Home Ownership and Social Mobility in Boston's Suburbanization.* New York: Columbia University Press, 1984.

Farrell, Betty G. *Elite Families: Class and Power in Nineteenth-Century Boston.* Albany: State University of New York Press, 1993.

Field, Peter S. *The Crisis of the Standing Order: Clerical Intellectuals and Cultural Authority in Massachusetts, 1780–1833.* Amherst: University of Massachusetts Press, 1998.

Fisher, David Hackett. *The Revolution of American Conservatism: The Federalist Party in the Era of Jeffersonian Democracy.* New York: Harper Torchbooks, 1965.

Foner, Eric. *Free Soil, Free Labor, Free Men: The Ideology of the Republican Party before the Civil War.* New York: Oxford University Press, 1970.

Formisano, Ronald P. *The Transformation of Political Culture: Massachusetts Parties, 1790s–1840s.* New York: Oxford University Press, 1983.

Formisano, Ronald P., and Constance K. Burns, eds. *Boston, 1700–1980: The Evolution of Urban Politics.* Westport, Conn.: GreenwoodPress, 1984.

Fredrickson, George M. *The Inner Civil War: Northern Intellectuals and the Crisis of the Union.* New York: Harper Torchbooks, 1965.

Freehling, William W. *Prelude to Civil War: The Nullification Controversy in South Carolina, 1816–1836.* New York: Harper Torchbooks, 1966.

Genovese, Eugene D. *The Political Economy of Slavery: Studies in the Economy and Society of the Slave South.* New York : Random House, Vintage Books, 1967.

———. *Roll, Jordan, Roll: The World the Slaves Made.* New York: Random House, Vintage Books, 1976.

———. *The World the Slaveholders Made: Two Essays in Interpretation.* New York: Random House, Vintage Books, 1971.

Genovese, Eugene D., and Elizabeth Fox-Genovese. *Fruits of Merchant Capital: Slavery and Bourgeois Property and the Rise and Expansion of Capitalism.* New York: Random House, Vintage Books, 1985.

Gilje, Paul J., and Howard Rock, eds. *American Artisans: Explorations in Social Identity.* Baltimore: Johns Hopkins University Press, 1995.

Gilman, Arthur. *The Story of Boston: A Study of Independency.* New York: G. P. Putnam's Sons, 1889.

Green, Martin. *The Problem of Boston: Some Readings in Cultural History.* New York: W. W. Norton, 1966.

Greenberg, Kenneth S. *Masters and Statesmen: The Political Culture of American Slavery.* Baltimore: Johns Hopkins University Press, 1985.

Gregory, Francis W. *Nathan Appleton: Merchant and Entrepreneur, 1779–1861.* Charlottesville: University Press of Virginia, 1975.

Hall, Peter Dobkin. *The Organization of American Culture, 1700–1900: Private Institutions, Elites, and the Origins of American Nationality.* New York: University of New York Press, 1984.

Hammond, Bray. *Banks and Politics in America, from the Revolution to the Civil War.* Princeton: Princeton University Press, 1957.

Handlin, Oscar. *Boston's Immigrants, 1790–1880.* New York: Atheneum, 1975.

Handlin, Oscar, and Mary Flug Handlin. *Commonwealth: A Study of the Role of Government in the American Economy: Massachusetts, 1774–1861.* Rev. ed. Cambridge: Harvard University Press, Belknap Press, 1969.

Hart, Albert Bushnell, ed. *Commonwealth History of Massachusetts.* 5 vols. New York: State History Company, 1928–30.

Holloran, Peter C. *Boston's Wayward Children: Social Services for Homeless Children, 1830–1930.* Rutherford, N.J.: Fairleigh Dickinson University Press, 1989.

Jaher, Frederic Cople. *The Urban Establishment: Upper Strata in Boston, New York, Charleston, Chicago, and Los Angeles.* Urbana: University of Illinois Press, 1982.

Johnson, Paul E. *A Shopkeeper's Millennium: Society and Revivals in Rochester, New York, 1815–1837.* New York: Hill and Wang, 1978.

Kazin, Michael. *The Populist Persuasion.* New York: Basic Books, 1995.

Kennedy, Lawrence W. *Planning the City upon the Hill: Boston since 1630.* Amherst: University of Massachusetts Press, 1992.

Kerber, Linda. *Federalists in Dissent: Imagery and Ideology in Jeffersonian America.* Ithaca: Cornell University Press, 1970.

Knights, Peter R. *The Plain People of Boston, 1830–1860.* New York: Oxford University Press, 1971.

———. *Yankee Destinies: The Lives of Ordinary Nineteenth-Century Bostonians.* Chapel Hill: University of North Carolina Press, 1991.

Kolchin, Peter. *Unfree Labor: American Slavery and Russian Serfdom.* Cambridge: Harvard University Press, 1987.

Lane, Roger. *Policing the City: Boston, 1822–1885.* New York: Atheneum, 1971.

Laurie, Bruce. *Artisans into Workers: Labor in Nineteenth-Century America.* New York: Noonday Press, 1989.

———. *Working People of Philadelphia, 1800–1850.* Philadelphia: Temple University Press, 1980.

Livermore, Shaw, Jr. *The Twilight of Federalism: The Disintegration of the Federalist Party, 1815–1830*. Princeton: Princeton University Press, 1962.

Luetscher, George D. *Early Political Machinery in the UnitedStates*. 1908. Rpt., New York: Da Capo Press, 1971.

McCaughey, Robert A. *Josiah Quincy, 1772–1864: The Last Federalist*. Cambridge: Harvard University Press, 1974.

McCormick, Richard L. *The Party Period and Public Policy: American Politics from the Age of Jackson to the Progressive Era*. New York: Oxford University Press, 1986.

Montgomery, David. *Citizen Worker: The Experience of Workers in the United States with Democracy and Free Market during the Nineteenth Century*. Cambridge: Cambridge University Press, 1993.

Morison, Samuel Eliot. *Harrison Gray Otis, 1765–1848: The Urbane Federalist*. Boston: Houghton Mifflin, 1969.

———. *The Life and Letters of Harrison Gray Otis, Federalist, 1765–1848*. 2 vols. Boston: Houghton Mifflin, 1913.

———. *Maritime History of Massachusetts, 1783–1860*. Boston: Houghton Mifflin, 1921.

Mulkern, John R. *The Know-Nothing Party of Massachusetts: The Rise and Fall of a People's Movement*. Boston: Northeastern University Press, 1990.

Nash, Gary B. *The Urban Crucible: Social Change, Political Consciousness, and the Origins of the American Revolution*. Cambridge: Harvard University Press, 1979.

North, Douglass C. *The Economic Growth of the United States, 1790–1860*. New York: W. W. Norton, 1966.

O'Connor, Thomas H. *Bibles, Brahmins, and Bosses: A Short History of Boston*. Boston: Trustees of the Public Library of the City of Boston, 1984.

———. *The Boston Irish: A Political History*. Boston: Northeastern University Press, 1995.

———. *Lords of the Loom: The Cotton Whigs and the Coming of the Civil War*. New York: Charles Scribner's Sons, 1968.

Patterson, Orlando. *Slavery and Social Death: A Comparative Study*. Cambridge: Harvard University Press, 1982.

Pessen, Edward, ed. *Jacksonian America: Society, Personality, and Politics*. Homewood, Ill.: Dorsey Press, 1969.

———. *New Perspectives on Jacksonian Parties and Politics*. Boston: Allyn and Bacon, 1969.

———. *Riches, Class, and Power before the Civil War*. Lexington, Mass.: Heath, 1973.

Peterson, Merrill D., ed. *Democracy, Liberty, and Property: The State Constitutional Conventions of the 1820s*. New York: Bobbs-Merrill, 1966.

Phillips, Urich B. *American Negro Slavery*. Rpt., Baton Rouge: Louisiana State University Press, 1966.

Purdy, Virginia Cardwell. *Portrait of a Know-Nothing Legislature: The Massachusetts General Court of 1855*. New York: Garland, 1989.

Ratner, Lorman. *Powder Keg: Northern Opposition to the Antislavery Movement, 1830–1840*. New York: Basic Books, 1968.

Richards, Leonard L. *"Gentlemen of Property and Standing": Anti-Abolition Mobs in Jacksonian America*. New York: Oxford University Press, 1970.

———. *The Life and Times of Congressman John Quincy Adams*. New York: Oxford University Press, 1986.

Robinson, William A. *Jeffersonian Democracy in New England.* 1916. Rpt., New York: Greenwood Press, 1968.

Rothbard, Murray N. *The Panic of 1819: Reaction and Policies.* New York: Columbia University Press, 1962.

Schneider, Eric C. *In the Web of Class: Delinquents and Reformers in Boston, 1810s–1930s.* New York: New York University Press, 1992.

Schultz, Stanley K. *The Culture Factory: Boston Public Schools, 1789–1860.* New York: Oxford University Press, 1973.

Seaburg, Carl, and Stanley Paterson. *Merchant Prince of Boston: Colonel T. H. Perkins, 1764–1854.* Cambridge: Harvard University Press, 1971.

Siracusa, Carl. *A Mechanical People: Perceptions of the Industrial Order in Massachusetts, 1815–1880.* Middletown Conn.: Wesleyan University Press, 1979.

Story, Ronald. *Harvard and the Boston Upper Class: The Forging of an Aristocracy, 1800–1870.* Middletown, Conn.: Wesleyan University Press, 1980.

Taylor, Alan. *Liberty Men and Great Proprietors: The Revolutionary Settlement on the Maine Frontier, 1760–1820.* Chapel Hill: University of North Carolina Press, 1990.

Taylor, William R. *Cavalier & Yankee: The Old South and American National Character.* Rpt., Cambridge: Harvard University Press, 1979.

Thernstrom, Stephan, and Richard Sennett, eds. *Nineteenth-Century Cities: Essays in the New Urban History.* New Haven: Yale University Press, 1971.

Thornton, J. Mills. *Politics and Power in a Slave Society: Alabama, 1800–1860.* Baton Rouge: Louisiana State University Press, 1978.

Thornton, Tamara Plankins. *Cultivating Gentlemen: The Meaning of Country Life among the Boston Elite, 1785–1860.* New Haven: Yale University Press, 1989.

Tyack, David B. *George Ticknor and the Boston Brahmins.* Cambridge: Harvard University Press, 1967.

Ward, David. *Cities and Immigrants: A Geography of Change in Nineteenth Century America.* New York: Oxford University Press, 1971.

Watson, Harry L. *Jacksonian Politics and Community Conflict: The Emergence of the Second American Party System in Cumberland County, North Carolina.* Baton Rouge: Louisiana State University Press, 1981.

———. *Liberty and Power: The Politics of Jacksonian America.* New York: Hill and Wang, 1990.

Whitehill, Walter Muir. *Boston: A Topographical History.* Cambridge: Harvard University Press, Belknap Press, 1959.

Wilentz, Sean. *Chants Democratic: New York City and the Rise of the American Working Class, 1788–1850.* New York: Oxford University Press, 1984.

Wyatt-Brown, Bertram. *Lewis Tappan and the Evangelical War against Slavery.* Cleveland: Press of Case Western Reserve University, 1969.

———. *Southern Honor: Ethics and Behavior in the Old South.* New York: Oxford University Press, 1982.

Dissertations, and Other Unpublished Works

Buckley, Peter G. "To the Opera House: Culture and Society in New York City, 1820–1860." Ph.D. dissertation, State University of New York at Stony Brook, 1984.

Crane, Theodore Rawson. “Francis Wayland and Brown University, 1796–1841.” Ph.D. dissertation, Harvard University, 1959.

Hilden, Michele M. “The Mayors Josiah Quincy of Boston.” Ph.D. dissertation, Clark University, 1970.

Sheidley, Harlow W. “The Politics of Honor: The Massachusetts Conservative Elite and the Trials of Amalgamation, 1824–1829.” Paper in author’s possession.

———. “Sectional Nationalism: The Culture and Politics of the Massachusetts Conservative Elite, 1815–1836. Ph.D. dissertation, University of Connecticut, 1990.

Zboray, Robert J. “Buckingham, Joseph Tinker.” Paper in author’s possession.

INDEX